355.0092

23.40

9/06

FOOTPRINTS OF HEROES

This painting is entitled *The Sentry*. It's from a series of recollections by Wilson Hurley, from his tour as a FAC (forward air controller) pilot in Vietnam when he was recalled to active duty. Hurley (West Point, '45) is one of the greatest landscape painters in the world.

Sitting in this lonely, empty teahouse in his poncho, with nothing but wet emptiness and the gigantic rainforest around him, this sentry symbolizes the grunts of our military history, the service personnel pulling guard duty in the thousands of remote areas where our wars have taken us. He could be yesterday's hero, or tomorrow's. He is one of the untold millions who have performed heroically in line of duty without fanfare or even recognition. He is the heartbeat of our honor and our existence.

(From the US Air Force Museum collection of thirteen paintings Hurley donated to that facility.)

ROBERT SKIMIN

FOOTPRINTS
OF HEROES

FROM THE
AMERICAN REVOLUTION
TO THE WAR IN IRAQ

Prometheus Books

59 John Glenn Drive
Amherst, New York 14228-2197

All sketches © Nacho L. Garcia Jr.

Published 2005 by Prometheus Books

Inquiries should be addressed to
Prometheus Books
59 John Glenn Drive
Amherst, New York 14228–2197
VOICE: 716–691–0133, ext. 207
FAX: 716–564–2711
WWW.PROMETHEUSBOOKS.COM

09 08 07 06 05   5 4 3 2 1

Library of Congress Cataloging-in-Publication Data

Skimin, Robert.
    Footprints of heroes : from the American Revolution to the war in Iraq / Robert Skimin.
        p. cm.
    ISBN 1–59102–281–9 (alk. paper)
    1. Heroes—United States—Biography. 2. United States—History, Military.
3. United States—Biography. I. Title.

E176.S25 2005
355'.0092'273—dc22

2004027192

Every attempt has been made to trace accurate ownership of copyrighted material in this book. Errors and omissions will be corrected in subsequent editions, provided that notification is sent to the publisher.

Printed in the United States of America on acid-free paper

CONTENTS

CHAPTER ELEVEN. THE KOREAN WAR

CHAPTER TWELVE. VIETNAM

US MILITARY MEDALS FOR VALOR

(IN ORDER OF PRECEDENCE)

1. Medal of Honor (MOH). Sometimes mistakenly called the Congressional Medal of Honor. Light blue field with tiny white stars. The medal is often worn on the ribbon around the recipient's neck. The recipient rates a salute regardless of rank.

2. Distinguished Service Cross (DSC) Army. Navy Cross—Navy, Marines. Air Force Cross.

3. Silver Star

4. Distinguished Flying Cross

5. Bronze Star Medal with "V" device

6. Air Medal

7. Soldier's Medal

8. Purple Heart. Awarded for wounds received in combat.

Full-size medals may be worn on a uniform at any time. Miniature medals and service ribbons may be worn on mess dress uniforms (retired personnel sometimes wear them on evening wear at military functions).

Service ribbons may be worn in lieu of medals. Foreign decorations follow all US awards.

PROLOGUE

HONOLULU, HAWAII
DECEMBER 7, 1941

They sounded like distant thunderclaps. The muted explosions coming from the naval base were quickly explained by the blaring radio in the seventeen-year-old boy's house: *"Pearl Harbor is being bombed by Japanese planes! This is no test! Japanese bombers are—"*

The boy, whose name was Dan, rushed outside with his father. They could see heavy smoke and black puffs of antiaircraft fire dotting the now dirty sky, and could make out dive-bombers wearing tiny red ball markings climbing out of the area where the fleet was anchored. Father and son stared in shock!

"I have to go to the aid station!" Dan exclaimed. He instructed First Aid there. Numerous other young Americans in Hawaii were caught up in the unbelievable crash of war that day, but Dan was different from many of them. His father had been born in a village in Japan and had come to Hawaii as a boy when his own father had arrived to work on a sugar plantation. Dan's grandfather had incurred the obligation, as eldest son, to pay off a debt of $400 Dan's great-grandfather had incurred decades before—an impossible sum to accumulate in those days. Both Dan's grandmother and grandfa-

13

ther had worked long hours for many years, often to send just a dollar a month back to the village. It was a matter of honor. As Dan pedaled away from the house on his bicycle, he shook his fist at the sky and shouted, *"You dirty Japs!"*

Dan had been born in near poverty on Queen Emma Street in Honolulu's Japanese ghetto, and was now a senior at McKinley High. But, like all of the other young Japanese Americans in the Islands, his life had just taken an abrupt turn. Anyone with slant or almond-shaped eyes was suspect—they were *Japanese*!

As America collected itself and began to fight back, Dan graduated from high school and enrolled at the University of Hawaii, deciding to be a doctor. But soon it was announced that an all-*Nisei* (second-generation Japanese Americans) regimental combat team was going to be organized, with vacancies for fifteen hundred young men. On the first day, one thousand Nisei volunteered!

Dan became a member of Company E, 2nd Battalion, of the 442nd Regimental Combat Team (RCT), and soon found himself in Camp Shelby, Mississippi, where the RCT went into rigorous training. At times, to make a few extra dollars, he ran one of the company's craps games. The regiment landed in the gutted harbor of Naples, Italy, in June 1944, and was soon in combat. Dan was now a buck sergeant, born to lead. The Nisei plunged into the heavy fighting with a vengeance, and many became casualties as the 442nd began heaping fame on itself. In November, Dan was given a battlefield commission and pinned on the bars of a second lieutenant. Platoon leaders didn't last long in combat, but Dan didn't worry about that.

On April 21, 1945, Lieutenant Daniel Inouye experienced a day that made him into a legend in the 442nd and changed his life forever. The citation for heroic acts that day reads:

> Second Lieutenant Daniel K. Inouye distinguished himself by extraordinary heroism in action on 21 April 1945, in the vicinity of San Terenzo, Italy. While attacking a defended ridge guarding an important road junction, Second Lieutenant Inouye skillfully

directed his platoon through a hail of automatic weapon and small arms fire, in a swift enveloping movement that resulted in the capture of an artillery and mortar post and brought his men to within 40 yards of the hostile force. Emplaced in bunkers and rock formations, the enemy halted the advance with crossfire from three machine guns. With complete disregard for his personal safety, Second Lieutenant Inouye crawled up the treacherous slope to within five yards of the nearest machine gun and hurled two grenades, destroying the emplacement. Before the enemy could retaliate, he stood up and neutralized a second machine gun nest. Although wounded by a sniper's bullet, he continued to engage other hostile positions at close range until an exploding grenade shattered his right arm. Despite the intense pain, he refused evacuation and continued to direct his platoon until enemy resistance was broken and his men were again deployed in defensive positions. In the attack, 25 enemy soldiers were killed and eight others captured. By his gallant, aggressive tactics and by his indomitable leadership, Second Lieutenant Inouye enabled his platoon to advance through formidable resistance, and was instrumental in the capture of the ridge. Second Lieutenant Inouye's extraordinary heroism and devotion to duty are in keeping with the highest traditions of military service and reflect great credit on him, his unit, and the United States Army.

Dan got out of the rehab hospital in 1948 as a captain. The medals on his chest included the DSC, the Bronze Star, and the Purple Heart with cluster. The DSC was later upgraded to the Medal of Honor. He married, finished college, got a law degree from Georgetown, and entered politics. The following was recorded in the *Congressional Record*:

Tuesday last was the third anniversary of the admission of Hawaii as a state. Today is the third anniversary of one of the most dramatic and moving scenes ever to occur in this House. On that day, a young man, just elected to Congress from the brand new state, walked into the well of the House and faced the late Speaker Sam Rayburn.

The House was very still. It was about to witness the swearing in, not only of the first Congressman from Hawaii, but the first American of Japanese descent to serve in either House of Congress. "Raise your right hand and repeat after me," intoned Speaker Rayburn. The hush deepened as the young Congressman raised not his right hand but his left and he repeated the oath of office.

There was no right hand, Mr. Speaker. It had been lost in combat by that young American soldier in World War II. Who can deny that, at that moment, a ton of prejudice slipped quietly to the floor of the House of Representatives?

As of this writing, Daniel Inyoue, long a United States senator, is still in office, and has given far more than his right arm to his country.

The Paladins*

> *It is in every man's mind to love honor, but little does he dream that what is truly honorable lies within himself and not elsewhere.*
> —Mencius (Chinese philosopher, 371–287 BC)

It is accepted fact that freedom and democracy are not eternal gifts. Periodically they have to be earned. Many Americans have done nothing to earn these precious gifts, and never will, but others have done much. In varying degrees, they are our paladins. They have given their lives, their limbs, or some other part of their beings, that all Americans may exist in freedom. Ethnicity and gender are not factors—all races and creeds have contributed and unflinchingly given of themselves for what they believe, for duty, honor, country, for patriotism, for whatever it is that being an American may foment. In every time of danger to their country, these paladins have stepped forward to give whatever is required to meet that threat.

---

*Paladin: Any knightly or heroic champion; any defender of a noble cause.

Their footprints are often deep and crisp, our heritage of valor.

And, as proven by the Afghan and Iraqi wars, there is no dearth of young Americans making footprints of their own, footprints that will stay etched in that heritage of ours beside the deepest of their forebears.

These earlier paladins of ours, many of whom are mostly unknown and whose remains are forgotten dust in some foreign grave, have given us more than can ever be measured, for can anyone quantify heroism? Is falling on a grenade to save one's buddies the ultimate example of heroism, or is it the skinny little draftee who has always been the worst soldier in his platoon and was scared beyond belief, rising out of his World War I trench at the shrill command of his captain's whistle and charging into the barbed wire and quite possibly death? Is it any member of a B-17 crew flying yet another hazardous mission over Germany in the daytime without a fighter escort, or a half-frozen Marine slowly raising his hand when his sergeant asks for volunteers to form a rear guard to cover the company's retreat in arctic Korea, or perhaps a sailor on the battleship *Arizona* trying to save whomever he can, rather than dive overboard as the huge, burning, dying ship begins to list?

I spent twenty years in the Army and have been in combat, and I've tossed the question to many experienced soldiers, both officer and senior noncommissioned officer, and I still don't have a consensus on what a hero is. Generally, a citation for a medal includes the phrase *"above and beyond the call of duty."* But what is the call of duty? What makes a person respond to a situation in such a manner that may save many of his fellow soldiers', sailors', marines', or airmen's lives—and often result in a decisive effect in combat? Is it a peer factor? "Oh, Lord, don't let me show cowardice in front of my buddies." With many, that's a definite element.

That leads us to *responsibility.* A soldier at the lower level of battle has a responsibility to not let his buddies down; a sergeant has a responsibility for the safety and leadership of his men, as does an officer but normally on a much larger scale. This sense of responsibility increases as we go up the ladder of command. In the movie *We Were Soldiers*, Lieutenant Colonel Hal Moore, portrayed quite believably by Mel Gibson, swore to his battalion he would be the first to go into battle and the last to come out. Further, he promised that he would leave no man behind, dead or alive. Based on the true story of the first major battle by an American unit in Vietnam, the heroism of those men in those few days was simply remarkable. And Hal Moore, who was miraculously unscathed while constantly in the middle of the battle, kept his promise. For his superb example of command and personal courage he was awarded the Distinguished Service Cross, the Army's second-highest award.

In the remarkable movie *Black Hawk Down,* based on a book by the same title by Mark Bowden—whose series in the *Philadelphia Inquirer* first brought the story to the world—the term *peer responsibility* was a key to heroism. Peer responsibility refers to the need to save fellow soldiers when they get into a threatening situation. In the Mogadishu, Somalia, battle, Rangers and helicopter crews performed various acts of courage in the ill-fated mission to capture warlords. One officer who was in the battle, Captain Gary Izzo, has written a vivid account stressing the peer effect. Two senior sniper sergeants were posthumously awarded the Medal of Honor, while six helicopter pilots won the Silver Star, the nation's third-highest award for valor. Other medals for that heroic battle, including many Purple Hearts for wounds, were scattered among the participants.

Again, *responsibility* was a major factor.

And we can't ignore the remarkable word *honor* that has caused many a serviceperson to perform with valor. The Brits spell it *honour,* and it has been such an integral part of their makeup since the days of mythical King Arthur that one might think they invented it. Yet honor is no stranger to the American fighting man and woman. It has been called "a mistress all mankind pursue." Honor knows no social level. A menial laborer's honor might be how well he uses his shovel. Remember Pruett, the talented bugler and boxer in *From Here to Eternity?* His honor lay in being a top-notch private soldier, no bugle blowing—though he was the best—no boxing, no rank, just "sol-diering" so well that it was his badge of honor, his pride. Now another term becomes part of the makeup of hero: *pride.* A person who is proud of his role in the military, who is fully unabashed at flaunting his pride in his military status or proficiency, or for that matter, in the way he lives his life, may be as heroic, given the opportunity, as anyone.

Heroism is a different act to different people. In the military, there will always be those who are glory seekers and will actually pray for an opportunity to earn a big medal. Is that motivation wrong? Not if it doesn't entail needless loss of subordinates. George Armstrong Custer, the golden-haired boy general in the Civil War (one-star at age twenty-three) constantly led from the front. His commands—both of brigade and division—always had heavy losses, but they nearly always took their objectives. His boss, the Union cavalry corps commander Major General Phil Sheridan (himself no laggard in battle), adored Custer because he could count on him to deliver victory. Officer heroes in that war and previous ones were usually rewarded by being mentioned in dispatches, and/or by receiving brevet (temporary) promotions.

I have written a novel of the Little Bighorn, the battle against the Sioux in 1876 in which Custer, along with a large portion of his Seventh Cavalry Regiment, was annihilated, and I know my Custer. There is no doubt that Custer was motivated to win a major battle against the Indians, to win more fame and get promoted back to general (he was a regular army lieutenant colonel at the time). And there is no doubt that Custer fought ferociously as long as it was humanly possible in that battle, as there is no doubt that he fought in part to save his men. But he was overwhelmed by the heavy numbers of highly motivated Lakota Sioux and Northern Cheyenne warriors who swarmed over that portion of his command like bees on a threatened hive...themselves earning heroic fame on that, the most famous day in Sioux history.

A retired Marine colonel reminded me that the Corps teaches its men to "give of themselves, of total commitment with no liability limits." But much of the bravery that has produced our heroes has not been taught; it is in the *essence* of the individual.

The bottom line is: there are simply different motivations for heroism, just as there are, unfortunately, varying degrees of apathy in appreciating it. The playwright George Bernard Shaw said, "Apathy is the worst sin toward our fellow creatures." I hope that some of our public apathy will disappear by bringing back a number of our heroes, both noted and unsung, to introduce them to our youth and to our other citizens who have no knowledge of them or who may have forgotten about them.

They are the heart of our heritage, of our courage.

They are the paladins.

CHAPTER ONE

THE REVOLUTION

Our first heroic figure, a Virginian, was to both the manner and the manor born. He was quite tall, broad-shouldered, athletic, and well-read for his time. He was also an excellent rider and a good shot. In 1755, after the outbreak of the French and Indian War, he joined the British commander, General Edward Braddock, as his aide-de-camp with the rank of honorary colonel, in the campaign to take Fort Duquesne (now Pittsburgh in western Pennsylvania). As the British army drew near the large French army and its Indian force, the young colonel was ill and confined to a wagon with a high fever. Nevertheless, he begged to lead the Virginian militia and their Indian allies who were attached to Braddock's Redcoats.

The next day, Braddock was ambushed and a fierce battle ensued. The tall Virginian's cool presence and raw courage enabled him seemingly to be everywhere, firing his pistols, exhorting his men, placing them to the best advantage, and slashing the enemy with his flashing saber. Two horses were shot from under him, but five were shot from under the brave Braddock—who died of wounds with the American colonel present at his deathbed. The Virginian, miraculously unhit, rallied his survivors and led them home through

Indian-infested country. He was rewarded with an appointment as commander of all of his colony's troops.

He was twenty-three years old.

His name was George Washington.

PAUL REVERE

Who could guess that a short two decades later in 1776 revolt would be seething and about to erupt against those same Redcoats in the colonies of North America? There were many factors that led to the American Revolution, primarily the heavy-handed taxation and arrogance of Britain's King George III. Added to this, the colonial population had matured and the desire for self-governance had hatched from its eggshell into an obtainable dream. All it took was courage and endurance to reach it. Boston, Massachusetts, was a cauldron of unrest, divided sharply between *Tories* (loyal to the crown of England) and *Whigs* (rebels). The famous Boston Tea Party, when chests of tea were dumped from the decks of three anchored English ships by Americans thinly disguised as Indians to protest the exorbitant British tax on that commodity, had occurred two years earlier, on December 16, 1773. With the war for independence imminent, Paul Revere made a courageous ride immortalized by Henry Wadsworth Longfellow in one of America's most famous and beloved poems. Here are excerpts of *Paul Revere's Ride*:

> *Listen my children and you shall hear*
> *Of the midnight ride of Paul Revere,*
> *On the eighteenth of April, in Seventy-five;*
> *Hardly a man is now alive*
> *Who remembers that famous day and year.*
>
> *He said to his friend, "If the British march*
> *By land or sea from the town to-night,*

Hang a lantern aloft in the belfry arch
Of the North Church tower as a signal light,—
One if by land, and two if by sea;
And I on the opposite shore will be,
Ready to ride and spread the alarm
Through every Middlesex village and farm,
For the country folk to be up and to arm."…

Meanwhile, impatient to mount and ride,
Booted and spurred, with a heavy stride
On the opposite shore walked Paul Revere.
Now he patted his horse's side,…

A hurry of hoofs in a village street,
A shape in the moonlight, a bulk in the dark,
And beneath, from the pebbles, in passing, a spark
Struck out by a steed flying fearless and fleet;
That was all! And yet, through the gloom and the light,
The fate of a nation was riding that night;…

You know the rest. In the books you have read
How the British Regulars fired and fled,—
How the farmers gave them ball for ball,
From behind each fence and farmyard wall,…

For, borne on the night-wind of the Past,
Through all our history, to the last,
In the hour of darkness and peril and need,
The people will waken and listen to hear
The hurrying hoof-beats of that steed,
And the midnight message of Paul Revere.

Paul Revere, the dissenting silversmith, set out on his famous ride to alert the countryside that British troops were coming, to warn

Samuel Adams and John Hancock in Lexington, then on toward Concord with his compatriots, William Dawes and Samuel Prescott, a doctor who had purportedly just left his mistress's warm bed. But Revere and Dawes were captured by the Redcoats, so only Dr. Prescott got through to issue the alarm. The following day, in the famous Battle of Concord, the alerted Minutemen routed a British force that outnumbered them more than three to one—igniting the War for Independence.

LADIES AND LEADERS

However, before we get to some of the Revolution's heroes, let's take a look at a woman who never wore a uniform or fired a musket but wielded a powerful pen for the cause of freedom. Mercy Otis was born in September 1728 in Barnstable, Massachusetts, the sister of James Otis, a lawyer and political activist against the Crown. Following her marriage to James Warren at the age of twenty-six, she began to write patriotic poetry, mostly for her friends' amusement. When her brother was mentally incapacitated by a Tory attack, Mercy's writing became more pointed. She risked the grave charges of sedition and treason in publishing numerous tracts, often humorous, that not only ridiculed the Tories and Brits, but enflamed the populace. *(Several women who were never actively in the military will enter this work, but their contribution to our wars, usually at severe risk, certainly earns them mention.)*

Along with Abigail Adams, the wife of John Adams, Mercy was one of the Revolution's most brilliant women. In 1772 she began writing plays that had to be published anonymously and were quite risqué for the time. In them, she continued to mock government leaders and their kin by loosely disguising them so they were easily recognizable by the masses. Some of her favorite stage names for them were: Crusty Crowbar, Dupe, Hector Mushroom, Hum Hunting, Brigadier Hareall, Sparrow Spendall, and Simple Sapling. Her most famous character was Mrs. Flourish, the popular synonym at the time for the F-word.

Mercy Otis Warren was unflinching in her writing support for independence. In one letter to a friend, she stated, "I cannot wish to see the sword quietly put up in the scabbard until justice is done in America."

LIGHT HORSE HARRY

> *How sleep the brave, who sink to rest*
> *By all their country's wishes blest!...*
> *... There Honour comes, a pilgrim grey,*
> *To bless the turf that wraps their clay;...*
> —William Collins, "How Sleep the Brave" (1746)

Following the Boston Tea Party, the British Parliament enacted legislation designed to punish the recalcitrant province of Massachusetts. Quickly dubbed the Intolerable Acts, they served the cause of independence by attracting mutual sympathy from the other American colonies. The First Continental Congress, convened on September 5, 1774, did not seek independence, but rather to effect a reconciliation with England without giving up any colonial rights. But by the time the Second Continental Congress met on May 10, 1775, the Battle of Concord had taken place and open hostilities with the Crown had broken out in Massachusetts. Boston was under siege by American militia. The Congress had little choice; it gave itself central government powers for "The United Colonies of America," adopted the militiamen in the siege of Boston as their Continental Army, and unanimously appointed forty-three-year-old George Washington commander in chief.

The war lasted six and a half years, and with major support from the French navy, ended with Washington's brilliantly executed defeat of General Charles Cornwallis at Yorktown, Virginia. Throughout, the Continental Army was outnumbered and lost its share of battles. But the British army simply couldn't exist in a hostile countryside and it, too, suffered defeats.

Heroes abounded, from a seaman on the deck of American frigate *Bonhomme Richard* to Lieutenant Colonel Henry "Light Horse Harry" Lee, the adventurous and controversial leader of Lee's Legion. From Prince William County, Virginia, Light Horse Harry was from one of the famous families of Lees. He graduated from Princeton (New Jersey College) in 1773 at age seventeen. Three years later he was a captain in Bland's Regiment of Virginia Cavalry. He distinguished himself at Spread Eagle Tavern on January 20, 1778, and was promoted to major-commandant. Given an independent command consisting of three troops of dragoons and three companies of infantry, he led a daring raid on Paulus Hook (now part of Jersey City). By this time, he was a favorite of Commander in Chief Washington. Following his promotion to lieutenant colonel in 1780, Lee joined General Nathanael Greene's forces in the South. He won further distinction at the Battle of Guilford Courthouse, after which his legion was detached from Greene to fight as an independent force. Personally fearless in battle, his forays brought him further fame as one of the great guerrilla leaders of the Revolutionary War.

Colonel Lee left the army in 1782, fatigued and unhappy. He felt that some contemporaries had been promoted ahead of him and that he hadn't received enough acclaim. Yet he was awarded one of only eight congressional medals.

Following the war, Light Horse Harry's life took on more controversy. He married a wealthy cousin, served in the US Congress and the Virginia legislature, and served three one-year terms as governor of Virginia. But during one of these terms he accepted a commission as a major general to command troops sent to Pennsylvania to put down the Whiskey Rebellion. During this absence, he was thrown out of office. Later he again served in the US House of Representatives and became famous for his eulogy of George Washington: "first in war, first in peace, and first in the hearts of his countrymen."

Many heroes are all too human, and Light Horse Harry was more so. A born gambler, he was forever looking for the pot of gold in land speculation. He often welshed on his debts. His first wife died, leaving him with three small children. But it didn't take long for him to find another rich young woman—Ann Hill Carter, seventeen years his junior. She bore him several children as he began to drink too much and continue his downward spiral. At one point Harry considered seeking a general's rank in the French army, and, while spending a period in debtor's prison, he penned his memoirs. He had a final heroic moment when he tried to protect a friend in an antiwar riot in Baltimore during the War of 1812; this left him badly crippled. With alcohol adding to his miseries, he escaped more debtors by fleeing to the West Indies in 1813. There he turned to yet another woman for monetary aid. He died in Georgia, while en route back to Virginia in 1818. Light Horse Harry went from hero to antihero, or more possibly from heroics to tragedy. He was intelligent, courageous, and a gifted leader—yet too impetuous, too covetous, and too desirous of fame. Yet he gave America one of its greatest gifts.

His youngest son was Robert E. Lee.

THE SWAMP FOX

During Harry's adventures in the South, his exploits intermingled for a short time with Francis Marion. Born in Winyah, South Carolina, in 1732, Marion first tasted combat as a private soldier fighting the Cherokee Indians in 1759. While a member of the first provincial congress of South Carolina, he was commissioned a captain of the newly formed state regiment in 1775. That September he was in command of the force that captured the British forts in Charleston. He was soon promoted to major, then to lieutenant colonel, and given command of the regiment. In 1780, his commander, General Benjamin Lincoln, surrendered Charleston to the British, but Marion would have none of it. Though he had suffered a broken ankle, he slipped away into the swamps he had learned to know years earlier while fighting the Cherokees.

He immediately gathered some of his former men and formed an irregular band of guerrillas that quickly became a thorn in the British command's side. Leading bold raids, he would strike, then dissolve into the swamps, causing the disgruntled British commander Banastre Tarleton to nickname him the "Swamp Fox." Nearly always outnumbered, his irregulars met with constant successes. In late 1780, he was appointed brigadier general of South Carolina's militia. He cooperated with Light Horse Harry Lee successfully in several attacks, then, near the end of the war, he teamed up with General Nathanael Greene at the Battle of Eutaw Springs. Their victory forced the British to retreat into North Carolina.

Marion then led a daring rescue of Americans who were surrounded by a huge British force at Parkers Ferry, South Carolina. For this heroic raid, he received the thanks of Congress. As the final curtain fell on the American Revolution, he was appointed brigadier general in the Continental Army, but he chose to return to state politics and later married the charming Mary Esther Videau when he was fifty-four.

He died in 1795, one of the most daring, bold, courageous, and heroic leaders of American history.

THE MOLLIES

While Mercy Otis Warren wielded a pen, two other women more directly related to military heroine-ism wielded a rammer staff for an artillery piece. The first was Margaret Cochran Corbin, a native of Chambersburg, Pennsylvania, who was orphaned by hostile Indians when she was five years old. Raised by an uncle, Molly, as she was called, married a Virginian named John Corbin when she was twenty-one. When he enlisted in the First Company of Pennsylvania Artillery, she followed him to camp. Some reports state that she also enlisted as a soldier, but it's more probable that she just accompanied him, doing cooking and laundry for him and others in his unit, as was sometimes the custom.

While he was stationed at Fort Washington on November 16, 1776, the British and their Hessian allies attacked. The gunner on Corbin's cannon was killed and Corbin took over his duties, with Margaret assisting him. Then Corbin was killed. Overcoming her shock, Mrs. Corbin simply took over the gun, loading and firing it herself. Suddenly a round of enemy grapeshot landed nearby, its jagged bits tearing into Molly's shoulder, chest, and jaw. She was carried to the rear where a surgeon did what he could for her and had her loaded onto a wagon with other wounded soldiers. When the British captured the fort, the American wounded were evacuated to Philadelphia. The heroine survived the jolting ride, but she never fully recovered from her wounds. Her left arm was useless for the remainder of her life.

She had celebrated her twenty-fourth birthday just four days before the battle.

The Continental Congress awarded her a pension of half the pay and allowances of a soldier in service in 1779 for her conspicuous bravery. Molly was carried on the regimental rolls until the war was over in 1783. She died at age forty-nine near West Point, New York, but in 1926 the Daughters of the American Revolution exhumed her remains from a practically unknown gravesite and had them re-interred behind the Old Cadet Chapel at West Point. Today's visitors at the Military Academy will find a monument erected to her. In Fort Tryon Park in New York City, a bronze plaque memorializes Molly Corbin as "the first American woman to take a soldier's part in the War for Liberty."

★★★★★

The other heroine was the Molly who's more well known. A long time ago when I was a corporal at a post in New Jersey, there was a nearby inn at Red Bank named for her: the Molly Pitcher. Actually her name was Mary Hays McCauly and though she was born in Trenton in 1754, she grew up in Carlisle, Pennsylvania. Of German descent, Mary worked off and on as a servant girl until, at sixteen, she married William Hays, a young barber. When he enlisted in the artillery, Mary traipsed along. The winter of 1787–88 was harsh at Valley Forge, where General Washington had his battered army in winter quarters, and while the redheaded, freckled Mary suffered along with the other camp-following women, she was a blithe spirit.

Spring finally arrived, then the flowers of May, and soon the wet, oppressive heat of an early New Jersey summer. General Sir Henry Clinton, the British army commander, decided to withdraw his eleven thousand troops from Philadelphia and move them to protect New York against a possible attack by a French invasion force. With one thousand loyalists and his huge baggage, Clinton's train stretched to twelve miles and moved at a snail's pace of just over five miles a day. Washington decided to attack the train on June 28. But his senior general, Charles Lee, was obstinately incompetent and nearly permitted the British to cut the American army in half. Grasping the peril, Washington brought the main part of his army into position in the nick of time and the day was saved by hard-fighting American valor.

In the midst of this combination of arrogant insubordination and the brilliant generalship that overcame it, an obscure artillery battery was struggling in the tug-of-war that became known as the Battle of Monmouth. In it, Private William Hays was serving in a gun crew, and his wife, Mary, was busy carrying cool springwater to the thirsty soldiers in a white porcelain pitcher she'd found. They quickly gave her the nickname "Molly Pitcher." She also tended to the wounded, and during one British charge, heaved a wounded American soldier on her back and carried him to the rear. This done, she went back to her water carrying. On one trip by her husband's gun, she watched in horror as she saw him fall wounded and overcome by the heat. She quickly poured the remainder of her water over his head, then grabbed the rammer and kept the gun in action in the face of heavy enemy fire.

For Mary Hays's heroic part in the battle, General Washington personally granted a noncommissioned officer's warrant to her. From that day on, she was known throughout the army as "Sergeant Molly." A monument to her, holding a rammer, was erected at a rest area on the New Jersey Turnpike near the battle site. Additionally, a cannon and a flagstaff stand by her gravesite in Carlisle, and numerous paintings depict her heroic day.

A FRENCH PALADIN

Strangely, one of the most valuable generals and heroes of the war wasn't even an American. He became a Continental Army major general before reaching his twentieth birthday, and displayed not only unswerving loyalty to General Washington, but a keen ability to lead soldiers. After two years of serving the commanding general, he went back to his native France, and raised not only money to aid the nearly bankrupt American states, but a French army to come to America and fight. On his return to the colonies, he continued to campaign until Cornwallis surrendered. He received the thanks of the American Congress and wrote a moving letter in response that ended with "Serving America is to my heart an inexpressible happiness."

He was the Marquis de Lafayette.

NATHAN HALE

Now for the story behind one of the most immortal sentences ever spoken by an American soldier. Nathan Hale graduated from Yale College at the age of eighteen and soon became a teacher in a quality school in New London, Connecticut. There, he advocated higher learning for women, and volunteered to teach an early-morning class to twenty young ladies in addition to his regular classes. But with the thunder of war rumbling, he joined the local militia in 1774. A year later, he was commissioned a first lieutenant.

After more than a year of exemplary service, he joined the elite Knowlton's Rangers, and was promoted to captain. In September 1776 Washington was hanging on with his army and needed vital intelligence as to British dispositions in New York. The general asked for volunteers to go into the city as a spy. One prospect, an older French NCO (noncommissioned officer), was purported to have replied, "I am willing to be shot, but not to be hung."

Captain Hale, recently turned twenty-one, volunteered. In the second week of September 1776 he donned civilian clothes and took along his college diploma to support his guise of being a school-master looking for work. Landing on Long Island, he arranged with the boatman to return at a certain time on the twentieth. After a week in the city, he made notes in Latin of the English troop place-ments and placed them in the soles of his shoes. But the boat that met his signal was from a British frigate and he was taken to the British commander, General William Howe. It was bad timing. New York had suffered a major fire the night before, believed to have been started by American sympathizers.

Howe was furious, and when Hale's Latin notes were shown to him, he demanded to know the circumstances. Hale's steely reply was, "Nathan Hale, Captain, Continental Army, sir." The British general ordered him hanged the following day without trial. Early the next morning, Hale wrote two letters that were destroyed. He then asked for a Bible, but the surly provost marshal refused the request. He was marched to an apple tree in a nearby orchard, and when asked for any final words, he uttered the speech that will for-ever spark American patriots, "I only regret that I have but one life to lose for my country."

His body was left to hang for three days before being buried in an unmarked grave, where a statue of him now stands in City Hall Park. Two other statues commemorate him in Connecticut, where he is the designated state hero.

A Man Named Jones

> *I wish to have no connection with any ship that does not sail*
> *fast; for I intend to go in harm's way.*
> —John Paul Jones to M. de Chaumont, November 16, 1778

It was early in 1776 when the fledgling Continental Navy sent its first squadron out to sea to begin its war against the most powerful navy in the world. Commander of this presumptuous group of five ships with a total of only ninety-eight guns was Esek Hopkins. His flagship was the *Alfred* with its twenty guns; his first lieutenant, John Paul Jones, a former captain with a checkered past on British merchant ships who had fled to the colonies to escape a trumped-up trial in England.

Jones served with distinction during the little fleet's campaign in the Bahamas, was promoted to captain, and was given command of the twelve-gun *Providence* in September of 1776. He soon proved his mettle, destroying eight ships and capturing eight others on a cruise of two months from the Bahamas to Nova Scotia. In the meantime, the other American captains were busy seizing a large number of British merchantmen.

But the largest contingent of American sea warriors were privateers, lightly armed vessels that were no more than legal buccaneers. In short, had it not been that they were licensed by the Continental Congress that garnered income from their prizes, they would have simply been pirates. Their success lay in the fact that the British merchantmen they victimized were practically unarmed. American merchants financed them and handled the goods from their prizes, and their crews shared in the loot. Even George Washington was part owner in one such ship. In other wars, privateers were known to shift their allegiances with the wind, but in this one, they were remarkably loyal. Their great value to the youthful nation they supported was in denying supplies to the British army in the colonies, and in ripping off the profits of British merchants. Eventually, as the war wore on, the howls of these merchants would be heard increasingly in Parliament to end the military conflict.

Between the young Continental Navy and the privateers, no fewer than 342 British vessels were captured in 1776 alone. Later, when the French fleet joined the cause, the colonies' Atlantic seagoing presence became a major factor in the war.

But on to the adventures of John Paul Jones—after commanding the *Alfred*, he successfully took the war right to the waters of the British Isles in the *Ranger*. In September of 1779 Jones led a four-ship American/French expedition out of Lorient in Brittany. Jones's flagship was then the forty-two-gun *Bonhomme Richard*. Encountering a huge British merchant fleet, stretching seaward from Flamborough Head and escorted by two ships of the line, Jones immediately made his decision and gave chase. As night began to fall, the *Bonhomme Richard* was within musket range of the HMS *Serapis*, and one of the most famous and desperate of sea battles began. The forty-four-gun *Serapis*, the flagship of the convoy, was commanded by Captain Richard Pearson.

The ships became entangled and Jones led his men in an attempt to board the English ship. As he was repulsed, Pearson, who couldn't see the ensign of the *Richard*, shouted, "Has your flag been struck?"

In one of the most famous statements in American history, Jones replied, *"I've not yet begun to fight!"*

They separated, but were soon broadside to each other, their gun muzzles touching. Jones shouted the order to lash the ships together and soon volley after volley was exchanged, pouring death and destruction into the guts of both vessels. Above decks, the crews fought valiantly, but soon the eighteen-pound balls of the *Serapis* had done their job. The *Richard* was badly wounded and her hold began to fill. But the marines in her round top kept pouring deadly fire onto the decks of the enemy ship. *Serapis* was on fire in a dozen places. By 9:30, as the moon arose, the *Richard* had use of only three nine-inch guns, and she, too, was ablaze.

Just as it seemed the fight was lost, Jones noticed that his guns had nearly severed Pearson's mainmast. He poured more rounds into it, and the tall mast teetered. Seeing his danger and not aware of the *Richard*'s mortality, Pearson struck his flag. Handing his sword to his victor and referring to the old charges against Jones, he snarled, "It is painful to deliver up my sabre to a man who has fought with a rope around his neck."

Jones chivalrously returned the sword, saying, "Sir, you have fought like a hero, and I have no doubt your sovereign will reward you in the most ample manner."

After both crews finally put out the fires, the sinking *Bonhomme Richard* was cut loose to sink into the depths of the North Sea. Aboard the barely seaworthy *Serapis*, the two crews tossed about for ten days until an American squadron rescued them.

Congress gave John Paul Jones its thanks and command of the seventy-four-gun *America*, in which he rendered further valuable service. His fame spread throughout the world and he was decorated by Louis XVI of France, Catherine of Russia, and the king of Denmark. Eight years later, the United States gave him a gold medal. (Captain Richard Pearson survived [acquitted by] a court-martial and was knighted by the king of England for his gallantry against Jones.)

The *Bonhomme Richard* will forever be one of the most memorable names of a fighting ship, and on John Paul Jones's tomb at Annapolis this inscription greets its visitors: "He gave our navy its earliest traditions of heroism and victory."

THE SUPERB WASHINGTON

In all wars, heroes abound, but few rise high enough afterward to lead a country. In the United States, Andy Jackson did it, and a few others: the Harrisons, Zach Taylor, Sam Grant, Dwight Eisenhower, and Jack Kennedy. But the most renowned of them all also earned the sobriquet "The father of our country." He was, of course, George Washington, the man whose portrait by Gilbert Stuart hangs in thousands of school classrooms throughout the country. We met him earlier with Braddock, when he seemed to set the table for what lay ahead in his remarkable life.

Tall, knightly, his only armor his valor...

Washington was born on February 22, 1732, in Westmoreland

GEORGE WASHINGTON

County, Virginia, the eldest son of Augustine Washington and his second wife, Mary. Large landowners, the family members were part of the colonial aristocracy. Upon his father's death, young George went to live with his elder half brother, Lawrence, at his large country estate of Mount Vernon.

Although he had little formal schooling, he was well-read for the time in agriculture, military history, geography, and composition. Simple mathematics and surveying were other skills he developed as he grew tall and strong. Moreover, he possessed high qualities of discipline, aristocratic and moral responsibility, and strength of character. He was also a superb horseman and excelled in the varied sports that young men of the planter society enjoyed. At the age of seventeen, he was appointed surveyor of Culpepper County, and at twenty-one he was commissioned a major and adjutant in one of Virginia's districts. After his earlier service on the Indian frontier, he wound up in the French and Indian fracas in the present-day Pittsburgh area.

His half brother, Lawrence, died in 1752, and Washington inherited Mount Vernon. In 1759 he married the wealthy widow and large landowner Martha Custis. The marriage, along with a remarkable rise in the price of tobacco, made him one of the wealthiest men in Virginia. His interest and success in agriculture would follow him the rest of his life. By the early seventies, he'd served in the Virginia House of Burgesses and then, in 1774 and the following year, as a delegate to the First and Second Continental Congresses.

He was ready when the call for his greatest duty came.

As the fighting around Boston enflamed the colonies, he took command of the fledgling and makeshift Continental Army. It would prove the most daunting challenge of his life. After early defeats by a superior British army in the New York and New Jersey areas, his ragtag army retreated into Pennsylvania. But on Christmas night 1776, he executed a daring and brilliant move.

The general's surprise attack on the enemy Hessians in Trenton early the next morning was immensely successful. He had not a single casualty. A week later he defeated the British at Princeton, restoring American morale and bringing him much-needed recruits. But the following winter saw Washington at his lowest point as he tried to keep his ragged army together in the harsh weather of Valley Forge. Often using his own money to keep the army supplied, he spent the next three years avoiding major battles against superior forces. It was the only way his small force could survive. The entry of France in the war, on land and mainly on the sea, gave him the strength that led to the last decisive battle of the Revolution—Yorktown.

Although it took two more years for Britain to recognize American independence, the new country had become a viable entity in the world of nations.

Washington's contributions to this war, not to mention his far-seeing brilliance as the first president, were remarkable. He learned his generalship quickly and became the equal of the British professionals. At a time when civilian volunteers could leave him and go home at the drop of a hat, he created and maintained an army that knew how to slug it out and win. Tactically, he was often brilliant, but above all, he never lost the respect of his men.

Washington was simply the father of our youthful country.

The term *heroic* can be applied to something grand, something impressive in size or scope. As many who have seen it know, the huge painting *George Washington Crossing the Delaware*, by Emanuel Gottlieb Leutze, that hangs in New York's wonderful Metropolitan Museum of Art, is heroic in many ways. Its size (12' × 21'), the commanding depiction of Washington standing in the lead boat as his small army makes its way through ice cakes, and the sheer manner in which it overpowers the gallery in which it hangs, join to create one of the most memorable paintings in American history.

An Average Soldier

> *Whatever courage is in the heart of a man, whether from*
> *nature or from habit, so much will be shown by him on the field.*
> —Cataline (62 BC), Roman politician and
> conspirator against the Republic who died
> in battle shortly after this speech to his soldiers

Before we depart from the Revolutionary War, let's look at an average soldier. Let's say he was a farmer from Pennsylvania named Caleb Brown. At age twenty-eight, he was married with a wife and three children. His mother also lived with him. When he was a boy, Caleb had helped clear the land of his farm with his now-deceased father. He needed to work long hours in the fields, planting or harvesting, and caring for his animals, just to eke out a living. To him, King George was a distant tyrant who had little effect on him or his way of life. Yet Caleb Brown believed in the liberty that the struggle against Britain promised. He believed in this Cause so much that he answered the call to arms and went to serve as a soldier with General Washington. He could shoot a musket well, and he could ride a plough horse. Surely, he could be a soldier.

The problem was, could his family make it without him? He would try it, and if it didn't work out, he could always walk home. After all, he was a Pennsylvanian, not a citizen of a *real* country, and he didn't know if he had the stomach to be a soldier.

How many Caleb Browns were there in the Continental Army in its six-and-a-half years of war for independence? Thousands. There were also many other young men with home responsibilities who answered the call to arms. They came from other colonies; they lived in the cities, and they lived in small towns.

How many of them were heroes? Many, if not most. What fortitude was necessary to face the cold steel of a battle-hardened, red-coated British infantry square with bayonets fixed? What grit did it take to stay at frigid Valley Forge with feet wrapped in rags, when a home fire beckoned? What mettle was required to fight the renowned and awesome British navy as a seaman on a ship's foredeck raked with fire? What backbone allowed a man to follow the Swamp Fox in his raids? Without these Caleb Browns, whose daily acts of heroism aren't recorded, there would be no American heritage, and most probably George Washington would be no more well known than any other rich Virginian.

They were the forebears of untold numbers of American heroes to follow.

CHAPTER TWO

THE WAR OF 1812

ENOUGH IS ENOUGH

And I heard the voice of the Lord say, "Whom shall I send, and who shall go for us?" Then I said, "Here I am. Send me."
—Isaiah **6:8**

Whether she was smarting from the fact that the rebellious colonies in America had won their war of independence, or whether mighty Britannia just wanted to entice the still-infant United States into another war, she began overt acts of aggression on the high seas such as the impressment of seamen of British origin. By stopping American merchantmen, the Royal Navy impressed, or forced the service of, nearly ten thousand US citizens in the decade before 1812. Finally President James Madison reluctantly banned trade with England.

In the meantime, the 1810 congressional elections had brought an energetic group of young men to Washington. Known as the "war hawks," they included John Calhoun, Henry Clay, and Felix Grundy. They wanted more land for settlement in the West and the annexation of Florida from English ally Spain, as well as the upholding of American honor against British maritime insults. They called for war with Britain. On June 18, 1812, they got their wish.

But let's pause a moment to look at these "war hawks."

John Caldwell Calhoun (1782–1850) was an American statesman and political philosopher. From 1811 until his death he served in the federal government, successively as congressman, secretary of war, vice president, senator, secretary of state, and again as senator. Always he was at the heart of the issues of his time, notably the conflict over slavery. Loyal to his nation, to his state of South Carolina, and, above all, to his principles, he sought to preserve the Union while advancing Southern interests. He was a proud American who, just before the War of 1812, thought of his country first.

Henry Clay (1777–1852) lost his bid for the presidency in 1824, 1832, and 1844. He was one of the most popular and influential political leaders in American history. He became known as "The Great Pacificator" for his skills of compromise. But in 1811, he sided strongly with Calhoun in bearding the British lion. But before the conflict was over, he negotiated the Treaty of Ghent that ended the war.

The third war hawk was Felix Grundy (1777–1840), the lesser-known of the three leading proponents of war with Britain. After a successful early career in Kentucky, Grundy (who was the same age as Clay) moved to Tennessee and was elected to Congress in 1811.

What made these three young leaders so fervently demand this war? My assumption is this: the recent revolution had created a rich democratic country, and in the breast of many young boys of the time was a thump of great pride. Patriots were heroes to them, and the first flag of our country depicted a snake with the slogan "Don't Tread on Me" emblazoned on its fabric. Three of these young boys were our war hawks. Nationalism drove them. The word wouldn't be invented for a couple more decades, but that was it—*nationalism.* This new pride in country would cloak the fires of war in different ways for the next two centuries. But we are straying…

Back to the war…

Following early American defeats, Commodore Oliver Hazard Perry gave the country's morale a shot in the arm in September of 1813. Perry, a Rhode Islander and the oldest son of a US Navy captain, signed on to his father's frigate as a midshipman when he was fourteen. Three years later, he was commissioned a lieutenant and served in the Mediterranean against the Tripoli pirates. After being given command of the schooner *Nautilus* (twelve guns) when he was barely twenty, he returned to the United States, where he learned the construction of gunboats and how to fight with them. He was in command of the Newport gunboat flotilla when the war broke out. Ordered to Lake Erie the following February, Perry took charge of the hasty construction of nine ships at Presque Isle (later Erie), Pennsylvania. In spite of a shortage of supplies and shipwrights, as well as officers and seamen, he got his little fifty-four-gun fleet into the water in late summer, but it was blockaded in port by Captain Robert Barclay's British fleet. After helping Colonel Winfield Scott take Fort George (later Niagara-on-the-Lake, Ontario, Canada), Perry returned to Presque Isle and slipped his nine small ships out into Lake Erie.

Engaging British Captain Robert H. Barclay's fleet of six heavier ships that carried sixty-four guns at noon on September 10, Perry led his undergunned command from his flagship *Lawrence*, with twenty guns and an ensign emblazoned with "Don't Give Up the Ship." The phrase was a testimonial to Captain James Lawrence of USS *Chesapeake* heroics. For some reason, the other eight boats lagged behind and the *Lawrence* took the brunt of heavy British firepower. With his ship fast becoming a battered hulk some two hours later, and most of its crew wounded or dead, Perry took to a small boat and moved his flag to the USS *Niagara*. From that nearly undamaged vessel, he renewed the battle, bringing all eight of his remaining ships aggressively into the fight. At 3:00 PM, Captain Barclay struck his colors, surrendering his flagship the HMS *Detroit* and the other ships. The remaining two English warships tried to escape, but were overtaken and commandeered.

An hour later, Commodore Perry sent another of the most famous messages in naval history to General William Henry Harrison, "We have met the enemy and they are ours."

It was the first major American victory of the war, and it kindled a much-needed morale boost for the still-young nation. Perry didn't get enough fighting on his ships, so he went on to lead a charge while ashore with General Harrison's army in the Battle of the Thames River in Ontario, Canada, on October 5, the engagement in which Chief Tecumseh was killed. He was barely twenty-eight years old. Promoted to permanent captain, he received the thanks of Congress and was given command of the forty-four-gun frigate *Java*. It was a few years after the war, in 1819, that he contracted yellow fever on the Orinoco River in Venezuela and died at sea.

One of the Navy's most charismatic, brave, and resourceful leaders had his brilliant career cut short at the age of thirty-four.

WILLIAM HENRY HARRISON

William Henry Harrison (1773–1841) was the youngest son of Benjamin Harrison, a wealthy Virginian and a signer of the Declaration of Independence. He studied medicine in 1790 and 1791, but opted for a military career and was commissioned an ensign in the First Regiment of Infantry. He quickly recruited a company of eighty men, persuading them to fight Indians for a resounding $2 a month. Marching his company westward and on down the Ohio River to Fort Washington (renamed Cincinnati in 1802) the eighteen-year-old made an auspicious start. He later became an aide to General "Mad Anthony" Wayne and was cited for bravery at the Battle of Fallen Timbers on August 20, 1794. A year later, he married Anna Symmes, the daughter of a judge who held title to huge Ohio Territory land patents. The good judge didn't particularly like the young captain's prospects, stating that "he could neither bleed, plead, nor preach, and if he could plow I'd be satisfied." Harrison would prove his impatient father-in-law quite wrong.

After resigning from the Army, Harrison developed farmlands in Ohio and was elected to Congress. He was appointed governor of the Indiana Territory by President John Adams following division of the Northwest Territory. But as white settlement expanded, the hostile local tribes banded together under Shawnee brothers Tecumseh and Tenskwatawa. We must pause here to look at these brothers.

Around 1660, the fierce Iroquois chased the Shawnee out of their homelands in Pennsylvania, southern Ohio, and West Virginia. Branches of the tribe moved west and south. By the turn of the century, the brilliant Tecumseh and his younger brother (who gave himself the name of Tenskwatawa—Open Door) were active in Indian politics. Sons of a Shawnee chief, both would play a major role in developments on the western frontier. Tecumseh was stalwart and noble, a brave war leader and a visionary who saw the value of the numerous bands and tribes gathering together as a great nation. He traveled far and wide, preaching his doctrine that all Indians were "children of the same parents." He was inspiring and persuasive, but he didn't quite sell his dream. Harrison stated that had Tecumseh done so, at another time, he might well have founded "an empire the rival of Mexico or Peru." This is one of his creeds:

> Live your life that the fear of death
> can never enter your heart.
> Trouble no one about his religion.
> Respect others in their view,
> and demand that they respect yours.
> Love your life, perfect your life,
> beautify all things in your life.
> Seek to make your life long
> and of service to your people.
> Prepare a noble death song for the day
> when you go over the great divide.
> Always give a word or a sign of salute when meeting
> or passing a friend, or even a stranger, when in a lonely place.
> Show respect to all people but grovel to no one.
> When you arise in the morning, give thanks for the light
> and for your life, for your strength.
> Give thanks for your food and for the joy of living.

If you see no reason for giving thanks,
the fault lies only in yourself.

Tenskwatawa, on the other hand, was described by Thomas Jefferson as a fraud. He claimed special powers deriving from a vision he had in 1803. He urged that all Indians should discard any white man additions to their lifestyles and return to the old ways. Because he once correctly predicted an eclipse, he became known as "The Prophet."

Harrison went back into uniform and defeated The Prophet at Tippecanoe, near present-day Lafayette, Indiana, on November 11, 1811. As a major general, following the naval victory at Put-in-Bay (on South Bass Island, Lake Erie), he led the American forces at the Battle of the Thames in 1813—the engagement in which Oliver Hazard Perry fought as an infantry commander, and in which Tecumseh was killed.

William Henry Harrison went on to become the ninth president of the United States, but he died from pneumonia after only a month in office.

The forty-five-year-old Tecumseh died bravely, demonstrating his code of valor. He is considered by many historians the greatest of all American Indian leaders.

DOLLEY MADISON

Can the First Lady be a military heroine? Well, the president is the commander in chief of the armed forces, and she's closer to him than anyone. Therefore, she's actually his *aide*, right? Now that we've established that, it's time to introduce the famous Dolley Madison, wife of President James Madison.

Dolley, a lively young Quaker widow from Philadelphia, married then congressman Madison in 1794. During the years of Thomas Jefferson's presidency, when Madison was secretary of state, the vivacious Dolley served as the unofficial hostess at White House social affairs. Jefferson was a widower. (In fact, the term "First Lady" was not used until it was applied to Mrs. Madison at her death in 1849.) When Madison was elected the fourth president of our fledg-

DOLLEY MADISON

ling country in 1809, Dolley quickly became the sparkling center of Washington society.

On August 23, 1814, the War of 1812 was still raging and the British army was closing in on Washington, torches in hand. No American army was close enough to prevent the nation's capital from being overrun. Dolley's letter to her sister, Anna Cutts, on that date best explains the frantic situation at the White House on that day:

> My husband left me yesterday to join General [William] Winder. He inquired anxiously whether I had courage or firmness to remain in the President's house until his return on the morrow, or succeeding day, and on my assurance that I had no fear but for him, and the success of our army, he left, beseeching me to take care of myself, and of the Cabinet papers, public and private. I have since received two dispatches from him, written with a pencil. The last is alarming, because he desires I should be ready at a moment's warning to enter my carriage, and leave the city; that the enemy seemed stronger than had at first been reported, and it might happen that they would reach the city with the intention of destroying it. I am accordingly ready; I have pressed as many Cabinet papers into trunks as to fill one carriage; our private property must be sacrificed, as it is impossible to procure wagons for its transportation. I am determined not to go myself until I see Mr. Madison safe, so that he can accompany me, as I hear of much hostility towards him. Disaffection stalks around us. My friends and acquaintances are all gone, even Colonel C. with his hundred, who were stationed as a guard in this inclosure. French John (a faithful servant), with his usual activity and resolution, offers to spike the cannon at the gate, and lay a train of powder, which would blow up the British, should they enter the house. To the last proposition I positively object....
>
> Wednesday Morning, twelve o'clock.—Since sunrise I have been turning my spy-glass in every direction, and watching with unwearied anxiety, hoping to discover the approach of my dear husband and his friends; but, alas! I can descry only groups of military, wandering in all directions, as if there was a lack of arms, or of spirit to fight for their own fireside.

Three o'clock.—Will you believe it, my sister? We have had a battle, or skirmish, near Bladensburg, and here I am still, within sound of the cannon! Mr. Madison comes not. May God protect us! Two messengers, covered with dust, come to bid me fly; but here I mean to wait for him.... At this late hour a wagon has been procured, and I have had it filled with plate and the most valuable portable articles belonging to the house. Whether it will reach its destination, the "Bank of Maryland," or fall into the hands of British soldiery, events must determine. Our kind friend, Mr. [Charles] Carroll, has come to hasten my departure, and in a very bad humor with me, because I insist on waiting until the large picture of General Washington is secured, and it requires to be unscrewed from the wall. This process was found too tedious for these perilous moments; I have ordered the frame to be broken and the canvas taken out. It is done! and the precious portrait placed in the hands of two gentlemen of New York for safe keeping. And now, dear sister, I must leave this house, or the retreating army will make me a prisoner in it by filling up the road I am directed to take. When I shall again write to you, or where I shall be to-morrow, I cannot tell!

Dolley was able to get safely through to join her husband, and together, from a safe vantage point, they watched their beloved White House and the Capitol burn. Only a severe rainstorm saved the rest of the city. The British, under orders not to hold any territory, withdrew.

Thus, Dolley Madison established her unmatched place in the annals of American heroics, and Gilbert Stuart's great portrait of George Washington survived to see its copies preside over hundreds of millions of students in the classrooms that followed. One can only wonder how many heroic acts were inspired by that portrait.

OLD HICKORY

> *I never had so grand and awful an idea of the resurrection as*
> *... [when] I saw ... more than five hundred Britons emerging*
> *from the heaps of their dead comrades, all over the plain, rising*
> *up, and coming forward ... as prisoners.*
>
> —Major General Andrew Jackson
> describing the Battle of New Orleans

One of the most controversial, irascible, and dominating leaders of our country ever to put on a uniform was the stormy, ever-intriguing Andrew Jackson. He was a giant both in war and in politics. His feistiness asserted itself at an early age, when it was rumored he never saw a fight he didn't like. Born on the banks of Waxhaw Creek on the North and South Carolina border on March 15, 1767, he was the third son of an immigrant Irish family. His father died just before he was born, and his mother raised him, making sure he learned how to read—not a normal achievement in those parts in those days. Shortly after the start of the American Revolution in 1775, thirteen-year-old Andrew served as a mounted messenger and an orderly. His brother Hugh was killed in a skirmish with British sympathizers. When an English force raided Waxhaw, Andrew and his brother Robert were taken prisoner. Assigned to a British officer, young Jackson angered his captor by refusing to shine his boots. The officer struck the impudent captive across the face and arm with his saber— a rash act that would dearly cost the British Empire, for it created in Andrew Jackson a hatred for the English that never fully subsided.

The boys were imprisoned in Camden, South Carolina. When a smallpox epidemic broke out there, Jackson's mother gained their release, but both she and Robert soon died of the disease. Fourteen-year-old Andrew was an orphan, but it didn't deter him. By the time he was twenty he had studied law and was admitted to the bar. Quickly gaining success, he moved his practice to the frontier settle-ment of Nashville, speculating in land and serving as public prosecutor for the western district of North Carolina. He was now tall and slender with the full head of bushy hair that would mark his appearance for the rest of his life.

Here, he fell instantly and madly in love with his landlady's lovely daughter, Rachel. There was only one problem; Rachel was married to a violently jealous man named Captain Lewis Robards. She had, however, left him for the refuge of her mother's house, and as far as the smitten Andrew was concerned, she was available. The handsome and aggressive Jackson quickly won her heart, and assuming that Robards had been granted a divorce by the Virginia legislature, the two were married in 1791. This assumption would cause the Jacksons much grief when it was discovered that Robards's divorce wasn't effective until two years later. Rachel and Andrew promptly remarried in January of 1794. But the unforgiving Robards, and later Jackson's political enemies, charged Jackson with wife-stealing and living with her in adultery from 1791 until 1794. But these opponents ran a high risk by doing so, because any suggestion of sinful conduct by his beloved Rachel brought a thunderous reaction from Andrew. His horsewhip and his dueling pistols administered the retribution. In one such duel, he killed a fellow Nashville lawyer. In another duel, knowing he was outgunned, he calmly took a round in the shoulder as he slowly steadied his aim and killed his opponent.

When Tennessee became a state in 1796, Jackson became its first congressman, and a year later, its US senator. Often critical of Washington policy, he was never a favorite with the political insiders. Money problems brought on his resignation and he accepted a nomination to the Tennessee supreme court, where his homey but respected opinions brought him new fame. His oft-repeated instruction to a jury was, "Do what is *right* between these two parties—that's what the law *always* means!"

In 1802 he was appointed head of the state militia with the rank of major general. But there was nobody to fight with his ragtag troops. In 1804 he left the court to build a mansion on his lovely farm, the Hermitage, a few miles northeast of the growing capital.

As time passed and war clouds formed in 1812, Jackson volunteered to lead an invasion into either Canada or British-held Florida. But the "Virginia Dynasty" remembered all too well his barbs and let him cool his heels. He was finally ordered to lead his command to Natchez, Mississippi, but with no Brits to fight, he soon headed back to Tennessee. His unruly troops proved a problem, but his iron will and strong discipline held them in check. That was when he acquired the sobriquet "Old Hickory."

But he didn't have to wait long before a serious call came. The Creek Indians, allies of the British, massacred some 250 settlers at Fort Mims in the Mississippi Territory in September 1813. Jackson headed for his real war. With a mixed command of mutinous militia, Old Hickory's resolve prevailed and he won several small engagements against the Creeks. Moving over into Alabama Territory, his command, poorly equipped and supplied by the federal government, arrived at a sharp bend in the Tallapoosa River where the enemy Indians had built a powerful fort accessible only by a narrow neck of land a little over three hundred yards wide. In the enclosure itself, large trunks of trees had been placed horizontally on top of each other, with portholes for defensive firing. Between one thousand and twelve hundred Creek warriors defended it.

Known as Horseshoe Bend, the place seemed an impregnable position, but Jackson quickly saw it as just the opposite: a trap. "They are penned up for slaughter," he told a subordinate. After allowing the Creek women and children to cross the river to where they would be out of harm's way, he ordered General John Coffee with the mounted men and the friendly Cherokee Indians to proceed to a ford two miles below the bend. Crossing to the enemy side, Coffee set up a blocking position to seal off the only escape route from the fort. Then Jackson stormed the fort at 10:30 AM. It was March 27, 1814, the worst day in Creek history. Jackson's command totaled nearly five thousand men, and many of them were heroes that day as frontal assaults against the fortress continued for several hours. One of them was a young ensign by the name of Sam Houston—who later became president of the Republic of Texas. In the end, Jackson was right; the Creek warriors were wiped out.

Jackson would exact further pain when he dictated a treaty that forced the Upper Creek nation to cede twenty-three million acres of their land to the United States—one-fifth of Georgia and three-fifths of Alabama.

(On one gentle note that belies Old Hickory's stern reputation, Jackson took a captured Creek boy home with him to the Hermitage and raised him.)

Jackson was now a national hero, and was rewarded with a commission as a major general in the regular army. Given command of the Seventh Military District—which consisted of Mississippi, Louisiana, and Tennessee—he drove back an attack by the British on Mobile in September of 1814. Two months later, Old Hickory was setting up the defenses of New Orleans, preparing for the invasion of a veteran British army and navy force of some fourteen thousand. As usual, Jackson's small army of nearly five thousand men was a hodgepodge of what could be gathered from the supply of manpower that was available. In this case, the militias were supported by the colorful companies of Louisiana, teamed with the First and Second Battalions of Free Men of Color (some six hundred blacks.) In fact, Louisiana was the first state in the Union to commission a black officer—as it authorized, in 1812, black militia units with black line officers.

Added to his Tennesseans and other ragtag units, Jackson had Major Pierre Jugeant's Choctaw Indians. Jugeant, who was part Choctaw, had been raised among them and was a natural to lead them against their longtime enemies, the Creeks.

Another interesting addition to the American force that has been romanticized on film was the legendary Baratarian pirates. Both Barataria Bay and Barataria Bayou are part of the Louisiana coast near the mouth of the Mississippi River—where Jean Laffite and his pirate ships were based. Supposedly Laffite spurned an offer from the British to use his ships in their invasion, an offer that included both a commission in the Royal Navy and cash. He asked Jackson for a pardon for his men in return for supporting the Americans. Old Hickory granted the pardons and Laffite's ships provided both supplies and fire support in the ensuing battles.

And there were several battles. In the first, the British captured five American gunboats on nearby Lake Borgne. The next one, on December 23, took place on plantations south of the city; this one was a bloody draw. On New Year's Day a large battle took place with Jackson winning and British casualties outnumbering the Americans 2 to 1. In the meantime, US and British commissioners had met in Ghent, Belgium, and a peace treaty ending the war had been signed on December 24, 1814. But no one knew it at New Orleans.

"Gentlemen," Old Hickory told his officers, "the British are below the city. We must fight them tonight!"

It was January 8, 1815, and Jackson had emplaced his command on a bottleneck between the Mississippi and a cypress swamp east of the city. Breastworks of logs and cotton bales protected his artillery and the expert Kentucky and Tennessee riflemen in the front positions. The settling of fog over the area was a bad omen to the British. Commanded personally by General Sir Edward Pakenham, the Redcoats marched into the withering fire from Jackson's well-placed fortifications. They reorganized and charged again, only to be cut to pieces. The next wave had to climb over the bodies of their fallen comrades to meet their own American lead. In thirty minutes, the British suffered 2,036 men killed and wounded, Pakenham and two other generals among them. Jackson lost just eight killed and thirteen wounded. The British retreated to board their ships, and the battle and the war were over. It was the worst defeat for an English force since Castillon in the Spanish campaign of 1453.

Of course, Old Hickory went on to become the seventh president of the United States, formulating what became known as Jacksonian politics and founding the Democratic Party. To this day, some staunch Democrats celebrate January 8 as a holiday.

Andrew's beloved Rachel saw him elected, but never got to be First Lady. She died shortly before the inauguration.

CHAPTER THREE

TEXAS,
THEN THE SEMINOLES

THE ALAMO

On one of my numerous visits to the Alamo in San Antonio, I was struck by the thought that no book on our military heroes would be complete without those who bravely fought to the end in Texas's "Cradle of Liberty." Millions of people have visited the Alamo, and millions more know its story, but it never loses its allure.

"Free men of Texas—to arms!! Now's the day and now's the hour!!"

This stirring circular called Anglo settlers to Gonzalez, Texas, where a small army of frontiersmen, farmers, and a few Mexicans started the Tejas war of independence. Led by Colonel Stephen F. Austin, the poorly equipped little force laid siege to San Antonio de Bexar. Early in December of 1835, a deserter informed the Texans that the town could be taken. Forty-seven-year-old Colonel Benjamin Milam sent out a ringing call for volunteers, "Who will go to San Antonio with old Ben Milam?" He was joined by 301 men and they entered the little city just before dawn the next morning. After four days of furious fighting, San Antonio fell to the Texans on December 7, but Ben Milam didn't share in the victory; he'd been killed by a bullet to the head.

When the cheering died down, the rebels realized that a token command couldn't hold the town if the Mexicans retaliated in force. General Sam Houston sent Colonel Jim Bowie to reenforce the small remaining garrison. Bowie was quite a well-known frontiersman, having fought some battles with the famous wide-bladed knife that his brother had invented. A big man and an adventurer, he had settled in Texas in 1828. He had married Ursula de Veramendi, the daughter of the wealthy lieutenant governor of Tejas and Coahuila, and had claimed vast landholdings. He also had become a Mexican citizen. But his beautiful young wife died, along with her parents, of cholera in 1833. Bowie could have remained apart from the revolt, but it wasn't his nature, so he plunged into the early fighting. In January of 1836 he brought a command of thirty men to join the force of about seventy in the Alamo. Soon, he and Lieutenant Colonel William Barrett Travis, a patriot lawyer from South Carolina, agreed to joint command of the small fortress that had been built as a mission in the early 1700s.

On February 8, the famous Tennessean, six-footer Colonel Davy Crockett rode in with twelve of his sharpshooters. A legendary backwoods hero who had commanded a battalion in the Creek War, he was a favorite of President Andrew Jackson. He had served as a Tennessee legislator and three terms as a member of Congress—all with a six months' formal education. Now, at forty-nine, he was about to serve Texas.

The Texans had stepped on the tiger's tail, and General Antonio López de Santa Anna, the president of Mexico, led a large army north to exact vengeance. Arriving at San Antonio on February 23, the Mexican army laid siege to the Alamo. Travis wrote an impassioned plea for reenforcements to "the people of Texas and all the Americans in the world." He stated, "I shall never surrender nor retreat.... I am determined to sustain myself... and die like a soldier."

His only response was received on March 1, when thirty-two men from Gonzalez bravely broke through the Mexican lines to enter the Alamo. Jim Bowie was now sick with what was believed to be a combination of typhoid fever and pneumonia, and was confined to a cot inside the fort. Travis purportedly had given his men an out; he had them formed up in ranks and drew a long line with his saber. "All who wish to die with me," he said, "come across the line—who will be first?"

Every man except two rushed across the line. One of those was Bowie, who supposedly said, "Boys, move my cot over the line."

Santa Anna was tired of being held off. It was time to do away with these upstarts.

The long rifles of Crockett's sharpshooters and some strategically placed cannon kept the Mexicans at a distance until the early morning of March 6, when well over two thousand Mexican soldiers stormed the four sides of the Alamo to the blaring of *"Deguello*—No Quarter!" The die was cast—the 189 defenders met the challenge with glorious, ultimate heroics.

The thinly manned outer defenses were overrun in short order, allowing the Mexicans inside the walls. Travis was killed by a single shot through the forehead near the guns at the north wall. Crockett and his Tennesseans died in the outside breastworks, swinging their long rifles and tomahawks. The defenders turned their guns inward at the attackers, the devastating fire killing them like flies. But the Mexicans' overwhelming numbers could not be denied. It's believed that Bowie fought to the end on his cot, dying, knife in hand, from several gunshots to his head. Finally it was hand-to-hand combat as the remaining rebels reached the chapel proper. There the last of the heroic defenders fell. For moments, the bloody structure was silent, then the victorious yells of the Mexicans pierced the air. The entire battle took about thirty minutes. After Santa Anna entered the Alamo, the bodies of the dead defenders were tossed on a large pile and burned. Some women were spared, including the pregnant wife of Lieutenant Almaron Dickinson. Santa Anna wanted them to spread the word, but the word quickly became something he grew to detest: *"Remember the Alamo!"*

MORE SAM HOUSTON

Exactly three weeks later, Santa Anna covered himself with more dubious glory. At his specific order, 342 American prisoners under the command of Colonel James B. Fannin were marched into an open field at Goliad, some ninety miles southeast of San Antonio, and shot. The bodies were given the same treatment as those at the Alamo—they were heaped into a pile and burned. Word of this infamous act blazed across Texas and a small army of about 740 men was assembled under one of the most interesting of American generals. To understand him, let's go back to the Battle of Horshoe Bend in the spring of 1814.

When General Andrew Jackson ordered the assault on the Creek fort, twenty-one-year-old Ensign Sam Houston sprang upon the parapet, urging his men on. An arrow buried itself in his thigh, but he ignored it, and leaped into the midst of the Indian warriors on the other side. Swinging his saber like a battle-ax, and continuing to bellow at his soldiers, he quickly cleared a space for them to jump into the fray. More than once he nearly fell on his wounded leg as he dodged attacking warriors. Seeing a lieutenant a few yards away, Houston called out for him to pull the arrow out of his leg. The officer jerked on the shaft, but failed to remove it. With his face distorted in pain, Houston growled, "Try again, and if you fail this time, I'll smite you to the earth!"

This time the arrow was jerked free, but the flesh was badly torn and it bled profusely. He had to go back across the breastworks, where a surgeon bound the hideous wound. At this time, General Jackson came up and, hearing the surgeon's quick description of Houston's condition, ordered him not to go over the logs again. But as soon as the general disappeared, the fiery young ensign grabbed a musket and jumped back into the battle.

Later in the day, after the fort had fallen, Jackson asked for volunteers to go after the Creeks who had escaped and were hiding under the overhanging bluffs of the riverbank. Ordering his platoon to follow him, Houston ran to the river's edge. But that was the end of the battle for him. Two bullets crashed into his shoulder, finally putting him out of action.

A huge, handsome man, Sam Houston stayed in the regular army after the war and was promoted to first lieutenant. But he resigned in 1818 to study law and was admitted to the bar in Nashville. With Jackson's blessing, he quickly entered politics and was chosen major general of the state militia in 1821. He was elected to Congress two years later, and four years after that, in 1827, at the age of thirty-four, he became governor of Tennessee. But in 1829, when his wife of three months ran away from him, he resigned from the governorship and went to live with the Cherokee. He was adopted by the tribe and fell in love with a tall Cherokee beauty named Tiana Rogers, the daughter of trader John Rogers. After Houston represented the Indians in Washington a number of times, President Jackson sent him to negotiate with several tribes in Texas in 1832. Houston got caught up in Texas politics and stayed. In November 1835, he was appointed commander of the upstart Texas army—which brings us back to April 21, 1836, and Houston's meeting with Santa Anna and immortality.

Outnumbered over 2 to 1, his 740 men clashed with the Mexican army at the San Jacinto River, near the present-day city of Houston, and defeated it—capturing Santa Anna and his mistress in the process. General Houston suffered a gunshot in his foot in the midst of the battle, but he recovered to become president of the fledgling republic that had gained its independence because of his victory.

When Texas joined the Union in 1845, Houston became one of its first senators. He served in the US Senate until 1859, when he became governor of Texas. He was serving in this office on the eve of the Civil War. While the hotheads around him clamored for Texas to join the Confederacy, the old hero steadfastly refused, insisting that he would not break his oath to the Union. In fact, there is a story that when the lieutenant governor came to plead with Sam for secession, Houston was sick in bed. Hearing the request, Sam turned his face to the wall and lowered his pants.

He was deposed by the Texas legislature in March 1861, and died July 26, 1863...one of the great American heroes.

THE SEMINOLE WAR AND OSCEOLA

The courage of the troops must be reborn daily.
—Field Marshal Comte de Saxe, 1732

There were three Seminole Wars in Florida, but the first one in 1817–18 didn't amount to much. The Seminoles are descended from Southern Creeks, who migrated into the territory in the 1700s, and a hodgepodge of other tribal elements, plus runaway slaves from Georgia. With western Florida territory still under the control of Spain, General Jackson led a campaign into the area to make it a part of the United States. In the process, he destroyed a number of Indian villages and easily overcame all opposition. In 1819 Florida belonged to the United States.

In 1835, when the Army arrived in Florida to enforce an 1832 treaty that required the Indians to move west to the Oklahoma Territory, some rebellious young Seminole leaders had their warriors ready to fight. The most prominent of these was Osceola, who was born in Alabama about 1804, the son of a Creek chief's beautiful daughter. His father is unknown, but he had Caucasian features and was also known as Billy Powell because his stepfather was a Scot named Powell. Realizing that the American Army could never be stopped conventionally, he took his warriors into the Everglades, coming out to strike whites with hit-and-run tactics reminiscent of the Swamp Fox.

The undeclared war actually began on December 28, 1835, when a column of 108 soldiers, led by Major Francis Dade, was ambushed and wiped out by Seminole warriors. Four days later, a column of some 750 men under General Duncan Clinch was attacked by Osceola commanding 250 warriors. Called the Battle of Withlacoochee, it firmly established Osceola's generalship. He stated he would fight the invaders "till the last drop of Seminole blood has moistened the dust of my hunting ground."

Along with other warrior chiefs, he continued to plague the growing US military force. But regardless of his vow, Osceola could no longer accept the constant loss of his warriors so he turned himself in at Fort Mellon (present-day Sanford, Florida) in May 1837. Hearing that US troops allowed Georgia slavers to come into Florida for the purpose of seizing blacks and Seminoles, he escaped and fled back into the swamps, where he continued to fight until he was taken prisoner while meeting Army officials under a flag of truce. He was imprisoned at St. Augustine, then moved to Fort Moultrie, South Carolina, where he died of malaria on January 30, 1838.

He was but one of many of our American Indian heroes.

ZACHARY TAYLOR

Now to the other side. Another hero had entered the stage in the form of Zachary Taylor. A member of numerous distinguished families, some dating from the *Mayflower*, and a cousin of President James Madison and a kinsman of Robert E. Lee, he was born November 24, 1784, and grew up in Kentucky. He was originally commissioned a first lieutenant at the age of twenty-four. He won distinction as a captain for his defense of Fort Harrison in September 1812. With only fifty men he held back a violent attack by four hundred Indians under the command of the famed Tecumseh. For this, Taylor became the first officer in the US Army to be promoted to brevet major. Thereafter his military career was relatively uneventful until he was promoted to colonel in 1832. He then participated in the Black Hawk War (the fracas in Illinois with the Sac and Fox Indians, who were led by a courageous chief named Black Hawk).

Taylor, who soon acquired the nickname "Old Rough and Ready," punctuated his arrival in Florida in 1837 with a Christmas

Day victory over the Seminoles at Lake Okeechobee. This brought him a promotion to one-star rank and command of the Florida War until 1840 (the war would drag on until 1842, and was revived on a minor scale in 1855).

But Taylor had bigger things ahead. Before we get to that, however, this is a good place to mention that one of his daughters became involved with a young officer who would leave an indelible mark on our country, and, for a few years, another country. Her name was Sarah Knox Taylor, but she preferred being called Knox. The year was 1832, the place Fort Crawford at Prairie du Chien, Wisconsin, where her father was the colonel commanding the new and comfortable stone post. She was eighteen, with long blonde hair parted in the middle and falling in ringlets to her shoulders, a tiny Scarlett O'Hara waist, very feminine, very Southern. She also had a mind of her own. The lieutenant was tall and slender, with sharp cheekbones, blond hair, and deep-set blue-gray eyes. He carried himself quite erect with a certain aristocratic reserve. He had graduated from West Point in the class of 1828, one year ahead of Robert E. Lee. It was at a dinner party that Knox and the lieutenant met, a case of love at first sight.

But it was far from love at first sight with Colonel Taylor. There have been many suppositions about why Old Zach, as he was sometimes known, didn't want the young officer for a son-in-law, but an acceptable one is that he didn't want his young beauty marrying a low-paid army officer. Without her father's blessing, young Knox became engaged to the lieutenant, a betrothal that lasted two years. Promoted to first lieutenant and separated by an assignment at another post, in one of his love letters he wrote, "I have kissed your last letter so often, I fear it will whither and fall to pieces.... Often I long to lay my head upon that breast which beats in unison with my own ... look in those eyes, so eloquent of purity and love.... *Adieu ma chere, tres chere amie.*"

They were married June 17, 1835, at the home of her aunt, outside of Louisville, Kentucky. Colonel Taylor and his wife did not attend, although he must have relented, because he sent her a large sum of money a short time later. The happy young couple went on an extended honeymoon, traveling around the country to visit relatives. (The groom had requested resignation from the Army on June 30.) While visiting his sister in Louisiana in September, both he and his bride were struck by malaria. They were nursed in separate rooms, but he heard Knox in delirium singing one of her favorite songs, "Fairy Bells." Realizing that she must be in critical condition, he somehow managed to get out of his sickbed and pull himself to her. A short time later, held in her husband's arms, she died.

He stayed in seclusion on the rough Mississippi plantation his brother gave him for most of the next decade. His name was Jefferson Davis.

CHAPTER FOUR

THE MEXICAN WAR

My wounded are behind me and I will never pass them alive.
—Major General Zachary Taylor

General Zachary Taylor had a relatively quiet few years after his departure from the Seminole War, at least until 1845. He spent a lot of time on his productive Mississippi plantation and still maintained his Army career. In the meantime, political forces, both nationalistic and power grabbers, were at work on both sides of the Rio Grande River. James K. Polk had been elected our eleventh president in 1844, an expansionist who looked with a hungry eye at the territories of New Mexico and California—both huge parts of Mexico that comprised the territory west of Texas and below the Oregon Territory. In 1845, Texas was granted the annexation it had requested and became the twenty-eighth state. Mexico still smarted at losing this huge area a decade earlier, and within its borders a struggle was going on between two major factions desiring to rule. As we all know, wars are often triggered by unimportant factors that could easily be worked out by negotiation. But Mexico wasn't in the mood. Texans had long considered their southern border to be the Rio Grande, but Mexico claimed the land north of that river to the Nieces River and sent troops to the region.

It was time to get Old Rough and Ready out of the cotton patch and back to soldiering.

Brigadier General Taylor was sent with a small army to the contested area near the mouth of the Nieces at Corpus Christi in August 1845, and then in early 1846 to build a fort at what would become Brownsville, Texas. On April 25 a force of some sixteen hundred Mexican soldiers crossed the river and wiped out an American detachment, and the new fort came under Mexican bombardment.

President Polk had his war.

Taylor, marching to relieve Fort Brown with an army of twenty-two hundred, ran into a Mexican army nearly three times its size on May 8 at a nothing place called Palo Alto, and the fur flew. The general, in his report, stated that his artillery, deploying brilliantly, was a major factor in the victory. In reality, the war's first significant hero was Major Samuel Ringgold, a brilliant artillery officer for whom a town in Georgia had already been named. Ringgold had developed tactics for light artillery that took the guns from the constraints of horse-drawn vehicles and made them highly mobile, hence the term *flying artillery*. But let's pause to regard Samuel Ringgold.

SAMUEL RINGGOLD

We learn about Samuel Ringgold from a remarkable memoir that was written by Dr. James Wynne and read by the author to the Maryland Historical Society on April 1, 1847. Ringgold was the eldest son of General Samuel Ringgold of Washington County, Maryland. His mother was the daughter of General John Cadwalader of Philadelphia, who had occupied an important post under George Washington. The boy was born in 1800 and at age fourteen he entered the United States Military Academy at West Point. He graduated number one in his class and was assigned as aide to thirty-two-year-old Major General Winfield Scott, the popular national hero of the War of 1812. After three years with Scott, he served as an engineer officer, then joined the Third Infantry as a captain. He later designed a military saddle for dragoons and artillery that remained in service until its popular replacement designed by Captain George McClellan came along. After being incapacitated by malaria while fighting in the Seminole War, he was assigned to Carlisle, Pennsylvania.

During his recovery, the brilliant officer, now in his forties and a brevet major, went to work developing the flying artillery tactics. Dr. Wynne wrote, "He was tall and commanding, quite spare; his countenance open, frank, and pleasing. His manners were easy and polite … his heart was full of human sympathy."

When Old Zach's army arrived at Palo Alto, Major Ringgold and his flying artillery battery were part of the complement. The action opened at about 3:00 PM with the Mexican artillery opening fire at a distance of a half mile. The barrage was answered by two American heavy pieces, while Major Ringgold took position with his light pieces—bronze 6-pounders firing solid shot and 12-pounder howitzers firing shell—some seven hundred yards from the enemy. He quickly opened fire with telling effect. He often pointed the guns with his own hand and achieved remarkable results. He said, "I feel as confident of hitting my mark as if I were using a rifle."

A regiment of enemy lancers threatened the American right, and Ringgold immediately dispatched two guns to meet the threat. With his remaining pieces, he continued to fire effectively, disregarding enemy counterfire, for three hours. Then a cannonball struck him in the thighs, severely wounding him. But even while one of his officers tried to evacuate him, he was still giving orders, "Never mind me, go ahead with your men."

The brilliance of the artillery that day was the major factor in the withdrawal of the Mexican army, which suffered 320 killed and 380 wounded. Taylor lost only nine men killed and forty-seven wounded. Samuel Ringgold, forty-seven, died the following morning, the first major hero of the war. One can only wonder what contributions that brilliant officer might have made had he survived.

The Toilet Paper Officer

The next day, the Mexican force positioned itself a few miles away at another obscure place, Resaca de la Palma. Taylor again attacked and, after a bitter fight, was victorious. The panic-stricken invaders fled back into Mexico, and when President Polk got the news, he promoted Old Zach to major general.

By September, Taylor's army had been beefed up to six thousand volunteers and regulars and had invaded northern Mexico. One of his mounted units was the First Mississippi Rifles, commanded by—guess who?

When the state of Mississippi was authorized just one regiment, a freshman congressman who had recently remarried and had lobbied hard for the command was elected its leader. Yes, his name was Jefferson Davis. It's not known how warmly Old Zach received the thirty-eight-year-old colonel, but no animosity is recorded. The easygoing general, who seldom wore a uniform and often sat sidesaddle on his trusty horse, Old Whitey, probably knew he was getting a commander and a legion he could count on.

He reached Monterrey, a city of stone in a pass of the Sierra Madres, on September 19, 1846, and found it strongly fortified. Three days later, his soldiers were in the city, battering down doors and tossing explosives inside in house-to-house fighting—tactics that would be repeated in WWII.

Many Americans were not sure Polk's War was justified. One young officer who subscribed to that belief was a second lieutenant in the Fourth Infantry Regiment. He was a quiet young man who usually kept his thoughts to himself. Yet he had a way with animals, a special communion he had discovered as an Ohio farm boy at the age of five. The horseback-riding record he established in his senior year at West Point would stand for a quarter of a century, yet he was unable to get a commission in the cavalry upon graduation. Now in the Battle of Monterrey, his duties were those of the regimental quartermaster, or as he called it, "the regimental drudge and toilet paper officer." He hated it, thirsting to be part of the action, and just the day before had managed to get away from the regimental rear and into the thick of battle. He had replaced the wounded adjutant, and was so capable that the commander couldn't send him back. On this afternoon, following a morning of fierce fighting in the city, the regimental commander's tone was tired as he stood in a doorway looking toward the heavily barricaded central plaza. "God, if those devils only knew how short of ammunition we are, they'd jump over those defenses and wipe us out. And the Third is just as bad off." Turning to his acting adjutant, he said, "Lieutenant, get a volunteer to ride back to headquarters for ammunition." Handing over a hastily scribbled message form, Colonel John Garland added, "And you'd better get somebody who's good on a horse. Those intersections will be deadly!"

"I'll go, sir."

The colonel sighed. "Well, if we don't get that ammunition, I guess I won't need an adjutant."

The lieutenant tightened the saddle cinch. His fine stallion had been killed the day before. "Well," he said softly to the gray mare, "we haven't known each other long, but we're going to make the most important ride of our lives. And you're going to take the brunt of it, pretty girl, because I'm going to be crouched on your side like a scared Indian. You just give it all you've got and we'll get through."

Moments later he urged Nellie forward. Gunfire was everywhere, with soldiers firing into enemy-occupied houses. The din was terrible in the narrow streets. The mare's speed was surprising to the lieutenant. As they flashed through the first intersection, a bullet tore through his right boot. He'd have to get down lower on the left side. Another intersection rushed by, and another. *"Move, Nellie! Atta girl!"* He caught the blur of faces as he roared through more intersections, each filled with a stream of lead that miraculously missed. And all at once, the firing subsided. They were out of it.

He swung into Taylor's command post and jumped out of the saddle, practically landing on a lieutenant colonel. It was Old Zach's chief of staff. "Sir," he panted, "Grant from the Fourth. I have a request from Colonel Garland for immediate resupply of ammunition for both the Third and the Fourth. The situation is desperate!"

The ammunition was sent to the beleaguered regiments immediately.

Yes, the second lieutenant was Ulysses S. Grant, and this was not his only heroic act as a young officer in the Mexican War. After the end of hostilities he received brevets to first lieutenant and captain. We will also hear more of him as this quintessential common man fights his way to command of the Union Army in the Civil War, where he finds some of his finest and most tragic moments—finally meeting the Mexican War's most important hero across a small table in a hamlet known as Appomattox Courthouse.

THE BATTLE OF BUENA VISTA

Taylor and others such as Davis and his lieutenant colonel, Alexander McClung, were also in the thick of it. On September 24 the Mexican commander in Monterrey offered to surrender on condition that his surviving troops be allowed to depart and that an eight-week armistice go into effect. Taylor agreed, eliciting condemnation from Polk. The president had allowed the ubiquitous Santa Anna to return from exile in Havana in hopes that the former general and president of Mexico would be able to bring about a treaty. Now Taylor learned that the general in chief, Winfield Scott, was coming to Mexico with a separate expedition, and that many of his troops would be sent to that command. Old Zach was furious. He now occupied the city of Saltillo, an important crossroads sixty-eight miles south of Monterrey, and had his force beefed-up by the arrival from San Antonio of twenty-five hundred men under Major General John Wool. The new command included a brilliant engineer by the name of Robert E. Lee.

In the meantime, the treacherous Santa Anna saw a possibility to regain his power and popularity. Assuming command of a large army in the south, he learned that Taylor's army was to be stripped for the oncoming Scott, and rushed north to Saltillo to demolish it. On Washington's birthday (that day the American password was "Honor to Washington"), the two armies met at a hacienda called Buena Vista. Santa Anna, with nearly twenty thousand men, sent a demand for the highly outnumbered Americans to surrender. In typical Old-Rough-and-Ready style, Zach replied, *"Tell him to go to hell!"*

The hardest battle of the war was on!

Again, an artilleryman would have a vital impact on the battle. Braxton Bragg, a tall West Pointer from the class of 1837 who had started the war as a first lieutenant and was now a brevet major, was one of the most unpopular officers in the army, but he was an outstanding cannon-cocker. Moving his guns brilliantly during the vicious fighting of the next two days, Bragg, on several occasions, delivered telling blows. Later, he was given high credit and promoted to brevet lieutenant colonel. But on the second day, with the Mexicans creating a near rout among the Americans, a mounted regiment arrived to stop a huge flanking movement by cavalry. It was Jefferson Davis and his Mississippians. Now down to half the number of men who had marched out of Biloxi, the Rifles were excellent marksmen and dedicated to their commander. They slashed into the Mexican cavalry, and played an important role in winning the battle. Davis suffered a foot wound that would keep him on crutches for two years, but he stayed in the saddle until the day's fighting was over. Referred to as "the hero of Buena Vista," he was the toast of Mississippi.

But the man who held it all together was the general with one leg hooked over the pommel of his saddle as he sat nonchalantly on Old Whitey in the middle of the battle. However, Taylor's heroism and great popularity weren't appreciated in Washington. As usual, politics was playing its insidious role. Polk was giving his full support to General Winfield Scott, whose army of nearly seventeen thousand men was headed for a seaborne invasion of Vera Cruz on the Atlantic side of Mexico.

OLD FUSS AND FEATHERS AND HIS ENGINEER

Scott, who was born in 1786, had enlisted as a private in a cavalry troop in 1807. He received an appointment as a captain the following year, and after the War of 1812 started, he secured a commission as a lieutenant colonel. Following several battles in which he was wounded, captured, and released, his brilliance and heroism brought him promotion to brigadier general at age twenty-eight. After his heroics at the Battle of Lundy's Lane (Niagara Falls, Canada), he became a national hero and received a brevet promotion to major general. The ensuing years brought roles in minor hostilities and numerous diplomatic successes, and Scott was appointed general in chief of the army in 1841. Loving pomp, fancy uniforms, and strict military protocol, he acquired the nickname "Old Fuss and Feathers." He was heavyset, with a commanding nose and mutton-chop whiskers, but he was far from a buffoon. He had a brilliant mind beneath his scowl and was not only a great organizer, but a shrewd tactician. And he knew how to use his subordinates.

Well aware of Captain Robert E. Lee's achievements as one of America's leading engineers in the years before the war, he also knew about the officer's brave and imaginative exploits in General John E. Wool's command on its way to join Taylor before Buena Vista. Scott had Lee brought up to join his "little cabinet," a private element within his staff that the general relied on quite heavily. Other members of that enclave were Colonel Joseph Totten, Second Lieutenant George B. McClellan, and other officers whose names would ring out as generals in the forthcoming Civil War. But in the campaign to take Mexico City and end the war, they were Scott's brain trust.

Captain Lee now would be working directly for him.

When the actual invasion took place, Scott, along with Lee, George G. Meade, Joseph E. Johnston, and Pierre G. T. Beauregard, ran close to the shore in a small boat to reconnoiter. A shell from the Mexican fortress landed close to the craft, splashing water on the occupants, each of whom would become a senior general in the Civil

War. We can only imagine how that conflict would have been changed had that round hit the boat!

It would also have had a major effect on the Mexican War.

In those days an engineer officer could be of tremendous value to a commander. He would reconnoiter possible routes of march, evaluate the terrain and disposition of the enemy, determine potential artillery emplacements, and often actually *lay* or place that artillery for its most effective use; sometimes he would build roads and bridges where no other passage was possible. But his highest value was in his analysis of what options lay ahead and his recommendations as a course of action for the commander. A brave and perceptive engineer with remarkable stamina was a gem. Such was Lee.

The Virginian had graduated second in his brilliant West Point class of 1829 with no demerits. There has long been a misunderstanding that he alone was "the perfect cadet." Actually, five of his classmates were also without a single demerit in their four years at the Academy. Upon graduation, Lee chose the engineers as his branch and was commissioned a brevet second lieutenant of that elite group. At the time, West Point was the only engineering college in the country.

Following marriage to Mary Custis, the young heiress of Arlington and a descendent of his hero, George Washington, Lee had a series of military engineering assignments, a stint as assistant to the chief of engineers, and some major civil engineering tours. Now, in 1841 at age forty, the handsome Lee was at the peak of his considerable powers.

The sixty-year-old Scott immediately entrusted him with important missions. Vera Cruz easily fell shortly after the American army landed, then it was on to Mexico City. His first major battle was at Cerro Gordo, a mountain pass in which the Mexican commander, General Santa Anna, had entrenched a larger army that was blocking the American advance. Scott dispatched Lee to determine the best means of defeating the Mexicans. The engineer's numerous actions in the following days of reconnoitering, placing artillery, and leading the flanking force around Santa Anna's left flank resulted in a remarkable victory. Lee received a glowing commendation from Scott and a brevet promotion to major. The army moved on toward the Mexican capital. Lee was conspicuous in three following battles, including the bloody fight for Churubusco. At one point, the engineer was afoot or in the saddle for thirty-six straight hours. Old Fuss and Feathers promoted him to brevet lieutenant colonel.

Ahead lay the battles of Molina del Rey and Chapultepec. At the latter, Lee was everywhere, and at one point went over forty-eight hours without sleep. His many contributions to that victory will never be fully known. With Chapultepec won, Scott rode victoriously into Mexico City on September 14. The war was over. A short time later, Robert E. Lee was promoted to brevet colonel. According to General Erasmus Keyes, "Scott had an almost idolatrous fancy for Lee, whose military genius he estimated far above that of any other officer of the army."

There were other heroes who would be heard from as Civil War generals: Don Carlos Buell gained three brevets to major, Joe Hooker received three to lieutenant colonel. George McClellan, the brilliant and boyish engineer from the West Point class of 1846, advanced to captain, as did U. S. Grant, the hard-fighting quartermaster.

There is little doubt that Robert E. Lee was, overall, the greatest hero of the Mexican War, and the major lessons he learned there would contribute heavily to his often brilliant victories in the Civil War, which was just thirteen years away.

Old Zach went on to be elected the twelfth president of the United States, but he died after less than a year and a half in office. A scandal involving three of his cabinet officers added to his conflict with Southerners over slavery, even though he was a slaveholder himself. Five days after collapsing from the heat at a Fourth of July celebration in 1850, Old Rough and Ready lost his last battle at the age of sixty-five.

Interestingly, his son, Richard, became a heroic lieutenant general in the Confederate Army, the commander-in-chief of which was President Jefferson Davis—bringing the Taylor/Davis entwinement full circle. Richard Taylor later wrote a memoir that brought him praise from noted historian Douglas Southall Freeman as "the one Confederate general who possessed literary talent that approached first rank."

CHAPTER FIVE

THE CIVIL WAR

Breathes there the man, with soul so dead
Who never to himself hath said,
This is my own, my native land!
—Sir Walter Scott, *The Lay of the Last Minstrel* (1805)

PRELUDE

The next decade had its difficult times, as the tempestuous South marched steadily toward secession. At issue were primarily states' rights, tariffs that could protect cotton growers, and that ever-darkening cloud of slavery. What most historians tend to avoid is the *patrone* factor, a way of privileged life in the South. Most of the politicians came from the wealthier class, many of whom were involved in King Cotton—and many of these were plantation owners. The only way cotton could continue to be grown on a large scale was with slave labor. If slavery were abolished, it would mean the death of the system. One must add to this the pride of Southern men, the privileged class who read the books of Sir Walter Scott and practiced chivalry and dreamed of honor and glory.

"DamnYankee" was becoming a single word, and secession was on the lips of many.

Winfield Scott continued as a popular general in chief of the Army, and Robert E. Lee served as superintendent of West Point. In 1853 Jefferson Davis became secretary of war and was instrumental in getting four new regiments added to the Army. One of these was the Second Cavalry to which Lee would later alternate between

ROBERT E. LEE

command and executive officer under Colonel Albert Sidney John-ston. Lee was home on extended leave at Arlington when a young lieutenant by the name of Jeb Stuart brought him a note from the War Department. Some men in Harpers Ferry, Virginia, had seized the federal arsenal and were inciting an uprising of slaves. Rushing there to take command, Lee found it was the infamous John Brown and some of his sons. With Stuart assisting, the little rebellion was soon squelched, and Old Man Brown was later hanged. Lee, as a per-manent lieutenant colonel, soon returned to his regiment in Texas.

South Carolina was the first state to secede from the Union when Abraham Lincoln was elected in the fall of 1860. In the next few months, six more states helped form the Confederate States of America, with the redoubtable Jefferson Davis assuming the presi-dency. The Confederate capital was initially in Montgomery, Alabama, but was soon moved to Richmond, Virginia, some one hundred miles from Washington, DC. The war began when Fort Sumter in Charleston, South Carolina, harbor was fired on by heavy rebel artillery on April 12, 1861.

The United States was about to be torn apart.

The Confederacy had a distinct advantage in that many of the Union Army's leading commanders were Southerners. Additionally, the better horsemen in Dixieland were formed into cavalry units that would wreak havoc on Union infantry. Top leaders, mixed with easily fired-up enlisted men fighting for what they considered to be their rights, under a president and commander in chief who had not only been a wartime commander and hero, but who had several years' experience as a capable secretary of war, made for a young, aggres-sive army in many ways superior to the boys in blue it would face.

General Scott offered Robert E. Lee field command of the Union Army, and while the hero of the Mexican War deliberated, he was finally promoted to regular full colonel. The struggle the patri-otic Lee had over his allegiance is one of the most dramatic an American ever faced. He was a proud Virginian, and when that state seceded, he sadly elected to join the Confederate Army. The heart-wrenching decision, he said, was because he felt he owed allegiance to his state more than the Union. Following initial command in western Virginia, he rose to the rank of full general, was the president's adviser for a short period, then was given command of the Army of Northern Virginia—where he would gain more fame than any other American general except Washington.

The Shooting War

The first major battle of the war took place close enough to Washington that thrill seekers could ride out with their ladies in carriages to get a front-row seat. It had two names: Bull Run and Manassas. Irvin McDowell, recently promoted from major to major general, commanded the Union Army, while command of the rebel army was shared by P. G. T. Beauregard and Joseph Johnston. Untrained soldiers on both sides fought incompetently, but heroically. William Tecumseh Sherman, commanding a brigade, had his first taste of battle. But the man who came to the fore in this battle was a brigade commander by the name of Thomas J. Jackson. Born in 1824, Jackson won brevets to major for bravery in the Mexican War as an artillery officer, but resigned from the Army in 1852 to teach artillery tactics and philosophy at Virginia Military Institute (VMI) in Lexington, Virginia. He was commissioned colonel of Confederate Volunteers right after Fort Sumter was attacked, and promoted to brigadier soon after. At Bull Run, his brigade stood fast at a critical time in the battle when another general said, *"Look at Jackson's brigade; it stands like a stone wall!"* The sobriquet stuck—Stonewall Jackson would become the second-most-revered leader in the Confederate Army after Lee, as well as the general who could best anticipate and execute his commander's aggressive tactics.

GRANT RIDES AGAIN

On the other side of the coin, a nondescript, quiet man with a history of failures and trouble with alcohol had come back into the Army as commander of an Illinois regiment and had soon been pro-

ULYSSES S. GRANT

moted to brigadier general. A West Point graduate of the class of 1843, his life had been difficult since he'd flashed through the bullet-washed streets of Monterrey on a horse named Nellie. His friends called him Sam, and his last name was Grant. Later referred to as a "bulldog," his mind was always geared to the offensive.

In early 1862 he conceived the philosophy of dividing the Confederacy by cutting off its use of two major rivers, the Tennessee and the Cumberland. The Rebels occupied two forts, Henry and Donelson, west of the major supply center of Nashville. He planned to first attack Fort Henry in concert with Commodore Andrew Foote, US Navy, and his four ironclad gunboats. He would then march some eleven miles overland and take Fort Donelson, while Foote moved his gunboats around to the Cumberland River to render support there.

The fifty-six-year-old Foote was a crusty temperance man who had once convinced his entire squadron, off the China coast, to take the pledge of abstinence—in a day when grog was issued! To add to his religious makeup, he was an archabolitionist. But none of these beliefs got in his way as a tenacious, offensive-minded commander, and a perfect fit for Grant.

The other exceptional member of Grant's team was Brigadier General C. F. Smith. Astonishingly, Smith had been a captain, commandant of cadets, when Grant reported to West Point as a five-feet-one-inch, 119-pound plebe in 1839. Grant had been in awe of the tall, soldierly Smith throughout his four years at the Academy, never dreaming that one day he'd be his commander. Smith was born in Pennsylvania in 1807, graduating from West Point in 1825. He was heroic in the Mexican War, earning three brevets to full colonel—later participating in explorations in the West and commanding the Utah Expedition. Lew Wallace, a division commander under Grant and author of *Ben Hur*, described C. F. Smith as "by all odds, the handsomest, stateliest, most commanding figure I'd ever seen." Regular officers considered Smith to be the best all-around soldier in the Army.

Yet, by a quirk, Smith had been delayed in getting his star at the onset of the war, and Grant was promoted to brigadier ahead of him. The unassuming Grant, though quietly sure of himself, couldn't help feeling humble in the situation. Smith, ever the gentleman, shrugged and told Grant he would serve him well. And he did.

☆☆☆☆☆

Back to Grant's river campaign. Fort Henry fell easily, outgunned by Foote's riverboats, but nearly all of the Confederate soldiers escaped to nearby Fort Donelson. Grant found the rebel army of some eighteen thousand firmly entrenched at that position when his army approached. Furthermore, Foote's gunboats were outgunned after coming up the Cumberland River, and the commodore was wounded. With the Navy practically out of it, the rebel fort had to be taken by land. Then the temperature plunged and heavy snow plagued the Union troops. At this point, the Confederates launched a counterattack that gravely threatened the federal right. While Grant was seven miles away seeing Foote, his adjutant, John A. Rawlins, came hurrying in on a lathered horse to inform him of the grave danger. Finding a lull in the battle when he galloped into his headquarters, Grant coolly ordered a counterattack on his right, then turned to his great brigadier to hit the rebel right. The following is excerpted from pages 146–47 in my book *Ulysses*, because it so vividly portrays the heroism that followed:

> General C. F. Smith eased to his feet as Grant reined in. Without dismounting, Grant said, "General, we've nearly lost the right in an all-out rebel effort. I think they've massed their forces there, so your front should be lightly held. You, sir, hold this army's fate. You must take Fort Donelson."
>
> Smith's hand unconsciously stroked the hilt of his saber. His deep voice was emotionless. "Then I'll do it." He turned to an aide. "Get the division in line with a column of regiments to attack at once. Turning back to Grant, he asked, "How bad is it?"

"Nearly a rout, but they've faltered. McClernand and Wallace should be counterattacking with everything shortly. And I've asked for supporting fire from the gunboats, so if your assault is successful, get word to the navy to cease fire."

The old ramrod body seemed to grow even taller as Smith looked coolly at his former cadet. "General, I told you I'd do it. Go on back to your amateur generals and don't worry about this end."

While Grant rode back to supervise the battle on his right, he missed a show that would have stirred the heart of any soldier. Smith rode his spirited mount up a small rise and drew his saber as his lead brigade quickly formed. His voice carried clearly, "Second Iowa, you must take the fort. Remove the caps from your guns, fix your bayonets, and I will support you!"

And with that, the tall, white-haired general raised his saber and spun up the slope toward the forbidding entanglements of felled trees and Confederate trenches. Immediately the Second Iowa regiment surged forward, knowing that their cold steel would somehow overcome enemy bullets. There would be no faltering, no indecision. Old Smithy, in his flowing white mustaches, would see to that!

And see to it, he did. Smith seemed to be everywhere—swinging that flashing sword, swearing, cajoling. Many heard him shout at one lagging element, "Damn you, gentlemen, I see skulkers! I'll have none here. Come on, you damned volunteers, come on! You volunteered to be killed for love of country and now's your chance. *Move your asses and be heroes!*"

Grant had been right; Smith's front was lightly held. But even a small force such as had been left there could be effective behind such fortifications—particularly with shotguns at bayonet range. The sheer drive of Smith's thrust, however, provided the deciding factor. The general was the first through the enemy trenches, almost asking to end his magnificent career in the utmost of glory. Yet, miraculously, he remained untouched as his inspired troops swept on to the edge of the fort, where enemy artillery fire finally stopped the assault. But he had rolled up the enemy right, making Grant's counterattack on the other end a rousing success.

In a war punctuated by heroic leadership, Smith's Donelson attack still lives in history as one of its most spectacular.

The overall Union counterattack sealed Donelson's doom. However, the cavalry command under Nathan Bedford Forrest wouldn't be captured. Then a lieutenant colonel, that dynamic leader led his Tennessee horsemen and some more who followed through three feet of water to fight another day—and many after that.

In another quirk of fate, Simon Bolivar Buckner, the Confederate brigadier who asked for liberal surrender terms, was an old friend who had loaned Grant money when the Union commander was a broke former captain back in 1854. But sternly, Grant replied, "No terms except unconditional and immediate surrender can be accepted. I propose to move immediately upon your works."

One of the most famous dispatches in American military history had just been penned. The Union had the major victory for which it had been thirsting, Lincoln had himself a general who could win, and "Unconditional Surrender" Grant became famous. The president rewarded him with a promotion to major general.

Grant recommended Smith for promotion as well, but it didn't come through until shortly after the white-haired hero died of infection from a foot cut he received going from one boat to another a few weeks later, an ignominious end for such a great man. It is believed by many that had Smith lived, he would have naturally overshadowed Grant and risen to head the Union Army.

SHILOH, BLOODY SHILOH

In the next major battle, the South lost a general who might have overshadowed Lee. The place was called Shiloh, and the general's name was Albert Sidney Johnston.

Johnston joined the Confederate Army with high laurels. Born in 1803, he graduated from West Point in 1826 and fought as a young officer in the Black Hawk War. He resigned in 1834 to take care of his ill wife and be a farmer in his native Kentucky. Following her death, he migrated to Texas and enlisted as a private in the war of independence against Mexico. A year later he was appointed senior brigadier general and later secretary of war in the new Texas Republic. Surviving a wound he received in a duel with a jealous rival, he heroically commanded the First Texas Rifle Volunteers under Zachary Taylor in the Mexican War. He reentered the regular army following that war and commanded the Second Cavalry before being brevetted brigadier general for his command of the Mormon Expedition in 1857–58. When the Civil War broke out, Davis appointed him his second-ranking officer.

Now in early April 1862, with a large army collected at Corinth, Mississippi, Johnston decided to attack Grant's army of six divisions that was bivouacked around Pittsburg Landing on the west bank of the Tennessee River. A little country meetinghouse called Shiloh, never dreaming it would become a famous name in history, stood quietly in the middle of the huge Union campground where soldiers were not dug in and didn't expect a massive attack from three corps of enemy infantry and heavy supporting artillery. Grant himself, hobbling around on crutches, was several miles downriver when Albert Sidney Johnston struck early in the morning on April 6.

The largest battle ever to roar on the American continent was beginning, and heroes would abound.

Brigadier General W. T. "Cump" Sherman, commanding a division, would bear some of the brunt and be wounded as three horses were shot from under him during the day. His aide would be killed right at his shoulder. But he stayed on the field and under his cool leadership, his untried troops managed to hold for hours under intense attack.

Perhaps the most violent and famous part of the daylong battle took place in a patch of woods along a sunken road that would become famous as "the Hornet's Nest," a name applied to the Union position by the Confederates trying to take it. It was a salient that, in spite of heavy attacks, the Union forces managed to hold in the center of the Union front as federal commands on each side of it were hurled back. The heroic Union force there was the 6th Division, commanded by Brigadier General Benjamin Mayberry Prentiss. An attorney, Prentiss had served as an officer during the Battle of Buena Vista in the Mexican War, and had been a militia colonel when the war broke out. He was now forty-three years old. The following are comments from his report of the battle:

> After having once driven the enemy back from this position, Major General US Grant appeared upon the field, I exhibited to him the disposition of my entire force, which disposition received his commendation, and I received my final orders, which were to maintain that position at all hazards. This position I did maintain until 4 o'clock p.m., when General Hurlbut, (on his left) being overpowered, was forced to retire.... General Wallace (W. H. L. Wallace) and myself consulted, and agreed to hold our position at all hazards, believing we could thus save the army from destruction; we having now been informed the first time that all others had fallen back to the vicinity of the river. A few minutes later, General Wallace received the wound of which he shortly afterwards died. Upon the fall of General Wallace, his division... retired from the field.
>
> Perceiving that I was about to be surrounded... I determined to assail the enemy, which had passed between me and the river, charging upon him with my entire force. I found him advancing in mass, completely encircling my command, and nothing was left but to harass him and retard his progress so long as might be possible. This I did until 5:30 p.m., when finding that further resistance must result in the slaughter of every man in the command, I had to yield the fight. The enemy succeeded in capturing myself and 2,200 rank and file, many of them being wounded.

The defense of the Hornet's Nest by General Prentiss and his remarkably courageous men is one of the most heroic events of the

Civil War. It probably did save Grant's Army of the Tennessee on that fateful day.

Meanwhile on the other side of the battle, what about all of the Confederate soldiers who staunchly attacked the Hornet's Nest, hour after hour, and died or were wounded? Certainly, they were heroic. The aggressive Braxton Bragg, who had urged General Johnston not to delay in the attack, was one of the rebel corps commanders. But in mid-afternoon the South would suffer a tremendous loss.

General Albert Sidney Johnston, for some reason known only to him, was using a tin cup to point directions, instead of his saber. Now at a little after two o'clock, he touched the tips of several bayonets with it as he leaned down from the saddle to speak to a group of dazed soldiers who had just been repulsed in an attack. "Men, they're stubborn. We must use the bayonet. These must do the work."

The Southern soldiers had just tried to take a strongly held peach orchard on the flank of the still-defiant "Hornet's Nest." The general had been personally involved in the battle all day long. Now, as anyone who knew anything about the great officer would expect, Johnston rode in front of the line of battle, stood tall in the stirrups, waved his hat, and shouted, *"I will lead you!"*

His uniform was torn in several places and the sole of one of his boots flapped loosely where a federal minié ball had struck it. His teeth flashed in a grin beneath his sweeping dark mustache. This was the epitome of leadership. The Confederates cheered, let out their yells, raised their flags, and stormed through heavy fire to the objective. Before long, Johnston watched proudly and quietly as the men he'd just led exulted in having taken the withered peach orchard.

Suddenly, his aide saw him sway in the saddle. "General—are you all right?" he cried out.

Johnston clutched his right thigh and leaned low over the pommel. The aide guided his horse close and held the general. "What is it, sir? Where are you hit?"

Johnston's eyes fluttered as he lost consciousness. *"Sir!"* the aide cried. "General, don't—" He leaped down from his horse and eased his commander to the ground. Frantically feeling around for a wound, he suddenly noticed a wide stain of blood spreading above the general's right boot. Moments later he found the wound, a bullet hole inside the thigh that had severed the femoral artery. Blood was gushing out with each pump of the heart, and the aide didn't know how to stop it. *"Help!"* he screamed, but the gathering soldiers just stared. Not a one knew how to apply a tourniquet. The gallant Texan's life was spilling out on the ground in a pool of crimson, and his staff doctor was a thousand yards away, attending to some wounded Yankee prisoners. Just thirty minutes earlier, Johnston had ordered him to stay with them.

It didn't take long.

A colonel from his staff arrived and knelt over the general. "O, my God, General don't... Oh, hang on, hang on!" He wiped a tear from his eye. "We need you too much, sir. Don't leave us."

But Albert Sidney Johnston couldn't hear him.

He was dead.

General Pierre Beauregard assumed command, but by sunset Grant had marshaled his forces and Union reenforcements were arriving. The Southern army had lost its opportunity and would have to retreat to Corinth after heavy fighting the next morning. One bright spot for the Rebels was the masterful way Forrest's cavalry fought as a rear guard. We'll hear more of Nathan Bedford Forrest later.

While Grant began the long and difficult campaign to capture Vicksburg and permanently take the Mississippi Run away from the Confederacy, Major General George B. McClellan, the boy wonder of the Mexican War, had assumed command of the huge Army of the Potomac in the East, and had been appointed general in chief of the army when Old Fuss and Feathers Scott retired. But when he finally did decide to fight, he was no match for what would face him. After Confederate general Joseph E. Johnson was wounded at the Battle of Seven Pines in Virginia in June of 1862, full general Robert E. Lee stepped into a limelight he would never escape. Lee, with his great subordinate generals, and his brilliant tactical mind, would prove the master of battle in the East, excluding Gettysburg, until Grant finally outlasted him near Richmond.

STUART AND MOSBY

Now for some more of the many heroes of the war that tore the heart out of America. Unfortunately, little has been recorded about the enlisted men who did so much. The leaders got the glory. John Ewell Brown "Jeb" Stuart, who accompanied Lee to Harpers Ferry to put down John Brown's little rebellion, took the reins of a cavalry command and soon rose to lead a cavalry corps. With his bushy red beard, the black plume in his hat, and a flair for the dramatic, the powerful Jeb was designated "the Knight of the Golden Spur" by one female admirer. And from that day on, he often wore golden spurs. He had his own banjo player, and once rode completely around McClellan's army with one other man of note—the famous John Singleton Mosby. Mosby, known as the "Gray Ghost," created great havoc behind Union lines with his famous rangers for the last three years of the war.

A lawyer, Mosby enlisted in the rebel army as a twenty-eight-year-old private and became a scout. Before long, Jeb got him a commission. Mosby showed remarkable courage and resourcefulness in unconventional operations and rose quickly in rank to colonel commanding partisan troops. He is considered the first modern leader of guerrilla special forces. To some he was ruthless, to most, imaginative. He caused Union commanders no end of worry in wondering where he would strike next. It will never be known how many federal troops were frozen in place to counteract what Mosby *might* have done. One belief was that the war might have ended some part of a year earlier were it not for his exploits. (I cast him as my protagonist and chief of Confederate intelligence in my novel *Gray Victory*, the 1988 "what if" in which the South has won the war.) Here are some excerpts from his autobiography.

We were incorporated into the First Virginia Cavalry, which Stuart had just organized, now on outpost to watch Patterson. I had never seen Stuart before, and the distance between us was so great that I never expected to rise to even an acquaintance with him. Stuart was a graduate of West Point and as a lieutenant in Colonel Sumner's regiment, the First Cavalry, (before the war) had won distinction and had been wounded in an Indian fight. At the beginning of the war he was just twenty-eight years old. His appearance—which included a reddish beard and a ruddy complexion—indicated a strong physique and great energy....

In his work on the outposts Stuart soon showed that he possessed the qualities of a great leader of cavalry. He never had an equal in such service. He discarded the old maxims and soon discovered that in the conditions of modern war the chief functions of cavalry are to learn the designs and to watch and report the movements of the enemy....

In June, 1862, McClellan was astraddle of the Chickahominy; his right rested on the Pamunkey, but there was a gap of several miles between his left and the James. The two armies were so close to each other that the cavalry was of little use, and it was therefore kept in the rear. [This was when Mosby was still a private, and a scout.]

John Singleton Mosby, letter to his wife (June 16, 1862):

I returned yesterday with General Stuart from the grandest scout of the war. I not only helped to execute it, but was the first one who conceived and demonstrated that it was practicable. I took four men, several days ago, and went down among the Yankees and found out how it could be done. The Yankees gave us a chase, but we escaped. I reported to General Stuart, suggested his going down, he approved, asked me to give him a written statement of the facts, and went immediately to see General Lee, who also approved it.

We were out nearly four days, rode continuously four days and nights, found among the Yankee camps and sutlers' stores every luxury of which you ever conceived. I had no way of bringing off anything. General Stuart gave me the horses and equipments I captured. What little I brought off is worth at least $350. Stuart ... told me before this affair that I should have a commission, on returning yesterday he told me that I would have no difficulty in doing so now.

I met Wyndham Robertson on the street to-day. He congratulated me on the success of the exploit, and said I was the hero, and that he intended to write an account of it for the papers. ... Stuart's name is in every one's mouth now. I was in both cavalry charges, they were magnificent. ... I have been staying with General Stuart at his headquarters. ... Richmond in fine spirits, everybody says it is the greatest feat of the war. I never enjoyed myself so much in my life.

This referred to Stuart's famous and audacious ride around McClellan's Army of the Potomac in which he destroyed considerable property, captured prisoners, and generally altered the Union general's plans.

James "Jeb" Stuart commenting on John Singleton Mosby's success in capturing Brigadier General Stoughton (March 12, 1863):

Captain John S. Mosby has for a long time attracted the attention of his generals by his boldness, skill, and success, so signally displayed in his numerous forays upon the invaders of his native soil. None know his daring enterprise and dashing heroism better than those foul invaders, those strangers themselves to such noble traits.

His last brilliant exploit—the capture of Brigadier-General Stoughton, USA., two captains, and thirty other prisoners, together with their arms, equipments, and fifty-eight horses—justifies this recognition in General Orders. This feat, unparalleled in the war, was performed in the midst of the enemy's troops, at Fairfax Court House, without loss or injury. The gallant band of Captain Mosby shares his glory, as they did the danger of this enterprise, and are worthy of such a leader.

Following the war, John Singleton Mosby supported U. S. Grant in his two presidential election campaigns, much to the chagrin of many Southerners, and served as US Consul to Hong Kong, 1878–85, and assistant US attorney, 1902–10. He died, remarkably, on Decoration Day (now Memorial Day) 1916 at the age of eighty-three.

John Ewell Brown Stuart is considered one of the greatest of American cavalry leaders. Daring and flamboyant, he became Lee's right arm in collecting intelligence and in leading his cavalry in battle. He was promoted to major general in July 1862. He was shot in close combat at the Battle of Yellow Tavern in May 1864 by one of Custer's cavalrymen, and died the next day at the age of thirty-one. Strangely, it was on the second day of the Battle of Gettysburg, when a brand-new brigadier general threw his Michigan brigade into Stuart's cavalry and thwarted him from making an impact on the battle. His name was George Armstrong Custer. He had long, golden curls, and he was twenty-three years old. He had been promoted from captain to brigadier, skipping three ranks, less than two weeks earlier. He had barely graduated at the bottom of his class of '61 at West Point, had won the hand of a vivacious and beautiful girl in Monroe, Michigan, and often wore an audacious uniform of black velvet. But it suited his persona of a *beau sabreur* cavalryman. In fact, as the darling of the media, he was referred to, as his fame grew, as the American Murat. Utterly fearless, Custer always led from the front, and almost always took his objectives. He was just under six feet tall, and weighed a hard 170; he thought himself indestructible. Eleven horses were shot from under him. His commands suffered heavy casualties, but his men adored him. His boss, Philip Sheridan, the Union cavalry corps commander, also adored him...mostly because they seemed cut from the same cloth when it came to combat. Little Phil also adored Libbie Custer and later gave her the desk that Grant used to sign the armistice at Appomattox.

George Armstrong Custer was conspicuous in all battles in which he was involved, but was specifically cited and brevetted for five major engagements. He became the Third Cavalry Division commander in October 1864, and led it to Appomattox, where he was one of the generals present in the small upstairs parlor where Lee surrendered his army. He was promoted to major general at the age of twenty-five.

Before we get very far away from "Little Phil" Sheridan, let's

GEORGE ARMSTRONG CUSTER

review his heroics. First of all, he was a banty black Irishman, short, feisty, and another natural cavalry leader at a time when the horseman's role was at its zenith. It took the belligerent Sheridan five years to graduate from West Point, and he was a second lieutenant for some seven years. He was a captain obsessed with the cavalry's role when he first came to Grant's attention. Soon he was a successful regimental commander, but before the eagles learned how to nest on his shoulders, he was given a brigade. Thirty-five days later, he pinned on a star, and was given command of a division, and before the year was out, he was a major general having won distinction in three major battles. In the fall of 1863 at Chattanooga, Tennessee, he led the charge up Missionary Hill that sent General Braxton Bragg reeling (yes, *that* Braxton Bragg, now a full general). His victories as an army commander in the Shenandoah Valley, Virginia, the following year, when he was thirty-three, were legend. At the Battle of Cedar Creek, Virginia, he returned from Washington to find his army in full retreat. Leaving the town of Winchester, waving his trademark little round hat and shouting encouragement, he personally turned his command around and forged a victory from sure defeat. The victory was a strong factor in Lincoln winning reelection in 1864, and in saving the Union. That magnificent accomplishment on his horse, Rienzi, was immortalized in a poem, "Sheridan's Ride," by Thomas Buchanan Read. The horse's name was changed to "Winchester," and, stuffed, he stands proudly in the American History Museum of the Smithsonian greeting millions of visitors to this day. Sheridan eventually succeeded General Sherman as commander in chief of the Army, but shortly after getting his fourth star, he died at the age of fifty-eight.

☆☆☆☆☆

We can't leave the cavalry without discussing one of the greatest natural cavalry leaders of any time or place in history. Barely literate, but an astute businessman who had accumulated over 1.5 million dollars by the time the war broke out, Nathan Bedford Forrest enlisted as a forty-year-old private and by the time the conflict ended, held the rank of lieutenant general. Shortly after enlisting, he recruited and took command of a cavalry battalion and used his own money to outfit it. In fact, he financed many of the needs of all of his commands, and at war's end he was broke. Tall, lean, and strong, Forrest executed classic maneuvers with his commands without ever knowing the terms describing them. He was quite simply a brilliant, natural leader who fought by instinct. And like Jeb Stuart, Philip Sheridan, and George Custer, he was fearless, always leading from the front. One story that any soldier can appreciate involves a river crossing his troops were trying to make. One of his artillery pieces was stuck in the mud, and Forrest was down in the water with its crew trying to dislodge it. Spotting a huge private sitting up on the riverbank watching, the general ordered him to come down into the water and help. When the big oaf refused, Forrest stormed up the bank, picked him up by the scruff of the neck, and threw him into the river. Operating often in his home state of Tennessee, he was the scourge of Union commanders. On more than one occasion, he charged federal positions alone and bluffed his way to victory. Once, when he was a two-star general, he told the troublesome General Braxton Bragg to kiss his ass, and stormed away knowing he was too important to be court-martialed. His heroics could fill a book, which they have. One of the best is *That Devil Forrest*, by John A. Wyeth. But this remarkable general's reputation is clouded by today's political correctness. On April 12, 1864, Forrest attacked Fort Pillow, a Union earthworks sixty miles north of Memphis on the Mississippi that was manned by over five hundred federal soldiers, about half of whom were Negroes. Forrest's command of about twenty-five hundred soon surrounded the fort in sharp fighting and he requested unconditional surrender. The surviving commander, an inexperienced young major, requested an hour to make his decision. Forrest offered him twenty minutes, which the Union commander refused. When the remainder of the Union troops rushed toward the landing, the

Rebels opened fire, killing many of them. Some two hundred of the dead were blacks. Following twisted facts by a biased congressional investigation, the battle was forever known as the Fort Pillow Massacre. Added to this, after the war Forrest helped found the Ku Klux Klan, from which he soon divorced himself. None of this, however, detracts from his record as one of America's bravest military heroes.

DRUMMER BOYS

> *On Shiloh's dark and bloody ground,*
> *The dead and wounded lay.*
> *Amongst them was a drummer boy,*
> *Who beat the drums that day.*
> *A wounded soldier held him up—*
> *His drum was by his side.*
> *He'd clasped his hands, then raised his eyes,*
> *And prayed before he died.*
> —Will S. Hays, "The Drummer Boy of Shiloh" (1863)

Now it's time for some little heroes, well, at least some young ones. It is reported that some forty thousand drummer boys beat cadence and orders in the Union Army. This seems exaggerated, but anything close to that number is amazing. More thousands served aboard ships, and were used to carry powder from storage areas to guns; thus their nickname: "powder monkeys." Much to the consternation of their mothers, boys were always begging to go along with units that were raised in local areas. Yielding to the pleas of a "bright little negro boy," the Second Ohio Infantry took him along to the Battle of First Bull Run, and before that fight was over, the little rascal was firing a musket "brave as the bravest."

The story of Private John W. Morgan as told by Helen Marie Melly More provides a good picture of what being a drummer boy in the Union Army was all about (it wasn't much different in the

Confederate Army). Morgan was older than many drummer boys—fifteen—when he enlisted in the 104th Ringgold Infantry Regiment just before Christmas in 1861. (The name "Ringgold" pops up again!)

> John Hargrave, the 104th drum major, took the drummer boys in hand, teaching them the manipulations of the fascinating drumsticks. All in due course...the rhythmic beating would set the marching pace and in trying times, bring cheer and boost the morale. The drums were heavy and the barrels of the regulation drums were too long for many of the boys to be able to carry them clear of the ground. Later, Colonel W. W. H. Davis (the regimental commander) won the hearts of the boys when he went to Philadelphia and ordered smaller drums for his smaller boys, of which John Morgan was one....
>
> John Morgan's prize possession was his drum, "I love it, though I recall to this day the over tired muscles after a long day's march over Northern fields and Southern miles, scorching sun and blinding storms, when the drum grew heavier and heavier until it took all the grit a fellow had, not to let the others know just how near a body came to collapsing. Then someone would shout, 'Lively there, boys!' and then the little fellows went at it with renewed vigor."

In addition to his adroit handling of the drumsticks, Private Morgan used his fine penmanship to sign discharges within his company. He signed his own in 1865.

Probably the most well known of the drummer boys was Johnny Clem. At the age of nine, he ran away from home and tried to enlist with the Third Ohio. The commander told him he wasn't enlisting "infants," so Johnny hightailed it over to the Twenty-second Michigan, where he got roughly the same response. But he tagged along with the Wolverines anyway, performing camp duties and finally getting a drum. At the Battle of Shiloh, his drum was smashed by an artillery round and he acquired the nickname "Johnny Shiloh." Later, at the Battle of Chickamauga that took place on the Tennessee-Georgia border September 19–20, 1863, tiny Johnny carried a musket trimmed down to match his size, as he rode an artillery caisson into battle. At one point, a Confederate officer was purported to have run after Clem's caisson shouting, *"Surrender, you damned little Yankee!"* Clem coolly killed him.

Now known as the famous "Drummer Boy of Chickamauga," Johnny served as a courier throughout the rest of the war, getting wounded twice. When the hostilities ended, Johnny applied for West Point, but was turned down because of educational deficiency. However, a personal appeal to President U. S. Grant got him a commission as a second lieutenant in the Regular Army in 1871. Now the story gets even more incredible—in 1903 he became the assistant quartermaster general of the Army, and in 1916 he retired as a *major general*, the last Civil War veteran on active duty! He died in San Antonio in May 1937 at the age of eighty-five.

So much for running away from home with a pair of drumsticks.

THE MEDAL OF HONOR

The Medal of Honor was the first military decoration authorized by the US government to be worn as a badge of honor. It was created by an act of Congress in December 1861 to be given to naval personnel for acts of bravery, imitating Britain's Victoria Cross and Germany's Iron Cross. Its first authorization was for enlisted men of the Navy and Marine Corps, then for enlisted men of the Army. Fifteen months later, Army officers were made eligible—although, strangely, Navy and Marine officers had to wait until 1915. In the Army, the criteria was for members who "shall distinguish themselves by their gallantry in action, and other soldierlike qualities"—pretty vague.

The first medals were given for one of the most bizarre of adventures. It is referred to as "Andrews' Raid," but is better known to movie buffs as *The Great Locomotive Chase*, starring Fess Parker. The story begins a year after the medal was authorized.

Washington, DC. March 25, 1863. Six soldiers, their hair long and unkempt while Confederate prisoners, stood before Secretary of War Edwin Stanton in his office at the War Department. The six had just been released in a prisoner exchange after participating in one of the most incredible events of the war. They were mostly Ohioans, volunteers for a mission that took them deep into the South; in time they would be known by another name: Andrews' Raiders.

Shortly after the Battle of Shiloh, thirty-three-year-old James Andrews, a Union spy who had moved boldly around the South, proposed a daring plan that was quickly approved by Brigadier General Ormsby Mitchell. The general would capture Huntsville, Alabama, with his command, while Andrews and twenty-two volunteers from Ohio regiments would take over a rebel train at Marietta, Georgia, and proceed north on the Western & Atlantic Railroad, tearing up track and burning bridges. The raid would enable General Mitchell to then take Chattanooga, Tennessee, with little opposition.

It was an audacious plan, but, with some luck, doable.

With his band of raiders that included several men skilled in handling locomotives, Andrews infiltrated north Georgia, and was in position at a place called Big Shanty, a stop with no telegraph key near Marietta, at the appointed time. When a locomotive known as The General (no relation to Mitchell) stopped so its crew and passengers could have breakfast on the morning of April 12, the Yankees grabbed the train and headed north. When the crew of the soon-to-be-fugitive train looked out in astonishment to see their cars rolling off, conductor William Fuller, engineer Jeff Cain, and another man named Murphy took off running after it. Two miles of chase led to a large handcar and two more railroad men to help pole and push.

Aboard The General, Andrews and William Knight, a young former engineer, stayed in the cab with two other raiders, while the rest of the Yankees fanned out across the commandeered train. Telegraph wires were cut, some rail ties were tossed into the roadbed as it proceeded north, but the rebel handcar wasn't deterred. At

Etowah, conductor Fuller took over the switch engine, Yonah, and charged on. Meanwhile, The General was held up by other northbound trains, so Andrews had his men tear up track behind them.

At this point, less than ten minutes behind the unsuspecting Andrews, Fuller and his men continued the chase on foot until they could commandeer a southbound engine, The Texas, that had come off a siding. Slamming it into reverse and heaping fuel into its boiler, the persevering Fuller made the new chase engine lurch backward up the track in pursuit of the thieves. Andrews was soon well aware of his pursuers, and first tried dropping crossties, then released two boxcars to deter The Texas. But Fuller's men kicked the ties aside and, pushing the cars to a siding, continued the chase. Reaching the wooden bridge over the Oostanaula River, Andrews tried to set fire to the remaining car and the wooden bridge, but all-day rains thwarted that effort.

Now, The General was running low on fuel.

And still the pursuers came on, whistle shrieking.

Fuller had gotten a telegraph message off to the Confederate commander at Chattanooga, and rebel soldiers were headed for Ringgold Gap (Ringgold yet again?) when The General heaved its last gasp there. Andrews and his men jumped off and tried to escape, but within two weeks they'd all been captured. Fourteen of them were sent to Confederate prison. Andrews and seven of his men were remanded to Atlanta, where they received a speedy trial and were hanged as spies. In October, the other fourteen pulled off a daring escape, but six of them were recaptured. The other eight made it to freedom, and the recaptured raiders were exchanged the following spring—which brings us back to six unkempt Union soldiers standing uneasily in Secretary of War Stanton's office on March 25.

Stanton scratched his head and turned to an aide. "Get me those new medals," he directed.

The aide returned in a couple of minutes with a box that held six five-pointed medals attached to light blue ribbons. Stanton pinned the first one on Private Jacob Parrott, the first recipient of the

Medal of Honor. Then he did the same with the other five soldiers, and told them to come with him over to the White House to meet President Lincoln. That set the precedent for the tradition that would begin some fifty years later and continue to the present.

Eventually nineteen of the raiders received the Medal of Honor, including four of those who were hanged. Civilians James Andrews and William Campbell were ineligible. Sergeant William Pittenger later became a minister and wrote an insightful version of the raid. (Another version can be found on the excellent Web site The Home of Heroes, maintained by Douglas Sterner [http://www.homeof heroes.com], at The First Medals of Honor from which I borrowed heavily for this account.)

THE CONFEDERATE MEDAL OF HONOR

A Confederate Medal of Honor never became a reality during the war. Financial problems, married with disagreement, kept it from happening. But in 1896 one of the few living senior officers of the Confederate Army, Lieutenant General Stephen Dill Lee, helped form the Sons of Confederate Veterans to preserve the memory and valor of the Confederate soldier. However, it took that organization until 1977 to bring the medal into being. Even though it was never official by any means, its recipients were certainly worthy. Private Samuel Davis of Coleman's Scouts was the first soldier to be posthumously presented with the Confederate Medal of Honor for bravery at Pulaski, Tennessee, on November 27, 1863. Some other recipients are:

> Seaman F. Collins—Attack on USS *Housatonic* outside Charleston harbor, S.C., 1864
> First Lieutenant Richard Dowling—First Texas Heavy Artillery, Sabine Pass, Tex., 1863
> Sergeant Adam Ballenger—Thirteenth South Carolina Infantry, Deep Bottom, Va., 1864

Father Emmeran Bliemel—Chaplain, Tenth Tennessee Infantry, Jonesboro, Ga., 1864

Brigadier General Richard Garnett—Pickett's Charge, Gettysburg, Pa., 1863

Juliet Opie Hopkins—Nurse, Seven Pines, Va., 1862

Private William Overby—Forty-third Virginia Cavalry, Front Royal, Va., 1864

David Llewellyn, MD—Surgeon, USS *Alabama*, off Cherbourg, France, 1864

Major John Pelham—Stuart's Horse Artillery, Fredericksburg, Va., 1862

Colonel Nathan Bedford Forrest—Forrest's Cavalry, Shiloh, Tenn., 1862

Sergeant Richard Kirkland—Second South Carolina Infantry, Fredericksburg, Md., 1862

SERGEANT KIRKLAND

Perhaps in the whole war, no soldier was ever such a remarkable hero to *both* sides as was Sergeant Richard Kirkland. Having recently transferred from Company E of the Second South Carolina to be First Sergeant of Company G, the nineteen-year-old Kirkland was in the thick of it when Kershaw's Brigade fought in the Battle of Fredericksburg. But let's first set the stage for Kirkland's incredible heroism.

On December 13, 1862, General Ambrose Burnside, who had assumed the reins of the Army of the Potomac from "Little Napoleon" George McClellan when Lincoln finally relieved him, attacked Lee's army at Fredericksburg, Virginia. Encountering stiff resistance by Stonewall's Corps on the federal left, Burnside ordered an all-out attack from the Union right against a hilly area known as Marye's Heights. Before the day was over, no fewer than fourteen Union brigades would try to get over a stone fence that guarded this hill. The gallant assaults of these waves of blue-clad soldiers were continually repulsed by General James Longstreet's I Corps. The federal brigades suffered massive casualties throughout the murderous attack.

The following day the ground between the lines was filled with a huge pile of wounded, dead, and dying Union soldiers from General George Sykes's division of Regular Army regiments. It was a bloody no-man's-land with snipers zeroed in from both sides. Cries from the wounded men split the air, "*Water! God, give me water!*" But no one dared go to their rescue. Enter young First Sergeant Richard Kirkland up on the Heights as General Kershaw was surveying the field below. Approaching the brigade commander, Kirkland said, "General, I can't stand this!"

Kershaw lowered his glasses. "What's the matter, Sergeant?"

"All night and all day I've heard those poor people crying for water and I can't stand it any longer. I came to ask permission to go and give them water."

The general regarded him admirably for a moment, then replied, "Kirkland, don't you know you would get a bullet through your head the moment you stepped over the wall?"

"Yes, sir," the sergeant replied, "I know all about that, but if you will let me, I'm willing to try it."

General Kershaw paused a moment before replying, "I ought not to allow you to run such a risk, but your request is so noble, trusting that God may protect you, you may go."

A short time later, armed with as many full canteens as he could carry, First Sergeant Kirkland edged over the top of the wall. Somehow, the shower of Union bullets that greeted him all missed, and moments later the young Samaritan was gently pouring water through the parched lips of the first wounded Yankee he reached. Putting him in a comfortable position and leaving a canteen with him, Kirkland moved on to the next wounded man. Federal riflemen, seeing what he was doing, ceased firing at him, as he left another canteen with a grateful Yank and moved on again and held a canteen to the mouth of a paralyzed soldier. More cries of "*Water, for God's sake, water!*" arose as Kirkland continued to the next man.

When he ran out of full canteens, he hurried back to the wall for fresh ones, which his eager comrades—who were forbidden to go down and help—handed him. For an hour and a half, the young sergeant hurried about his mission of mercy—until he had given relief to every wounded enemy soldier in his sector. When he finally climbed back over the stone wall, a huge *cheer* went up from the Union line.

But Kirkland wasn't done with the war. He was promoted to lieutenant at the Battle of Gettysburg, and fell on the field of battle at Chickamauga just as a Confederate victory was assured. General Kershaw wrote, "He was but a youth when called away and had never formed those ties from which might have resulted a posterity to enjoy his fame...but he has bequeathed to American youth, yea, to the world, an example which dignified our common humanity."

An excellent statue showing Sergeant Kirkland administering water to a fallen soldier stands at the foot of Marye's Hill, and a museum in his memory is connected to a Civil War library and publishing company bearing his name in Spottsylvania, Virginia.

The Angel of Marye's Heights has not been forgotten.

GETTYSBURG

> *In great deeds something abides. On great fields something stays. Forms change and pass; bodies disappear; but spirits linger, to consecrate ground....*
> —Union General Joshua Lawrence Chamberlain,
> Dedication speech for the Twentieth Maine monument,
> Gettysburg, October 3, 1889

Anyone who has ever read Michael Schaara's *The Killer Angels* or watched the miniseries *Gettysburg* knows of the gallant Joshua Lawrence Chamberlain's contribution on Little Round Top on July 2, 1863. Gettysburg, a sleepy little town in southeastern Pennsylvania, was where the Army of the Potomac, just handed from Major General Joseph Hooker to Major General George Meade, ran into Lee's Army of Northern Virginia on July 1, 1863. Lee was on his way to Harrisburg to strike enough fear into the already war-weary North to hopefully bring it to the peace table with terms favorable to the South—in short, to win the war for the Confederacy. But through a number of blunders, primarily by Lee's corps commanders, Ewell and Longstreet,* Meade was able to defeat the rebels on day three of the battle. Uncharacteristically, Lee himself did not make sound decisions, partially because he was suffering from severe dysentery. On July 2, the southern flank of the Union army ended at the two Round Tops, south of the town. Chamberlain's Twentieth Maine was rushed to Little Round Top as the vanguard of a band-aid effort to stop General John Bell Hood's division from inflicting major damage to the federal left.

Chamberlain was born September 8, 1828, in Brewer, Maine. He graduated from Bowdoin College in 1852. Although his male forebears had fought in America's earlier wars, Chamberlain had little military experience when the Civil War erupted. He soon became the lieutenant colonel of the Twentieth Volunteer Regiment of Maine. He was colonel of the regiment when it reached Gettysburg and everlasting fame at Little Round Top. Although many of his men's enlistments were running out, he managed to lead them in one of the most incredible acts of valor of the war. In the face of hard-charging rebel troops late on that hot July afternoon, with ammunition running out, he knew there was only one thing to do. He ordered his men to fix bayonets and charge down the hill into the face of intense fire. His action held the south face of Little Round Top until reenforcements arrived, and had a major effect on the battle.

Chamberlain fought in twenty-four battles and many skirmishes in the war; he was wounded six times and had six horses shot from under him. He rose to the rank of major general, and was chosen by

---

*See my *Gray Victory*.

General Grant to accept the formal surrender of colors and weapons three days after Appomattox. He chivalrously had his men salute the defeated Confederates as they marched by in that ceremony. General Chamberlain returned home to become governor of Maine, and, later, an innovative president of Bowdoin College for many years.

In 1893 Congress finally awarded him the Medal of Honor for his gallant leadership at Little Round Top.

Tom Custer

For some reason, Civil War heroics seem more vivid than those of other wars. Perhaps it's because new weapons of destruction such as rapid-firing carbines and rifles, better artillery, ironclad ships, the telegraph, and the observation balloon came into play, yet the personal side of combat remained. Capturing the enemy's colors was a major individual achievement, mainly because it meant getting into the well-defended heart of an opposing command, and because those colors weren't given up easily. It was a disgrace for a command to lose its colors. Then there is the aspect of a family feud, sometimes brother against brother, that added to the personal side of the war— and certainly may have had an effect on the number of brave acts.

During our wars, fourteen men have received the Medal of Honor twice for separate actions. One of them was Tom Custer, and who knows if he might not have earned a third at one of the most famous battles in American history? One of the reasons George Armstrong Custer was so successful as a cavalry leader was that he was fearless in battle. Apparently, being in the forefront of an engagement was a family trait. The golden-haired boy general's brother, Tom, was five years younger. At age sixteen, lying about his age, Tom enlisted as a private in the Twenty-first Ohio Infantry in September 1861. He soon became a general's orderly and fought at Chickamauga, Chattanooga, and Kennesaw Mountain in the entourages of several generals.

In October 1864 Corporal Tom Custer was appointed a second lieutenant upon Brother George's request, and soon became his aide. But nepotism in this case would be far from detrimental. In the closing campaign of the war, Custer's division fought at Waynesboro, Dinwiddie Court House, and Five Forks—where Tom had his horse shot from under him. For "distinguished and gallant conduct," Tom was brevetted to first lieutenant, captain, and eventually major. At Namozine Church on April 3, 1865, he led the charge of the Second Brigade, had another horse shot from under him, and captured the color-bearer and his flag, as well as a dozen prisoners including some officers. This action earned him the Medal of Honor.

Three days later, on April 6 at the fierce Battle of Sayler's Creek in Virginia, Tom Custer was again in the thick of it. The rebels occupied a good position with two lines of breastworks. Tom jumped his mount over the first breastwork, and in the face of heavy musket fire, was in the midst of the defenders when he saw the enemy flag. He seized the rebel colors and demanded that the enemy surrender, but the butternut-clad color-bearer shot him through the face from a position so close that Tom got powder burns. Young Custer held on to the rebel flag, drew his revolver, and shot the soldier dead. Racing back to his brother's command post, blood pouring from his face wound, Tom jammed the flag into the ground and wheeled around to return to the fight. But General Custer stopped him by threatening him with arrest. Tom recovered from his wound, with only a small scar as a reminder. For this action, twenty-year-old Tom Custer was awarded his second Medal of Honor, and, a couple of years later, a brevet to lieutenant colonel.

He was the first to be awarded two of the medals.

But the next time he was in battle as his brother's aide, he would not be as fortunate.

Introducing a MacArthur

Flags were important in the Civil War. As evidenced by Tom Custer's exploits, capturing the enemy flag was a major accomplishment. But troops tended to "rally round the flag" and follow it on the offensive side of battle, which brings us to Arthur MacArthur, "Boy Colonel of the West." MacArthur was commissioned a first lieutenant, adjutant of the Twenty-fourth Wisconsin Infantry Regiment, just two months after his seventeenth birthday. Two months later, he was brevetted captain for gallantry at the Battle of Perryville. After two more months passed, he distinguished himself at Stones River, and in late November of that same year, at Mission Ridge in the Battle of Chattanooga. There, he grabbed the regimental colors and stormed up the steep hill, leading the Twenty-fourth Wisconsin all the way to the top in the Union victory that ended Braxton Bragg's command years. He was later awarded the Medal of Honor for that act. Soon he was a major commanding the regiment. He was promoted to colonel before his twentieth birthday. He entered the regular army after the war, and had a long and distinguished career that included the military governorship of the Philippines in 1900. But his heart remained with the Twenty-fourth Wisconsin. Having retired as the senior lieutenant general in the Army, MacArthur was addressing the veterans of the regiment in Milwaukee in 1912 when he collapsed and died at the rostrum. Imagine—he joined the regiment as a boy adjutant, led its members to fame, and died among his old comrades while speaking to them fifty years later. Remarkable!

And, by the way, he had a son.

Chaffee

We just have to mention Adna Romanza Chaffee. Being a soldier with that name alone qualifies a young man for bravery. However, Chaffee, another Ohioan, enlisted as a private in the Sixth Cavalry in June 1861, at the age of nineteen. Soon promoted to sergeant, he served heroically at the Battle of Antietam and was made a first sergeant. In May 1863 Secretary of War Stanton personally granted him a commission as second lieutenant. After fighting with distinction in several battles, including Gettysburg, he got out of the army when the war was over. But it didn't last long. Returning to uniform, he fought in several Indian skirmishes and was brevetted major in 1868. Two more promotions slowly followed. The Spanish-American War brought him a star and he commanded a brigade in Cuba. As a major general, he commanded the US force that relieved the legations at Peking in 1900. *Now comes the big one:* from January 1904 to January 1906, he was chief of staff of the US Army—rising from private soldier to its top post, a remarkable achievement. Furthermore, his son, Adna Romanza Jr., West Point class of 1906, became the Army's brilliant developer of armor, but died prematurely, of cancer, as a major general in 1941. Quite a contribution overall, Private Chaffee!

ADMIRAL DAVID GLASGOW FARRAGUT

This US Navy officer deserves a line of his own. He entered the naval service at nine-and-a-half years of age, and assumed command of a prize ship when he was *twelve.* Adopted by Commodore David Porter, a famous naval officer in his own right, young Farragut sailed with his foster father during the years when an average lad of his age was learning his ABCs. His foster brother was David Dixon Porter, who would also make a big name for himself on the deck of Union ships in the Civil War and later. Farragut had a distinguished career at sea prior to 1861, when he had to make the same fateful decision that Robert E. Lee faced. But the naval officer, then residing in Virginia with his second wife—"a very superior woman in character and cultivation"—decided, according to his words, that he was "sticking to the flag."

In January 1862 Farragut was picked to command a squadron to capture New Orleans, then the biggest city in the South. His fleet consisted of nearly fifty ships of varying sizes and types, carrying some two hundred guns. In a brilliantly planned and executed attack up the Mississippi River, he destroyed the Confederate fleet, captured the Crescent City, turned it over to General Benjamin Butler's army, and further cleared the vital river. After helping Grant in the Vicksburg campaign, Farragut was a famous Union hero. He received the Thanks of Congress citation and was promoted to rear admiral, two-star rank.

He then turned his sights to Mobile, Alabama, but first he took his flagship, the *Hartford*, north for repairs. The big sloop had been damaged some 240 times from shot and shell. Returning to the Gulf Coast a few months later, he was faced with another major test. Mobile Bay was extremely well guarded by two forts, the formidable ironclad ram *Tennessee*, and a field of torpedoes (mines). Undaunted, Farragut lined up his ships and went in. The battle was fierce, with all of the rebel defenses causing severe damage. When the captain of one of his ships complained about the mines in his way, the admiral, who was lashed to the upper rigging of his flagship to best observe everything, barked, *"Damn the torpedoes! Full speed ahead!"*

Intense as he was, Farragut was far from insensitive. With the battle won, and the last major rebel port in Union hands, a ship's officer reported that the admiral, upon seeing the bodies of his killed crewmen stretched out on the deck of the *Hartford*, began to cry, "…tears came into his eyes like a little child."

Returning to New York, the sixty-three-year-old Farragut, who was in failing health, was the biggest naval hero of the war. He was the first officer to be promoted to vice admiral (three stars) and a year later to full admiral. He died in 1870.

One biographer referred to him as "the world's greatest naval commander—ever."

Hood

The gallant rebel General John Bell Hood led his commands strapped to the saddle after losing a leg at Chickamauga and the use of an arm at Gettysburg. At that vital battle in Pennsylvania, Hood struggled with his boss, General James Longstreet, for permission to flank the Union left at Gettysburg on the second day. Had the stubborn corps commander listened, Hood (and his Texans—he always had hard-fighting Texans in his commands) would have torn up the federal rear, Chamberlain never would have gained fame at Little Round Top, and the whole outcome of Gettysburg, and very probably the outcome of the war, would have been different. Hood married after the hostilities ended and fathered eleven children in ten years in New Orleans. He and his wife died within a day of each other after contracting yellow fever in 1879. Fort Hood, Texas, is named for him.

The Red Cross Lady

Clara Barton and many other nurses on both sides were heroic in various ways, not necessarily in combat. But Barton's work was often on the battlefield, where she carried supplies and nursed wounded men. As she attracted more and more attention in the North, she became known as the "Angel of the Battlefield." In the next-to-last year of the war she was appointed superintendent of nurses for the Army of the James.

Clara Barton was born in 1821 in North Oxford, Massachusetts, and was a teacher before turning her interest to the field of health. When the war was over, the forty-four-year-old nurse formed an organization to search for missing soldiers. It marked over twelve thousand graves in the Andersonville National Cemetery in Georgia. In 1869 Barton went to Switzerland for a rest and discovered the International Red Cross. Joining, she went on to the battlefields of the Franco-Prussian War, where she served bravely again. Back home in the States, she established the American Red Cross in 1881. She was its president for twenty-two years. Barton rendered aid in several more wars and disasters, and found time to write a number of health-related books.

She died in 1912. Her thirty-eight-room house in Glen Echo, Maryland, was designated as the Clara Barton National Historic Site in 1974.

☆☆☆☆☆

Now to wrap up some of our threads, General Braxton Bragg served as a personal advisor to President Jefferson Davis in Richmond in the period following his major defeat at Chattanooga. Fort Bragg, North Carolina, the home of the famed 82nd Airborne Division, and the Special Warfare Center, where the Green Berets get part of their training, is named for him.

Jefferson Davis, who reigned over the Confederacy with a certain amount of "imperious temper" as Mark Boatner mentions in his useful *The Civil War Dictionary*, fled from Richmond with his cabinet shortly before its fall in early April 1865. He was captured in Irwinville, Georgia, on May 10 and held as a prisoner for two years at Fort Monroe, Virginia. He was never brought to trial. In his brief history of the First Battle of Bull Run, written after the war, General Beauregard said of the Confederacy's problem, "We needed for President either a military man of a high order, or a politician of the first class without military pretensions.... The South did not fall, crushed by the mere weight of the North; but it was nibbled away at all sides and ends because its executive head never gathered and wielded its great strength under the ready advantages that greatly reduced or neutralized its adversary's naked physical superiority."

APPOMATTOX

Hundreds of pages could be written about heroes in the Civil War, but we must move on to the dramatic meeting at Appomattox that not completely but essentially ended the war. Robert E. Lee had dynamically and, at times, brilliantly commanded the Army of Northern Virginia since 1862. And he had commanded all Confederate troops in the last year of the war. His terribly difficult decision to turn his back on the flag he loved and, instead, go with Virginia when she seceded in 1861 gave the South the leader General Whinfield Scott thought was the best officer in the country. His brilliant tactics, his ability to analyze a situation swiftly and accurately and then act on it with dispatch, as well as his strength of character and high sense of duty during those four years of war established him as one of the great generals in history. He was half god and half myth to the ranks of the Confederate Army, often being referred to as "Marse Robert."

The meeting of Lee and the Union Army commander for surrender would prove to be Grant's highest point of moral rectitude. The following, though from my biographical novel of Ulysses S. Grant (*Ulysses*, chapter 55), is accurate. President Lincoln had given Grant a specific order prior to the capitulation: the general was to resolve only military matters, not delve into anything political that could affect pending high-level government surrender terms. To set the stage, when Petersburg, Virginia, finally fell in early April of 1865, Lee tried to slip the Union noose with as many troops as possible. But it was to no avail. After losing some final, quick battles, Lee's army had little ammunition and no food. He had no recourse within his honor to do other than meet with Grant to discuss terms. Brigadier General John A. Rawlins was Grant's feisty and utterly loyal adjutant general. Chaplain John Eaton Jr. was the minister he had appointed to oversee the freed blacks some time earlier. Cincinnati was Grant's favorite horse. The parlor on the west side of the upper floor of the McLean house was about to become the site of one of the most momentous days in American history.

★★★★★

… The red brick McLean house in the hamlet of Appomattox Courthouse was the site that was quickly selected for the surrender. By a strange twist, the owner of the house—Wilmer McLean—had owned the farm on Bull Run near Manassas Junction where the first major battle of the war had been fought. Wanting to get away from shot and shell, he had later moved his family to the rural hill country well west of the capital and apart from the railroads and other features of military value. Now, inexplicably, the very war he was trying to escape was about to culminate in his living room.

Young Walter Taylor, Lee's adjutant, had been so overcome by the thought of forthcoming surrender that Lee had excused him from attending the ceremony. Lieutenant Colonel Charles Marshall, his secretary, and Lieutenant Colonel Orville Babcock, the aide Grant had sent ahead, accompanied the silver-headed Lee into the house to await the arrival of the Union commander.

Some thirty minutes later, Grant, accompanied by Rawlins and part of his staff, rode Cincinnati into the little village. Somehow, on the move from City Point, the trunk containing his fresh uniforms and ceremonial sword had been misplaced, so he wasn't dressed for the occasion. This would never have worried him, except that he didn't want to offend Lee. In any case, he wouldn't have worn the sword—and it was the occasion that mattered, not one's appearance. Mud had spattered his worn, plain uniform and had covered his boots. The braid on his epaulets was tarnished and barely proclaimed his rank. Even the slouch hat looked as if it had been thrown in too many corners.

Sheridan was waiting. He saluted.

Grant touched his hat brim. "How are you, Sheridan?"

"First-rate, thank you. How are you, General?"

"All right. Is Lee here?"

"Up in that brick house."

"Well then, let's go up."

It all seemed so casual, but Grant felt a rushing in his ears, a tightness in his stomach, as he swung down from the big horse. He had prayed for this moment, had always been sure it would arrive— perhaps not in this manner, but in some way. Now, as if in some surreal pantomime, he was moving toward his country's most historic moment. A horse neighed in the bright sunlight. Leather creaked. Out of the corner of his eye he saw his red flag with the three white stars suddenly flap, as if to urge him on. For a brief second he saw himself in an old army overcoat driving a wagon full of wood through the snow. For some odd reason, his next thought was of Chaplain Eaton.

Was it really Palm Sunday?

His staff and escort sat quietly on their horses.

He noticed Lee's gray horse, Traveller...that fine horse he'd read about in the Richmond papers. He had his saddle off and was eating grass. An orderly stood by his side.

The wind stopped and for a moment it was totally silent.

He looked up into the spring sky and squinted at the sun, remembering that Easter wasn't far away. But that had nothing to do with the present, with ending a bloody war.

The rushing was in his ears again.

Reaching the top step of the porch, he looked into Babcock's smile. The colonel said, "Come in, sir. General Lee is waiting."

Removing his hat as he entered, Grant followed his aide up the stairwell to the parlor on the west side of the house. He was greeted by a relatively small room that held chairs, a sofa, and two small marble tables—one round, the other rectangular. Standing in front of the fireplace was the erect, patrician figure of Robert E. Lee. How white he was, so different from the hazy major he recalled from a glimpse of yesterday.

As Lee came forward, extending his hand, they exchanged greetings.

Babcock motioned toward the round table in the middle of the room as Lee returned to the other one. Leaning over as Grant seated himself, the aide quietly asked, "Don't you think it would be a good idea, sir, to invite the senior staff and generals in?"

Absently, Grant nodded. Moments later, Sheridan, Ord, Rawlins, and others clanked in amid the noises that boots, spurs, and sabers always make. They quietly lined up along the wall behind Grant. Lee's only aide was Charles Marshall, who stood silently behind the waiting general.

Grant drew in a breath.

The air seemed charged. It was time.

He cleared his throat and spoke in his normal quiet tone, "I met you once before, General Lee, while we were serving in Mexico. I've always remembered your appearance, and I think I should have recognized you anywhere."

"Yes," Lee answered tonelessly, "I know I met you, and I've often tried to recollect how you looked. But I've never been able to recall a single feature."

A slight smile softened Grant's expression. "Most people don't. You were a major and I was a second lieutenant. It seems eons ago."

Lee nodded, obviously anxious to get on with it. "I suppose, General Grant, that the object of our present meeting is fully understood. I asked you to ascertain upon what terms you would receive the surrender of my army."

Grant looked into the dark eyes for a moment before replying. "The terms I propose are those stated substantially in my letter of yesterday. That is, the officers and men surrendered are to be paroled and disqualified from taking up arms again. And all arms, ammunition, and supplies are to be delivered up as captured property."

Lee nodded without breaking the gaze. "Those are about the conditions I expected."

Grant spoke of peace, loss of life and property, and the hope that their actions of the day would be of mutual benefit. Then, on Lee's urging, he proceeded to write out the terms in his manifold order book. Pausing now and then for a word or a phrase, he scratched away with a pencil. He labored over the ending, knowing he might be stepping on Lincoln's toes. But he wanted to make sure that brave soldiers who believed in a cause—no matter how wrong—would never be tried for treason. He wanted to include something that would forestall any government reprisal, that would have the effect of a general amnesty. Finally, he motioned to Rawlins, who came over and read the two pages. Rawlins nodded, then stepped back against the wall, where Sheridan uneasily shifted his weight from one foot to another.

Even the breathing in the room was hushed.

Grant arose and walked to Lee, handing him the order book. After pointing out a missing word, Lee reread the draft. He lingered over the final sentence, which read, "This done, each officer and man will be allowed to return to his home, not to be disturbed by the United States authority as long as they observe their paroles and the laws in force where they may reside." His expression softened some-what. "This will have a very happy effect on my army."

"Then I'll have a copy made in ink and sign it."

Lee removed his spectacles and frowned. "There is one thing. The cavalrymen and artillerists own their own horses in our army. I'd like to understand whether these men will be permitted to retain their horses."

"The terms as written do not allow this, General. Only the offi-cers are allowed to take their private property."

Lee replaced his glasses and read the second page of the foolscap again. Looking up again with a touch of fleeting pain, he said, "No, I see the terms do not allow it. That's quite clear."

Grant felt Lee's discomfort. The great man would not beg, not even for his men. And Lincoln had said, "Get them back to their farms." Again he saw himself in that wagon, hauling wood from Hardscrabble. How would he have survived without horses? No, it would be bad enough for these men *with* the animals. He stroked his beard, replying, "Well, the subject is quite new to me. Of course, I didn't know that any private soldiers owned their animals, but I think this will be the last battle of the war—at least I sincerely hope so—and the surrender of this army will soon be followed by others.

"And I take it that most of the men in the ranks are small farmers, so I will arrange it this way. I will not change the terms as written, but I will instruct the officers I shall appoint to receive the paroles to let all the men who claim to own a horse or a mule to take the animals home with them to work their little farms."

Lee nodded, relaxing. "This will have the best possible effect on the men. I believe it will be very gratifying and will do much toward conciliating our people."

Grant turned to Rawlins to have the letter copied. While this was being accomplished, Grant presented a somewhat aloof Lee to his officers. Lee moved back to the table when the introductions were complete. After a minute, he said, "General Grant, I have about a thousand of your men as prisoners. I shall be glad to send them back into your lines as soon as it can be arranged, for I have no provisions for them. I have, indeed, nothing for my own men. They've been living for the past few days on parched corn, and are badly in need of both rations and forage."

"Yes, by all means," Grant replied. "I should like our men back as soon as possible. How many men are in your present force?"

"I can't say. I have no means of ascertaining our present strength."

"Suppose I send over twenty-five thousand rations. Will that be enough?"

Lee nodded. "I think that will be more than enough."

General Lee then turned to Colonel Marshall, and the two spent the next twenty minutes on the draft and then the ink copy of Lee's acceptance. This done, Lee signed the letter and handed it back to Marshall, who sealed the envelope and exchanged it for Grant's letter.

It was 3:40 on the 9th of April 1865.

Lee's surrender was complete.

The gray-bearded general rose stiffly from his chair and moved to Grant, hand outstretched. Grant shook the hand, looking directly into Lee's unseeing eyes, feeling for this magnificent soldier, torn in the climax of victory by the sadness. Lee nodded to the other federal officers, and, with shoulders back, walked out the door. Several officers sprang to their feet and saluted.

Moments later, Lee mounted Traveller and turned back for a final look at the McLean house—just as Grant stepped out onto the porch. Grant removed his hat and stood at attention, as did the other officers present. Erect in the saddle, Lee raised his hat and barely nodded his head, then turned his horse to return to his vanquished army.

Yes, it was Grant's greatest moment—through the words of that surrender, he absolved all soldiers of the Confederacy of treason against the United States and kept them from ever being tried under that charge... a remarkable stroke of fairness and understanding, considering Lincoln's admonition that he deal only with military matters in such an event.

LINCOLN

> *Military glory—that attractive rainbow that rises in showers of blood....*
>
> —Abraham Lincoln, speech on
> Declaration of War on Mexico (January 12, 1848)

> *The mystic chords of memory, stretching from every battle-field and patriot grave, to every living heart and hearthstone, all over this broad land, will yet swell the chorus of the Union...*
>
> —Abraham Lincoln, First Inaugural Address (March 4, 1861)

Who was more eloquent than this remarkable man? How can anyone ever define Abraham Lincoln's bravery? To be president in the years of the Civil War required staggering strength—and not just physically. During the first two years of the war, he had no generals on whom he could count. He had to, with no previous experience, learn the essentials of command. While in reality running the war, he had to spend many hours every day receiving visitors at the White

House, visitors who mostly wanted something. This requirement alone sapped his energy. He lost a favored son during his presidency, and had to fight through that grief. Often his working days reached to eighteen hours, eighteen hours of usually jam-packed stress and activity. And when he was finished, he had to face a wife who, if not mad, was certainly exceptionally eccentric. Lincoln's day-to-day bravery, his heroism, can never be measured. Many books have been written about this magnificent president, and there will be more. I simply can't do him justice with merely a capsule. He cared for his servicemen, he cared for his civilians, he cared for the enemy, but mostly he cared for the Union. And he, through his staunch will and the use of a general who didn't back up, saved that Union.

His reward was an assassin's bullet.

CHAPTER SIX

THE INDIAN WARS

I n the aftermath of the war, America's growth—aside from its remarkable new industrial muscle—was its thrust westward. California had been settled to a great extent, as had Texas and New Mexico. But huge expenses of raw country lay open to the pioneers who thirsted for a new life and their own land. They were mostly hardy and hardworking, and usually invested everything they owned to chance new settlement.

There was only one major drawback; a major portion of that land was occupied by the American Indian. The numerous tribes of Indians in the West were hunter/warrior types, rovers who followed migrating game. And the buffalo was king; practically every part of that remarkable animal found a use in Indian life. Different tribes followed this nomadic existence in borderless areas referred to as their homelands. Often these areas overlapped, creating conflict. Some tribes became the perennial enemies of others. And naturally, some tribes were stronger in their making of war than others, most notably the Comanches in Texas, the Apaches in New Mexico and Arizona, and the Lakota Sioux on the Northern Plains.

As would be expected, the intrusion west by the settlers was contested by the Indians, particularly the fiercest of the tribes. The settlers, in turn, needed protection, so the US Army rode and marched west to give them security. This conflict, known as the Indian Wars, actually began many years before the Civil War, and lasted until the turn of the century. A policy of forcing tribes onto reservations, often large areas of land, was adopted by the government. But to the warrior chiefs, this wasn't acceptable. The buffalo didn't know the boundaries of any reservation, and to the proudest of these often great leaders, such confinement was utterly unacceptable. Furthermore, the policies of the Bureau of Indian Affairs varied, and the Indians were cheated and mistreated on the reservations. Graft and broken treaties were prevalent. To those considerate of the Indians, the term "stealing of the Indians' land" became popular. Before we go on, let's examine this controversy.

Before the coming of the white man and afterward, the Indians didn't *own* land in the exact meaning of the word. By right of domain, they lived and roamed on certain lands. Now comes the problem: if a stronger tribe wished to move into that area, that homeland, it made war upon the occupying tribe and simply *took* it. An example is the Lakota Sioux. Around the turn of the eighteenth century, the Lakota Sioux resided in the southern Minnesota area. Another tribe using the northern Minnesota area as a homeland was the Ojibwa, more commonly known as the Chippewa. The Sioux and the Chippewa, quite naturally, were enemies. Two elements changed western Indian life forever—the arrival of the horse, and the arrival of the gun. The Chippewa sold furs to the French, who provided them with the first guns. Armed with this weapon, the Chippewa forced the Sioux southwesterly into present-day South Dakota, where they ran into the Arikaras, who had been kicked out of the Nebraska area by the Iowas and Omahas. The Sioux expelled the Arikaras, making permanent enemies of them. Later the Sioux, now armed with the gun, took over western Montana and northern Wyoming in the Crows' homelands. The gun and the warrior ferocity of the Sioux made them the supermen of the Northern Plains. So there isn't much truth in the ownership theory.

Warriors. The warrior tribes maintained a fighting psyche unknown to any other culture. At present-day kindergarten age, young boys began serious training. By the time they were twelve, many were capable of holding their own in combat. By fifteen, most had gone on raids against their enemies. Some became noted war leaders well before they reached their twentieth birthday. And they could fight! And they could ride! The only thing they couldn't do was get replacements. There were no "repo depots." As a result, Indian war parties seldom fought toe-to-toe battles, and almost never attacked a superior force. When the American Army brought war to them, they usually had their elders, their women, and their children with them, and normally eschewed direct combat.

MacKenzie

Transitioning from the Civil War to the Indian Wars was a matter of changing ranks for many Union officers. The rapid promotions and earned brevet ranks created by heroism and wartime expansion of the Army had to be exchanged for whatever rank those wishing to continue a military career could get. Perhaps the biggest reduction in grade was a brigadier general who accepted sergeant's stripes. Most officers, however, were able to find positions at two, three, sometimes even four grades below the rank they held at the end of the war. It's interesting to note that these officers could always be addressed by their highest rank. George Armstrong Custer had to accept a position as the lieutenant colonel of the Seventh Cavalry, but he was addressed as "General Custer."

With Custer's shadow looming so large, an exceptional young officer in both the Civil War and the following campaigns was pretty much overlooked. He was Ranald Slidell MacKenzie. Born July 27, 1840, he graduated first in his West Point class of June 1862, compared to Custer, who graduated last in his class a year earlier. Additionally, he was younger than Custer was when they were promoted to major general. And finally, Custer's press and his own promotional capability made the golden-haired one into a big Indian fighter, although he did very little to warrant that fame.

MacKenzie shot up in rank during the war, distinguished in numerous battles for his bravery. Grant described him as "the most promising young officer in the army." In 1867 he was appointed colonel of the Forty-first Infantry Regiment. Later he took command of the Fourth Cavalry at Fort Concho, Texas. Fighting the fierce Comanches and Kiowas, it soon became one of the top regiments in the army. On one occasion, he covertly pursued warring Apaches 160 miles into Mexico on a thirty-two-hour raid. He was known as "Bad Hand" by the Indians because one of the *seven* times he was wounded in both wars he lost two fingers on his right hand. MacKenzie won battle after battle against several of the great Indian leaders and dealt successfully with Red Cloud, Dull Knife, and Crazy Horse. He joined with General George Crook to avenge Custer's defeat by the Sioux, and got a general's star back. Illustrious could be his synonym. And now the sad part...

In 1875 he was thrown from a wagon and remained dazed for several months—which may have been the cause of later health problems. In 1883, when he arrived in San Antonio to command the Department of Texas, he resumed a love affair that had lapsed for fourteen years. He and his former lover, now a widow, were making their wedding plans when he was struck by what was known as "paralysis of the insane." He was sent to an asylum in New York, and after suffering for nearly five more years, he died in 1879 and was buried at West Point.

CROOK

George Crook graduated thirty-eighth out of forty-three in his West Point class of 1852. Another Ohioan, he had a brilliant Civil War record, taking part in over a dozen battles, mostly as a brigade or division commander. He was a major general when the war ended, but reverted to lieutenant colonel of the Thirty-second Infantry. He was all over the place fighting different Indian tribes for the next thirty years. Known by them as the "Gray Fox," he took the time to learn much about them. He seldom wore a uniform and usually rode a mule named "Apache." He was reappointed a brigadier general in 1875 and is well known for his battle with Crazy Horse at the Rosebud that helped set the stage for the Little Bighorn. He dealt successfully with the Apaches in Arizona in the early 1870s and later, when he made promises to them upon which the government reneged. Crook is considered by most military historians as "the most successful Indian fighter the army ever produced."

AND WHAT ABOUT THE GREAT INDIAN WARRIORS?

Unfortunately, the American Indians have no authentic written history. Some efforts at historical recording were made in the latter part of the nineteenth century and continue through the present, but they aren't truly factual. With only drawings depicting such history, one must depend on stories that have been passed down around many campfires before it can be written. And storytellers have always embellished their tales to make them more interesting. (Except me.) Sources sometimes get sudden recall many years later, and the result is usually unreliable. Many historians have tended to believe these reports because they *want to.* An example is the scout Curly recalling the Battle of the Little Bighorn years later. Millions of words have been written about that battle, with writers ready to jump on anything with a slight odor of being new. Then we get to two recent factors: political correctness and revisionist history—the latter often used to support the former. *Slant* is the forming of a report in a certain subjective direction; slant is the favorite tool of the revisionist. Therefore, many historical Indian stories are simply not totally true.

But we do know that there were remarkable Indian heroes, and since so many of them became prominent in the Indian Wars, they are the ones we know the most about. To become a chief in most Apache clans (there were no nations), one had to prove himself in combat; the mantle of leadership was not inherited. This was also true in other tribes. Therefore, the heroes we know about were leaders as well. One such was Mangas Colorados (Red Sleeves), chief of the Mimbreno Apaches. At six feet six inches, he was far taller than the average Apache, but he didn't find himself until his wife and son were killed in a massacre by scalp hunters. Then he became a heroic chief, leading his warriors on raid after raid into Mexico. He was also the first Apache chief to recognize the value of political alliances. One example is his marrying off a daughter to the famed Chiricahua chief Cochise. After a humiliating flogging by some miners, he turned his wrath on Americans for a time. Under peaceful conditions, Mangas was deceived by the American general Joseph R. West, killed, and beheaded.

Due to the popular TV series *Broken Arrow*, Cochise became quite famous. He was born about 1812, and while he lead his warriors repeatedly against their natural enemies, the Mexicans, he didn't fight against Americans until he was wrongfully accused of kidnapping a white child. He escaped from prison and took hostages to trade for his own people who were in custody. When the exchange failed, all-out war resulted. For the next few years, raids on white settlements made Cochise and his Chiricahuas the scourge of Arizona. A brave and noble chief, he was trustworthy, highly respected, and only after the Army hired Apache scouts under General Crook was he defeated. He died in 1874.

At this point, a few words about the Apache warrior are in order. As in other tribes, the warrior began rigorous training at a very early age. In addition to fighting skills, he soon became a superb horseman. He was perhaps the hardiest of the western warriors, capable of riding sixty miles in one day, and doing battle. He took few male prisoners, and those he did take were turned over to the Apache women to be beaten to death. Female prisoners were made slaves or wives. He hated Mexicans and had a fierce code of honor. It was claimed that northern Mexican haciendas were merely farms for Apache stock since the raids were often years apart, giving the Mexicans time to rebuild their herds.

Geronimo is considered a hero by some of today's Apache descendents, but he was more of a renegade. He was a Bedonkohe Apache, born in 1820. Near the Mexican village of Janos in 1858, his mother, his wife, and three children were killed by Mexican soldiers. His rage fueled years of retaliatory raids. Then he shifted to raiding Americans, leading various-sized bands of followers. General George Crook finally brought him in, and later a general named Nelson A. Miles. Each time he made a promise to behave, but it was just a means to get out of custody, and his word was worthless. At one time, much of the US Army in the Southwest was chasing him. He was finally shipped off to Florida, and later transferred to Fort Sill, Oklahoma, where he was somewhat of a rascally old celebrity until his death at age eighty in 1909. He was never a chief.

SITTING BULL

The Yellowstone was the white man's name for the usually swift-flowing river that watered a broad, grassy valley set off by the often snowcapped and imposing peaks of the Bighorn Mountains. Here and there thick groves of willow and cottonwood trees accented the river's edge or other places where seeds had fallen long before the arrival of the *wasicus*, the whites. Broad and rolling plains on either side could range from hunter green to burnt orange, or to crackling hip-deep white in mid-winter. Off to the south, the Tongue, Powder, Rosebud, and Bighorn rivers fed the Yellowstone and provided the water for the buffalo and other game that thrived there. It was the heartland of the Lakota.

They called the river the Elk.

It was the domain of one of the most powerful men to ever stride the American stage, a Lakota whose name could demand ink on the front page of any newspaper in the country and strike fear into the hearts of traditional enemies he might face. He considered himself invincible. He was Sitting Bull.

In 1876, the year his Lakotas would meet Custer, he was forty-four years old. Going by his boyhood name of "Slow," he'd counted his original coup at fourteen, when he killed a Crow warrior with a tomahawk. His bravery and feats of arms were legend, and he'd become the foremost warrior and war leader in the Lakota world.

He was the main chief of the Hunkpapa Sioux—tall and every inch a man who was used to the mantle of authority. He had a heavy, muscular build, a big chest, and a large head. His face was broad, with a prominent hooked nose, and his half-bloodshot eyes gleamed alertly from beneath arching black brows. His dark hair, braided on one side with otter fur and hanging loose on the other, was thick and reached down to his shoulders. It was severely parted in the middle, where it glistened with a heavy streak of crimson paint. By always being in the forefront in battle, and seemingly impossible to hit, his name struck fear in the enemy. His horsemanship was legendary; without using a saddle or bridle he could flatten himself on either side of the animal. Gripping the horse's mane, he was amazingly accurate with a firearm.

By the time Custer and his Long Knives came to the Yellowstone to meet their fate, Sitting Bull had put aside his weapons and had become the spiritual leader of the Sioux. He could prophesy and make powerful medicine. His dream about "soldiers falling out of the sky" would reach far and wide in Siouxland that eventful summer, drawing thousands of reservation Indians to his encampments and motivating Crazy Horse to attack Crook on the Rosebud.

CRAZY HORSE

Crazy Horse was the other great Sioux war leader whose fame was never-ending. Mystical, yet one of the greatest natural generals America has ever produced, he was never a chief, and was, in fact, a loner. Let's look at him...

Born in the Black Hills (the *Paha Sapa*) in the Year of the Big Horse Steal—1841—he was marked by light skin and brownish, curly hair. His mother was Brulé Sioux; his father, Crazy Horse, was an Oglala Sioux medicine man. Called Curly, the boy began his warrior training as soon as he could pull a bowstring. He sneaked off on his first war party a month after his twelfth birthday. But Curly was different from the other young Oglala warriors as he grew into his teens. Reticent and introspective, he disdained many of their boisterous ways. He reached medium height, was thin and wiry with a narrow face, a high-beaked nose, light skin and hair, and dark eyes that seldom looked straight at anyone.

A vision he induced in his midteens deeply influenced him. A *vision quest* was vital to a male's life in the Sioux world. It was usually preceded by fasting and purification rites, and was brought about by remaining awake in a holy place until a vision came to him. It was a man's power; it set his life course—warrior, hunter, healer, horse catcher. Generally, though, it was the life of a warrior that was perceived in the vision.

In Curly's case, a man enveloped in mist and wearing a stone behind each ear rode a horse out of a lake and told him to pass dust over his body and that of his pony for invincibility in battle. "Never wear a headdress and never take anything from the enemy for yourself," the man in the vision said. At that moment a storm broke and a little zigzag mark of red lightning appeared on the rider's cheek; hail spots dotted his body. And, as suddenly as he had appeared, the rider was gone.

From that day on, Curly followed the instructions of the mystic rider. Having counted first coup, he wore a single feather straight up in the back of his light hair. He tied a small stone behind each ear before going into battle, sprinkled dust over himself and his pony, and painted a zigzag red line from his forehead to the point of his chin. He added one other effect—regardless of weather, he would fight with a bare torso dotted with white spots to represent hail.

On a raid against the Arapahoes during his sixteenth summer, Curly single-handedly charged a hill in the face of heavy gunfire and a barrage of arrows. He was unharmed, and the exploit brought him enduring praise. It also marked a pattern of brave exploits. It was at this point that his father bestowed his own name on him; henceforth he was known as Crazy Horse. He soon became a war leader warriors wanted to follow. In battle over the next decade, his brilliant leadership became legend. At the Fetterman massacre in 1866, he sucked the cavalry in, then slashed into them on the flank— a common Crazy Horse maneuver.

The war leader had a powerful love affair at the age of twenty-one with a woman named Black Buffalo Woman. But she married another man and gave birth to three children. However, in the white man's year of 1871, she eloped with Crazy Horse. Divorce under such circumstances was easy and normal, but the husband was the jealous type and he shot Crazy Horse through the jaw, leaving a nasty scar. Black Buffalo Woman eventually went back to her husband, but soon gave birth to a light-haired, light-skinned daughter.

THE BATTLE OF THE ROSEBUD

With migration of the roving and reservation bands of Sioux attracted to Sitting Bull's powerful medicine in the early summer of 1876, the number of available warriors grew quickly. On June 17 Crook's force of some 1,325 was encamped on the Rosebud River in southern Montana. His command included about 170 Crows and Shoshones, and 85 civilians. Crazy Horse had approximately 1,000 Sioux and Cheyennes—the largest Indian fighting force ever assembled to attack a huge army. He slashed into Crook's command and repeatedly deployed his warriors to meet Crook's responses. Much bravery on both sides marked the seesawing six-hour battle that was finally terminated when Crazy Horse decided to withdraw. He had won his victory. To attack and hold a huge force of Long Knives to a draw that *he* decided, with minimal casualties, was not only an incredible feat that would be retold around campfires for generations, but would feed the feeling of invincibility that was surging in Lakota land, part of the remarkable medicine that would partially fire the most famous Indian battle in American history.

General Crook justifiably also claimed a victory; he had been attacked on ground not of his choosing, or in any way favorable for defense against such an inspired, competent enemy. And he had held the field when Crazy Horse withdrew.

Whenever the Little Bighorn is mentioned, the Rosebud gets some ink as well. To add to the drama, Custer was headed for his destiny at the very time of that battle. With communication limited to courier, there was no way that Yellow Hair (Custer) could know a confident Sioux force had just won a great battle, or about Sitting Bull's medicine, *or* that by June 25 more and more Sioux would join the great leader's campfire, bringing the total Sioux and Cheyenne fighting strength on the Little Bighorn River campsite to nearly two thousand confident, experienced, and well-led warriors.

THE LITTLE BIGHORN

Intensely wanting his general's star back, and believing himself and his Seventh Cavalry invincible, Custer probably would have charged into that Indian buzzsaw even if he had known what he was up against. As it was, he met the most fired-up and well-trained Indian force the US Army had ever faced. He made other mistakes, primarily because he had poor intelligence (his Indian scouts lost their nerve and didn't serve him well) and he split his command. Captain

Frederick Benteen, a hard-bitten Civil War colonel, was sent on a reconnaissance in force with three companies off to the south, and Major Marcus Reno, a former brigadier, with only about 100 fighting men, was ordered into the southeastern end of the nearly three-mile-long village. Meanwhile Custer rode off with some 260 troopers above the encampment to *cut off* a possible Sioux escape.

In short, Reno got clobbered and lost his ability to command effectively. Benteen finally arrived with his three companies to take over, and no one knows exactly what happened to Custer and his five companies. What is known is that while Custer was heavily engaged on that hot late Sunday afternoon on the bluffs, Crazy Horse came crashing into him from the other end of the village. A short time later, not a soldier was alive up on those hills.

Back at the other end, Benteen had reorganized what was left of Reno's command, joined it with his own, and had formed a perimeter on what would become known as Reno Hill. That position would soon be encircled by the enemy, and would entrench against the heavy attack that came the next day. Heroes abounded, with several troopers volunteering to go alone down the hill to the river to bring back much-needed water. Twelve were later awarded the Medal of Honor. Benteen himself was heroic throughout, and was the main reason that portion of the command had as many survivors as it did. All the while, they had no knowledge of what had happened to Custer and his five companies.

When the Indians finally broke off the fighting the afternoon of the second day, it is believed they did so because of the staunch resolve of the troopers on Reno Hill, and the fact that Sitting Bull had earlier planned to move on to another camping ground that would provide grazing for their twenty-thousand-odd horses. For whatever reasons, the survivors of the Seventh Cavalry suddenly found themselves without a foe. Later they moved west to find the grisly evidence of Custer's defeat. The bodies of most of the troopers, noncommissioned officers, and officers were stripped and terribly mutilated by the women of the tribes. Tom Custer, whose body was recognizable only by a tattoo, was found lying by his brother's naked remains. One of the few who were not mutilated was George Armstrong Custer, raising speculation that a Cheyenne woman who supposedly had had an affair with him a few years earlier had saved him from the knife.

In fact, speculation as to what really happened on that fateful day continues to run rampant. Book after book continues to be written, including mine. The Army losses were, in effect, minuscule compared to Shiloh, Gettysburg, Fredericksburg, and other battles. But the Battle of the Little Bighorn, or "Custer's Last Stand," looms above them, perhaps because of the fact that it was the most complete victory by American Indians ever, perhaps because an entire command was killed to the man, or perhaps because of the mystique of Custer—the most well-known officer in the Army.

Little Bighorn buffs number in the thousands, and groups exist as far away as Britain. Some are Custer fans who like to blame Reno and Benteen, others are strongly anti-Custer. Libbie, his beautiful wife, is revered by all; she lived to four days short of her ninety-first birthday, until her final breath supporting the flamboyant man she so loved and fighting against those who would defame his name.

Crazy Horse surrendered with his people at the Red Cloud Agency two years later. He was shot and killed in unknown circumstances a few months afterward. Sitting Bull took his people to Canada, but brought them out, the worse for wear, in 1881 and surrendered to the Army. He was imprisoned for two years, then toured for a time with Buffalo Bill Cody's Wild West Show. He never quit fighting for what he considered his land, and was killed by tribal police in 1890. Two weeks later, the Battle of Wounded Knee took place.

That battle was an accident, as so many are. The Sioux on the Pine Ridge reservation had been incited by an emotional movement called the Ghost Dance, and the Indian agent called on the Seventh Cavalry for protection. As the soldiers were disarming the Indians, a Sioux rifle was accidentally discharged, leading the skittish participants into a full-fledged firefight. Due to the packed location, women and children were among the 150 Indians who were killed; another 50 Sioux were wounded. Twenty-five soldiers were killed and thirty-seven wounded. Wounded Knee became a rallying cause for late-twentieth-century activists, who called it a massacre in spite of its happenstance origin.

Major General George Crook died in Chicago in 1890 at the age of sixty-one, so overall, it wasn't a very good year. But it did mark the end of the Indian wars.

CHAPTER SEVEN

THE SPANISH-AMERICAN WAR

"REMEMBER THE *MAINE*"

S ome eight years would go by before another real battle by Americans would take place. In that period, the United States would further flex its muscles in the international political world, and the Spanish heel on Cuba would become a concern not only to revolting natives of that island, but to freedom-minded Americans as well. In support of Cuban insurgents, the battleship *Maine* was sent to anchor in Havana harbor in January 1898. Shortly after, Undersecretary of the Navy Theodore Roosevelt ordered Commodore George Dewey to move his Asiatic squadron to the Spanish-ruled Philippines. Then the zestful Teddy donned an olive drab uniform, pinned on the silver leaves of a lieutenant colonel, and put together the First Volunteer United States Cavalry Regiment. It consisted of cowboys, hunters, lawmen, numerous Eastern sportsmen, and graduates of Ivy League universities. Quickly becoming known as the "Rough Riders," it was the most exclusive regiment in the Army. Enough applicants clamored to get in it to fill more than three like-size units. Roosevelt declined command because he felt he was lacking in the administrative side, so he had his friend, Leonard Wood, a noted surgeon and veteran of the

137

Apache campaign (where he had been awarded the Medal of Honor for heroism), as the colonel.

On February 15 the *Maine* was blown up, killing some 260 men. The American reaction was outrage, with *"Remember the* Maine*"* becoming a popular slogan as war was declared.

When Dewey reached Manila Bay, he defeated the ten-ship Spanish fleet without the loss of a single American life.

And in Tampa, a large expeditionary force, V Corps under three-hundred-pound Major General William Shafter, assembled to invade Cuba. Included among its hodgepodge of units were all of the black regiments in the army and Teddy's Rough Riders. Landing east of the fortified city of Santiago on June 23, V Corps assembled and moved eastward to attack the hilltop city on July 1. By this time, Colonel Wood had moved up to command the Second Brigade, and Roosevelt had assumed command of the Rough Riders.

In an anomaly of war, Fighting Joe Wheeler, another of the Confederate Army's great cavalry leaders, was appointed a one-star general and commanded the US Cavalry division in V Corps. He had become a congressman after the Civil War, where he was quite effective, and was sixty-two years old when the invasion took place. (As a sidebar, the 1997 miniseries *Rough Riders* quite mistakenly portrayed him as an oversized buffoon, even though he was diminutive, and heroically refused to be taken out of the battle for Santiago even though he was extremely ill. So much for Hollywood and facts.) During the battle for Santiago (San Juan Hill) during the hottest fighting, it is told that General Wheeler momentarily forgot his whereabouts and, as the enemy showed signs of weakening, cried out impulsively to his troops: "Give those Yankees hell now, boys!" His aides and those standing near burst into laughter and told him what he had said. "Oh, well," he explained with a smile of deprecation, "I just forgot a moment—but you all know I meant the Spanish. I'm a Yankee myself now."

The Second Brigade was under Wheeler. And in it, besides the Rough Riders, were the two regular regiments, the First Cavalry and the Tenth Cavalry (of Negro Buffalo Soldiers).

The Navy was doing its part off the Cuban coast, as well as in the Philippines. Rear Admiral William Sampson's North Atlantic Squadron had Admiral Pascual Cervera's Spanish fleet bottled up inside Santiago Bay, just hoping it would try to make a run for it.

TEDDY ROOSEVELT AND THE ROUGH RIDERS

The San Juan Hills above Santiago were composed of the main hill and a lower one on the right, which later became known as Kettle Hill. Fat General Shafter, virtually prostrate from the heat, deployed Brigadier General Jacob Kent's infantry division on the left and Wheeler's cavalry on the right. Although the attack was launched at dawn, it was stymied for a number of reasons until noon. Even then, there was quite a bit of disorganization—and Teddy was right in the middle of it, much to his flamboyant satisfaction. He had planned to dismount at the foot of the hill and lead his dismounted troopers to glory on foot, but he quickly found he could see better and cover more ground on horseback—enemy fire be damned!

Spurring "Little Texas," his favorite horse, among the ranks of his charging Rough Riders, Roosevelt soon found himself the ranking officer in a group of troopers from all three regiments. After finally dismounting, under heavy Spanish fire, he ran ahead and with just five men neared the top of the hill. Wisely running back, he berated his men for not following, but quickly learned they hadn't heard him when he ordered the second charge. Teddy waved his hat as he exhorted his men to follow. Firing a pistol from the *Maine* that had been given to him, he killed a couple of Spanish soldiers as he continued to cheer the combined command on.

Swarming behind him were the mixture of volunteer cowboys, lawmen, and Ivy Leaguers who made up the Rough Riders; the Regular Army professionals of the First, Third, and Sixth Cavalry; and the proud Buffalo Soldiers of the Ninth and Tenth Cavalry. Teddy's raw courage was at times reckless, but his valiant courage was conspicuous as he grabbed the reins of command of six regiments at a crucial time in the attack, presumably being the most important influence in taking Kettle Hill.

In the meantime, Color Sergeant J. E. Andrews of the Third Cavalry was shot in the stomach. As he fell back down the hill, Sergeant George Berry of the Tenth Cavalry was moving up the hill with the

THEODORE ROOSEVELT

colors of his own regiment when he saw Andrews down. Grabbing the colors of the Third Cavalry and raising both flags bravely, he shouted, *"Dress* [form up] *on the colors, boys, dress on the colors!"*

As the Americans reached the blockhouse at the top of the hill, they found the Spanish soldiers had just fled into Santiago. The Rough Riders planted their flags, while Sergeant Berry drove in the two flags of the Third and Tenth Cavalry. Other flags were stuck in the top of the hill as well. To this day controversy continues as to who took Kettle Hill.

To the left, General Kent's infantry was still fighting its way to the top of San Juan Hill. But soon, the battle for the heights was over.

But it would take several days to end the war in Cuba. Admiral Pascual Cervera was ordered to break out of Santiago Bay, only to have his entire fleet sunk or run aground by Admiral Sampson's squadron. It took even longer to defeat the Spanish forces in the Philippines.

Thirteen members of the combined forces that attacked San Juan and Kettle Hill were awarded the Medal of Honor. But Teddy wasn't one of them. He did emerge, thanks to being the darling of the media, from the Spanish-American war its most well-known and beloved hero. His book *Rough Riders* was an instant best-seller, and he was selected to run as governor of New York. Too reform-minded for the politicos, he was shunted over to become the vice president under William McKinley in 1900. When the president was assassinated in September 1901, Teddy moved into the White House, America's youngest president ever.

Regarding the obviously deserved Medal of Honor, Roosevelt wrote scathing reports of poorly planned and inept efforts to properly equip and supply soldiers in the war, and it was felt those responsible exacted their revenge by blocking his award. Over a hundred years after the last shot of the war was fired, Congress finally approved it. It was the only posthumous grant of the medal from the entire Spanish-American War.

Three others, all lieutenants, stand out. As the Sixth Infantry in

General Kent's First Brigade waited, pinned down at the bottom of San Juan Hill, Lieutenant Jules Ord was a member of Brigadier General Hamilton Hawkins's staff. Tired of the heavy Spanish fire that rained down from the enemy positions above, the impatient young officer approached the general and said, "Sir, if you will order a charge, I'll lead it!"

The general, a Civil War veteran who knew the carnage that would result from a frontal attack on a fortified position, didn't answer. Ord insisted, "If you do not *forbid* it, I will start it. I only ask you not to refuse permission."

The general finally responded, "I will not ask for volunteers, I will not give you permission, and I will not refuse it. God bless you and good luck!"

Wearing no shirt in the damp morning heat, Ord hitched up his pants, drew his saber and pistol and rose up. *"C'mon, you men. We can't stay here. Follow me!"*

His soldiers slowly got to their feet, inspired by the young officer, and followed him into the enemy fire. Soon the front of the Sixth Infantry rose to join them. It was the beginning of the successful assault on the hill. But Lieutenant Ord didn't see the success of his heroic example; he was killed shortly after he inspired it.

US Military Academy lore includes this young cadet. Colonel Roosevelt wrote in his book:

> A young West Point cadet, Ernest Haskell, who had taken his holiday with us as an acting second lieutenant, was shot through the stomach. He had shown great coolness and gallantry, which he displayed to an even more marked degree after being wounded, shaking my hand and saying: "All right, Colonel, I'm going to get well. Don't bother about me, and don't let any man come away with me." When I shook hands with him, I thought he would surely die; yet he recovered.

And again from The Home of Heroes Web site, this interesting story: The first lieutenant was thirty-seven years old and an 1886 graduate of West Point. He had forcefully requested transfer from his position as an instructor at the Academy to V Corps prior to the invasion, threatening to resign if his transfer was not effected, and had further written to the commander of the Tenth Cavalry, requesting assignment to his former Buffalo Soldiers regiment. Thus he was regimental quartermaster of the Tenth, who, like Ulysses S. Grant in the Mexican War, couldn't stay out of the fire. He was called "Black Jack," and this is what he later wrote about the battle:

> Each officer or soldier next in rank took charge of the line or group immediately in his front or rear and halting to fire at each good opportunity, taking reasonable advantage of cover, the entire command moved forward as coolly as though the buzzing of bullets was the humming of bees. White regiments, black regiments, regulars and Rough Riders, representing the young manhood of the North and the South, fought shoulder to shoulder, unmindful of race or color, unmindful of whether commanded by ex-Confederate or not, and mindful of only their common duty as Americans.

His name was John Pershing and he was destined for greatness. (A fine two-volume biography, *Black Jack*, was written about Pershing by Dr. Frank Vandiver, former president of Texas A&M and one of America's outstanding historians.)

And finally, Colonel Leonard Wood, who got his first star in Cuba, became the only doctor to become chief of staff of the US Army and is considered one of its finest soldiers.

When Teddy became president, it was suggested to him that much more attention should be given to the awarding of the Medal of Honor—providing a formal and impressive ceremony. Teddy, of course, was all for it, and signed an executive order that stated, "…the recipient will, when practicable, be ordered to Washington, DC, and the presentation will be made by the President, as Commander-in-Chief, or by such representative as the President may designate." With great pleasure, Teddy made the first presentation at the White House to Assistant Surgeon James Robb Church, a Rough Rider. The citation read, "In addition to performing gallantly the duties pertaining to his position, he voluntarily and unaided carried several seriously wounded men from the firing line to a secure position in the rear, in each instance being subjected to a very heavy fire and great exposure and danger."

JUST GOTTA STICK SMEDLEY IN SOMEWHERE

When your name is Smedley Darlington Butler, you just *have* to be able to fight. And you might as well become a Marine. That's just what Smedley did. Born on July 30, 1881, in West Chester, Pennsylvania, he was a major in Vera Cruz in 1914 when he earned the Medal of Honor. In 1915, in Haiti, he led the battalion he commanded in an attack on an enemy fort and received his second Medal of Honor. He retired from the Corps as a major general in 1931. Maybe naming one's son Smedley isn't so bad, after all.

CHAPTER EIGHT

WORLD WAR I

Our game was his but yesteryear;
We wished him back; we could not know
The self-same hour we missed him here
He led the line that broke the foe.
　　　　　　　　　—Sir Henry Newbolt, "The Schoolfellow" (1914)

BLACK JACK AND GEORGIE

With powerful Otto von Bismarck no longer around to control Germany's destiny, Kaiser Wilhelm II (Cousin Willie to King George of England) saw himself as the emperor of a powerful German state that would rule Europe. And he was ready to prove it. In the summer of 1914 Europe was virtually an armed camp with many hurts, both real and imagined, to be assuaged by its most powerful nations. Alliances were formed, and in 1907 saw the formation of the *Triple Entente* made up of France, Britain, and Russia. The *Triple Alliance* consisted of Germany, Austria, and Italy, but Italy decided to join the Triple Entente, which became the *Allied Powers*. Smaller countries jumped in on both sides, and the situation was, as Colonel Edward M. House, President Wilson's personal advisor, called it, "militarism run stark mad."

All the tinder needed was a match.

On June 28 a Serb student provided that match. He assassinated Prince Ferdinand, heir to the Austrian throne. A month later, Austria declared war on Serbia. Due to the entangling alliances and the bulging arsenals, all of the major powers entered the war. The tinder ignited a giant powder keg.

Eagerly ready to attack old enemies France and Russia, the German general staff had a great plan in which a huge army would pour across the lowlands, the staff of a massive hook, that would strike southwest of Paris and ensnare the French army, its capital, and win the war in one fell swoop—one of the most daring single envelopments ever planned. Its architect was Germany's brilliant chief of staff, Count Alfred von Schlieffen. The problem for Germany was that von Schlieffen died. His successor, von Moltke, weakened that northern army so repeatedly that the hook never enveloped anything. By early winter, the huge opposing armies settled down into a stalemate along the Ainse River that would turn into the most devastating trench warfare in history. Soon the improved machine gun and poison gas would rule the battlefield, with the fast-developing airplane adding its newfound power. On the sea, and under it, another new weapon began to wreak havoc: the submarine, known in the German navy as the U-boat. It was this predator that first made Americans realize they couldn't keep their heads in the sand while Europe tore itself apart. An American freighter was sunk, but it was the sinking of the British liner *Lusitania,* with the loss of 1,198 lives, including 128 Americans, that shocked the United States.

But while millions of soldiers in Europe were becoming casualties in the Great War, an incident occurred in the sleepy little border town of Columbus, New Mexico, that also jolted the American public. A band of Mexicans belonging to General Pancho Villa rode in, shooting and killing civilians and US soldiers stationed there.

Word flashed to Fort Bliss at El Paso, Texas, where Brigadier General "Black Jack" Pershing was in command. His volunteer aide was First Lieutenant George S. "Georgie" Patton, whose sister, Nita, was also at Fort Bliss, keeping company with General Pershing and helping him cope with the inconceivable pain of losing his wife and three daughters in a recent fire at the Presidio in San Francisco. (His wife was the daughter of Senator Francis E. Warren, who received the Medal of Honor in the Civil War.) Pershing quickly got orders to take a command on a punitive expedition into Mexico to run Villa down. It was the first campaign in which automobiles, trucks, and the new-fangled flying machines the Signal Corps had acquired were used.

Pershing had jumped over 862 officers senior to him when he was promoted from captain to brigadier general in September 1906, and had spent many of the intervening years in the Philippines. Ten years later, he was poised to become one of America's greatest military leaders. And Georgie Patton was going right along with him.

Patton began his swashbuckling combat career by shooting it out with some banditos. Leading a small detail (and looking for trouble), the tall, very blond lieutenant ran into Villa's chief bodyguard, General Julio Cardenas, and three other armed men at a ranch. All of the Mexicans were killed in a shootout that would have made Hollywood proud. Patton claimed just one. He then had them tied to the front of the touring cars and brought them in to Pershing. The pistol Georgie used was a single-action colt on which he later added pearl handles (with an appropriate notch, of course). A success-hungry media jumped on the story and Patton's name was emblazoned in newspapers across America.

Otherwise, the whole ten-month Mexican expedition was fruitless. Pancho thumbed his nose at the modern American might, and Black Jack came home empty-handed. But lessons were learned by the Americans, lessons that would prove worthy in the very near future. War at sea escalated as the Germans built more U-boats, and President Woodrow Wilson issued stern warnings about attacks on neutral ships —to no avail. Then a secret diplomatic message from Berlin to Mexico City was intercepted by British intelligence. Essentially, it proposed that in the event of war with the United States, Mexico would align itself with Germany and take up arms against its northern neighbor. In return, Germany would provide generous monetary reward and, after victory, Mexico would get back Texas, Arizona, and New Mexico.

That did it! On April 6, 1917, the United States declared war on Germany.

At first, the US Navy had all the glory. Its destroyers began escorting convoys of merchant ships, then five of its battleships made their presence known in the Atlantic. It didn't stop the wolf-packs of U-boats, but the loss of Allied shipping fell off measurably. Meanwhile the understrength Army had to whip up some kind of a fighting machine. In mid-June, the Big Red One—the First Division—shipped out for France, but it would need to be trained. President Wilson gave command of the American Expeditionary Force (AEF) to Black Jack Pershing, who headed for France three weeks after the appointment. He participated in a parade of the Sixteenth Infantry on the Fourth of July in Paris, where a quartermaster colonel uttered the famous comment, "Lafayette, we are here." A repayment from the American Revolution had begun.

MacArthur and the Rainbow

Soon three other divisions arrived; one was the 42nd Rainbow, so named because it had members—many National Guard—from every state in the Union. Its chief of staff was a flamboyant young colonel named Douglas MacArthur. Naturally, in the sense of good storytelling, he was the son of *that* MacArthur of Civil War fame. He had graduated first in his West Point class of 1903, and as first captain had in fact been the most outstanding cadet since a previous first captain—John J. Pershing in 1886. He had served as aide to his father on a tour of the Orient, and to President Teddy Roosevelt, and had made high marks as a junior officer—a fast start in peacetime. As a captain on the general staff, he was Chief of Staff Leonard Wood's special observer in the Mexican fracas at Vera Cruz in 1914. He got involved in a hazardous private adventure there, and was nominated for the Medal of Honor—which was turned down.

In battle in France, he refused to wear a tin hat or a gas mask, and was absolutely fearless whether it was in leading troops or going on individual forays behind enemy lines. After a few months he was promoted to brigadier general and given command of the Rainbow's Eighty-third Brigade. He struggled with Pershing's General Headquarters (GHQ), but his men loved him. And he took objectives

JOHN J. PERSHING

against heavily fortified positions. Obviously he was reckless, but he felt glory was his destiny. When it came to medals, only WWII's heralded Audie Murphy came close in sheer numbers. MacArthur was awarded two DSCs, *seven* Silver Stars, the Distinguished Service Medal, two Purple Hearts (when the medal was finally authorized in 1932), and nineteen foreign honors. His strong nomination for the Medal of Honor by his corps commander was turned down at GHQ, possibly because of toes he'd stepped on.

His father would have been proud of him.

THE FIGHTING SIXTY-NINTH

Some two million Americans would fight in France, and many of them didn't live to see the Statue of Liberty again. A proud regiment of US Marines glorified itself as part of the Second Division, and few people know that 11,880 women enlisted in the Naval Reserve and the Marine Corps between 1917 and 1918. Of course, thousands of other women served in different capacities, many of whom, particularly nurses, saved countless lives through their unswerving dedication. But since medals for heroism were awarded for action under enemy fire, their bravery has gone uncited.

Stern and demanding Black Jack Pershing was quickly promoted to full general so he had the rank to deal with all of those French marshals who wanted to have red-blooded young Americans fed into their depleted divisions as replacements—not that he needed it, because he staunchly insisted on US soldiers fighting in US units.

The most famous infantry regiment in America's history covered itself with glory on the battlefields of France. It was New York City's proud Fighting Sixty-ninth. After a heroic record in the Civil War and other combat stints, the Sixty-ninth was called to active duty on July 15, 1917. Redesignated the 165th Infantry, the "Fighting Irish" was sent overseas to become a vital cog in Douglas MacArthur's Rainbow Division. Before it returned to march proudly up Fifth

Avenue in steel helmets with bayonets fixed, it would take part in six major campaigns. It would be in contact with the enemy for 180 days and would suffer 3,501 casualties. Its members would receive two Medals of Honor and 133 DSCs along with two more its commander was awarded.

In 1940 a movie was made entitled *The Fighting 69th*, starring James Cagney and Pat O'Brien as the famous Father Duffy.

(There is far too little space in this short narrative to cover the many chaplains who have served heroically in American wars. May this account of perhaps the most famous of their calling serve in their name and honor them.)

A handsome, bald-headed Roman Catholic priest by the name of Francis P. Duffy was the Sixty-ninth's regimental chaplain. Born in 1871, he was assigned to the Sixty-ninth in 1914, surely a match made in heaven. Father Duffy was certainly born to wear a uniform besides the one with a white collar. For those members of the regiment who were non-Celtic in heritage, Duffy classified them as "Irish by adoption, Irish by association, or Irish by conviction."

In France his exploits became legendary. In combat, he was constantly at the front, conspicuous in battle, fearlessly tending to his charges, helping with the wounded, offering solace and encouragement, and administering, where necessary, last rites. His flock never tired of telling his deeds. His only weapons were his steel helmet, his faith, and his sacraments.

Beloved by all, wearing the DSC he so surely earned, along with the Distinguished Service Medal, the French Legion of Honor, and the Croix de Guerre, Lieutenant Colonel (Chaplain) Duffy was one of the three men who led the regiment up Fifth Avenue in that postwar Manhattan parade.

After the war, Father Duffy was assigned as rector of Holy Cross Church, a nearly bankrupt parish that contained the notoriously poor Hell's Kitchen and Times Square areas. An outspoken advocate of tolerance, he was much in demand as a speaker. Everything he earned—and his fees could be high—went to his troubled church. He kept a small kitty for any needy soldier who might show up at his door, and his housekeeper was given a strict order: "Never turn away a soldier."

When he died in June 1932, at the age of sixty-two, he was given a requiem mass at St. Patrick's Cathedral. The Fighting Sixty-ninth accompanied the horse-drawn caisson that bore his casket in the funeral procession. Tens of thousands of mourners lined its route, and Alexander Woolcott, his writer friend, wrote, "Father Duffy was of such dimensions that he made New York into a small town."

A statue of him in an army trenchcoat in front of a Celtic cross graces Times Square. Much of the money for its installation was donated by members of his beloved Sixty-ninth. As long as there is an Irishman in New York, Father Duffy will live on.

★★★★★

*I think that I shall never see
A poem lovely as a tree.*

These famous lines opened one of the most famous poems ever written by an American poet. Unfortunately, he would be one member of the Fighting Sixty-ninth who would not march up Fifth Avenue in the regiment's victory parade. For the body of this poet-soldier lay in an isolated grave in France.

For those who don't know who wrote the poem "Trees," it was Joyce Kilmer—*Sergeant* Joyce Kilmer—on that fateful thirtieth of July in 1918. As an intelligence NCO on the regimental staff, he was no stranger to forays into No Man's Land, but in this battle of the Ourcq, the Sixty-ninth's objective was Muercy Farm. He could have stayed back at regimental headquarters, but he was acting adjutant to the First Battalion's Major "Wild Bill" Donovan, because the adjutant had been killed the day before. A sniper's bullet ended the poet's life, and he was buried at age thirty-one in a creek bed below the farm. He was posthumously awarded the French Croix de Guerre for bravery. Kilmer could have stayed out of the war because he was married with children, but he felt he should serve and was able to get into the proud Sixty-ninth. Camp Kilmer in his native New Jersey is named for him, and his legacy of writings please many to this day.

★★★★★

The leader of that Manhattan victory parade was William J. Donovan, who had been promoted to colonel at war's end and given command of the Sixty-ninth during its few months of occupation duty after the end of hostilities. Wild Bill had earned the DSC at Ourcq when Kilmer was killed, and was promoted to lieutenant colonel. When he was about to be moved up to GHQ on the staff of the provost marshal general, he got MacArthur to intervene so he could stay with the regiment for the final offensive. It was the bitter Meuse-Argonne campaign.

Wild Bill assumed direction of the Sixty-ninth's frontline operations while the commander coordinated at the regimental post of command. It was October 14, 1918. Knowing the battle would be tough, and that it would inspire the men, Donovan put on every silver leaf of rank he could find—making himself a visible target for every German sniper. He seemed to be everywhere, directing dispositions and encouraging the men. The nearly impregnable enemy defenses included interlacing fire and imbedded positions. At daybreak the following morning, Wild Bill was in a frontline position when his leg was shattered by a German rifle round. He managed to crawl into a shell hole, refusing to be evacuated, and directed the attack for over five hours. When the Germans counterattacked, he called in mortar fire that stopped them cold, and wouldn't return to the rear until the regiment was relieved.

His heroics on those two days earned him the Medal of Honor.

But Wild Bill Donovan wasn't finished serving his country. When WWII drew America into its grasp, he formed the Office of Strategic Services (OSS), which had behind-the-lines operations in both major theaters (some of its military members later formed the core of the army's famed Green Berets). Donovan finished the war as a major general, and the OSS became the forerunner of the Central Intelligence Agency.

In 1953–54, Wild Bill was serving as ambassador to Thailand. Finishing this assignment, he was awarded the National Security Medal, thus becoming the first American to win the Medal of Honor, the DSC, the DSM, and the top civilian award.

A Mountain Man

*A Simple Soldier**

He was getting old and paunchy
And his hair was falling fast,
And he sat around the Legion,
Telling stories of the past.
Of a war that he had fought in
And the deeds that he had done,
In his exploits with his buddies;
They were heroes, every one.

And tho' sometimes, to his neighbors,
His tales became a joke,
All his Legion buddies listened,
For they knew whereof he spoke.
But we'll hear his tales no longer
For old Bill has passed away,
And the world's a little poorer
For a Soldier died today....

It was at Pall Mall in the Valley of the Wolf in Fenstress County that one of Tennessee's most famous men was born on December 13, 1887. He wouldn't become a West Pointer, or a senator, or a president, not even a movie star or a country singer. He would become a three-stripe sergeant. In his midtwenties, he was a hard-drinking, hard-gambling, hard-fighting day laborer on the railroad—a gandy dancer —and a mountain man. Mountain men lived by their rifles and he was a crack shot. But in 1915 his best friend was killed and his mother helped influence him to "get religion." He joined the little Church of Christ in Christian Union and quit his hell-bent ways for good.

By then, word had filtered into those hills that there was a big war going on against a feller named the Kaiser across the Big Pond. The man who was to be famous registered for the draft and was soon selected to go. He was thirty years old, redheaded, six feet two, with little schooling, and although he later denied it, he was a conscientious objector. But he got drafted, took it in stride, and went on down to Camp Gordon, Georgia, for training. However, he had a dilemma: he wanted to be a good Christian and a good American. While he was trying to sort this out, he was assigned to Company G, 328th Infantry, 82nd Infantry Division and sent to France.

His name was Alvin C. York.

And he got it sorted out. He finally decided, based on a passage in the Book of Ezekiel, that fighting under certain circumstances was all right, that killing the enemy would be justifiable. From that point on he became a capable soldier, convinced he was "doing it for the good of mankind." He even made corporal. His encounter with the glory that he never sought came on the morning of October 8, 1918, in the Argonne Forest. His company was in the assault with orders to take Hill 223, then drive across a valley surrounded on three sides by hillside machine-gun emplacements. Under intense fire, the attack staggered to a halt and a patrol of seventeen men, commanded by a sergeant, was directed to outflank the hill on the left and hit the machine-gun nests from behind. Corporal York was one of those men. After the sergeant was hit, York was the senior man.

The patrol killed a couple of Germans and then—but let's have Alvin York tell us what happened. From his diary:

> They was about fifteen or twenty Germans jumped up and threw up their hands and said, "*Kamerad!*" So the one in charge of us boys told us not to shoot; they was going to give up anyway. (These prisoners included a major and two other officers.)
>
> By this time, some of the Germans on the hill was shooting at us. Well, I was giving them the best I had, and by this time the Germans had got their machine guns turned around and fired on us. So they killed six and wounded three of us. (The sergeant was hit, leaving York in command.) So that left just 8, and then we got into it right by this time. We had a hard battle for a little while, and I got hold of the German major and he told me if I wouldn't kill any more of them he would make them quit firing. So I told him all right if he would do it now. So he blew a little whistle and they quit shooting and come down and gave up. I had killed over 20. . . . After he blew his whistle, all but one of them came off the hill with their hands up, and just before that one got to me he threw a little hand grenade which burst in the air in front of me. I had to touch him off.
>
> The rest surrendered without any more trouble. There were nearly a hundred of them. We had about 80 or 90 Germans there disarmed, and had another line of Germans to go through to get out. . . . In this battle I was using a rifle and a .45 Colt automatic. So I lined the Germans up in a line of twos and I got between the ones in front, and I had the German major before me. So I marched them straight into those other machine guns and I got them. So when I got back to my major's PC . . .

Brigadier General Lindsey was there and said, "Well, York, I hear you've captured the whole German army."

York softly replied, "No, sir, I have only 132."

In the taking of this critical strongpoint, essential to the 82nd's mission, Alvin York had taken 132 Germans prisoners, overcome about thirty-five machine guns, and killed no fewer than twenty-five of the enemy. In the division's official history, York's exploit in the Argonne "will always be retold in the military tradition of our country. It is entitled to a place among the famous deeds in arms in legendary or modern warfare."

Promoted to sergeant, York was awarded the DSC in February at a division review. And at a review at St. Silva, France, on April 18, the Medal of Honor was pinned on his tunic. Six days later, Marshal Ferdinand Foch himself added the Croix de Guerre. York's honors were just beginning: on his return to the States, he received one of New York City's huge ticker-tape parades. With that over, all the modest mountain man wanted to do was get home to Pall Mall and that little mountain girl who was waiting for him. But he still had to be honored by a joint session of Congress and the secretary of war. But finally it was discharge time and marriage time. Pall Mall in the Valley of the Wolf would never be the same.

York's gigantic fame could have made him the richest veteran in Tennessee, but accepting the fabulous offers that filled his mailbox just didn't feel right to him. Then he got what he decided was his "calling." He decided to open some small schools so that mountain kids would be able to get a better education than he did, but it became one large institution that eventually was called the York Agricultural Institute. He was much in demand as a speaker and donated most of his fees to the school—which sent him into debt.

He finally signed a contract with Warner Brothers for the movie rights of his life story. Starring the soft-spoken Gary Cooper, *Sergeant York* is still a popular film that would be enjoyed in many a classroom throughout the country.

Though in failing health, York contributed in several ways during WWII. He died on September 2, 1964, at the age of seventy-six. Eight thousand people, including General Matthew B. Ridgway, one of the WWII commanders of the famed 82nd Airborne Division, and Tennessee's governor Frank Clement attended the services of one of the most famous of America's mountain men.

THE TANK MAN

> *Courage is the art of being the only one who knows you're*
> *scared to death.*
> —British prime minister Harold Wilson (1916–1995)

Wars always provide a rich testing ground for many new weapons. Accelerated technological developments, plus the ingenuity provided by actual combat, combine with stepped-up manufacturing impetus to create remarkable results. One such tool of war was the tank.

When Pershing went to France to lead the American Expeditionary Force, Georgie Patton was still his aide. Although it had no military connection, because Pershing was all business, he and Patton's sister, Nita, had talked about marriage. They had decided, however, to hold off because of Black Jack's heavy responsibilities. Patton, promoted to captain, was essentially headquarters commandant both in Paris and in Chaumont, a small city 150 miles east of the capital, when Pershing moved the headquarters to get away from the distractions of the City of Light. Georgie was also the adjutant and had no qualms about fiercely dressing down both officers and enlisted men who were derelict in military courtesy and discipline, who were dirty, or who failed to salute.

Chafing to get into combat, Patton became interested in tanks and put his name in for consideration in the event a tank service were organized. His qualifications were numerous: he knew weapons, had commanded a machine-gun troop, had repaired automobile engines, spoke and read French fluently, thought tanks could perform a cavalry mission, and believed in getting close to the enemy.

Patton got the job. He was appointed director of the new American tank school at nearby Langres, and promoted to major. He was elated, confiding in a letter to his wife, Bea, that it was a golden dream; he would set up and run the school, become the Army's expert on tank warfare, and command a tank battalion in combat. He also confided in his wife that he hoped he might rise higher in command, and that, since tanks were a novelty, he'd get more publicity in the press.

Taking a two-week familiarization course at the French tank-training center, he fell in love with his newfound toy. He enthusiastically drove the small two-man Renault vehicle, imagining different battle scenarios. In it, the driver sat on the floor, while the gunner stood in the turret, directing the tank by pressure on the driver's head and shoulders with his foot. He went to Cambrai and talked to the British about their heavy tanks, and learned more. By this time, applications to join the new combat arm were flooding GHQ while Patton's ardor for his new babies grew by the day. Then it was back to his training center and his first two hundred tanker recruits. With the strict discipline in which he firmly believed, he led them through his concept of the training that would make them successful in battle. He barked at them, swore at them, and could never figure out why his tankers liked him. They composed a song about him that had a line, "We'll follow the colonel through hell and out the other side." Promoted to lieutenant colonel, Patton got his own tanks and finally formed his first battalion. Shortly after that, the 1st Light Tank Brigade was his to command.

But he agonized further about getting into battle before the war was over. He had always seen himself reincarnated from having served in Caesar's Roman legion, and felt he was destined for glory. How could he stand and watch it pass him by?

Convinced that tanks should work in full cooperation with infantry, he lectured on their use at the Army General Staff College in France, which he also attended. He believed in lightly armored tanks that would be highly maneuverable, in keeping with his cavalry upbringing. In August 1918 he commanded fifty officers and nine hundred men. He had 25 tanks, but another 119 were on their way when he was notified that the first large-scale American offensive was to kick off in September and his tank brigade was to be part of it!

Georgie Patton had his battle. It began on the twelfth, after Patton had already been out in No Man's Land reconnoitering the ground on foot. Now he set up his command post on a hill between the Big Red One and the Rainbow divisions, each of which was in the assault with a tank battalion in support. When some tanks bogged down, he hurried the two miles on foot to get them going. Leaving his rank on his shoulders in defiance of German snipers, he later strode rapidly through heavy shellfire to another holdup. His puffing pipe seemed to mark his contempt.

At the town of Essey, Patton ran into a calm Douglas MacArthur, who saw no objection to his moving on. Georgie climbed on a tank and pushed his men on to the town of Pannes. It seemed the German riflemen simply couldn't hit him. He continued to direct his pets until four tanks captured four German artillery pieces and sixteen machine guns. Out of gas, Patton's new charges were finished for the day, but they had handled their baptism of fire superbly—as had Georgie.

Next, it was the Meuse-Argonne offensive, where Patton once and for all proved his coolness under extreme danger. His tanks were fighting with I Corps. He had rounded up enough gasoline and stored it close to the front for 140 of them. The battle kicked off in dense fog, so Patton, with a couple of staff officers and a dozen runners, followed the sound of battle ahead. Once, under heavy fire, he stopped and collected about a hundred panic-stricken infantrymen and led them back toward the enemy, where he emplaced them.

He found several of his tanks blocked by deep trenches at one point, and pitched right in with the digging to break down the walls and fill them in. He hit one recalcitrant soldier over the head with a shovel when the man refused to dig. It was Patton at his most passionate: *no man could endanger others by not doing his job!*

A short time later, when his tanks went down the forward side of a hill, Georgie led a handful of soldiers into more intense fire. His orderly, Joe Angelo, soon told him, "We're alone, Colonel."

It was moments later that Patton's invincibility expired. An enemy bullet hit him in the left thigh and came out near his rectum. Angelo helped him crawl into a shell hole and bandaged his bleeding wound. But Patton hadn't come this far to be finished; he directed his orderly to point out the locations of enemy machine guns forty yards away. He sent a runner with word for a battalion commander to assume command, and refused to be carried to the rear. He continued to use Angelo to give directions as more tanks arrived and passed by. When that part of the battle subsided and he was finally carried on a litter two miles to the rear, he insisted on first going to division headquarters to render an action report. Only then did he allow himself to be taken to an evacuation hospital.

Miraculously, Patton's wound did not involve anything vital and he recovered rapidly. He attributed this fact to fate, his fate from ancient Rome. He was promoted to full colonel just before his thirty-third birthday, the date on which the war ended. After all, shouldn't such a war come to a close on the birthday of such a warrior—November 11?

His orderly, Joe Angelo, received the DSC.

George Patton received the DSC for bravery and the DSM for fathering the new tank service. But he had not yet found his fate.

Time for the Fliers!

It would become perhaps the most famous bar in the world, and even its address would later become well known: 5 rue Daunou, pronounced *Sank Roo Doe Noo*. It was Harry's New York Bar, but in 1916, while Harry was off flying for the Royal Navy, it was just the New York Bar. It was the Paris haunt of many exceptional people, but in particular the famous and hard-drinking pilots of the *Lafayette Escadrille*, the Americans who flew unbelievably fragile fighter planes over the Verdun front. The freewheeling Yanks further enhanced their country-club image by having two lion cubs named "Whiskey" and "Soda" as their mascots.

Originally, the organization was called the *Escadrille Americaine*, but that name was changed and the squadron became part of the Lafayette Flying Corps, named for the young noble who came to

America to fight in the Revolution. Filled with adventurers from all walks of life, including Ivy Leaguers, the squadron was a glamorous, silk-scarfed batch of intrepid fliers, whose flimsy Nieuport 17 biplanes rose to meet the German Fokkers on many cold mornings. Late in 1916 they flew the more advanced Spads against the Germans.

The most well-known member of this group was Raul Lufberry, an American soldier of fortune of French lineage. He had served in China and in the French Foreign Legion, and had joined the French Stork Squadron in 1914, where he serviced planes while taking flying lessons. He accumulated the most kills in the Escadrille. When Pershing's American Expeditionary Force came to the war, Lufberry transferred over to the American Air Service and commanded the 94th Aero Squadron, the famed "hat-in-the-ring" bunch of aviators. All told, he had seventeen victories in the war, but died in an aerial dogfight in June 1918, with Colonel Billy Mitchell, the chief of AEF aviation watching from the ground below.

All told, some two hundred Americans flew with the Lafayette Flying Corps. Sixty-five were killed. The Escadrille's aces accounted for ninety-nine kills.

But before them, even before Pershing used Jennys on his Mexican Punitive Expedition, Billy Mitchell paid for lessons and learned to fly. Mitchell, born of well-to-do American parents in Nice, France, left college before graduation to enlist in the Army for service in the Spanish-American War. As an officer, he served in Cuba and the Philippines and was attached to the Signal Corps in 1901—the branch of service that bought the first 1909 Wright Military Flyers. Mitchell was already in France as an observer when the Yanks declared war, and in June 1917 he was named air officer for the AEF. Later, as a colonel, he became air officer of I Corps. He was the first American officer to fly over enemy lines and seemed to be on combat patrols as often as his junior pilots. In September of 1918 he led the largest number of aircraft ever assembled—fifteen hundred American and French planes—on a bombing mission over the Saint-Mihiel salient. He was promoted to brigadier general and led another huge raid in the rear of enemy lines during the Meuse-Argonne offensive. Again, his aircraft was more often in the air than on the ground in those final days of the war.

Billy Mitchell received the DSC and many other medals for his bravery and fearless leadership, but he is best known for his postwar activities. As a proponent of air power, he was insistent and sometimes abrasive in his pursuit of aviation readiness and the development of a separate air force. He angered old-line Naval officers when he stated that the airplane had made the battleship obsolete, then sought to prove his point by sinking the former German dreadnaught *Ostfriesland* with his lumbering aircraft. He was reduced in rank to colonel, and when the lighter-than-air ship *Shenandoah* went down in a thunderstorm, he accused both the War and Navy departments of "incompetency, criminal negligence, and almost treasonable administration of the National Defense."

That got their attention and it got Mitchell a general court-martial for insubordination. Found guilty, he was sentenced to a five-year suspension from active duty. He stayed out of the army and continued to flog the military about aviation preparedness (one of his warnings was that Japan would bomb Pearl Harbor).

The visionary who is considered the father of the US Air Force died in New York City in February 1936.

Gary Cooper, after being promoted from three stripes in *Sergeant York*, starred in the 1955 movie *The Court-Martial of Billy Mitchell.*

★★★★★

The tank was one of the great developments of WWI, but it was just a machine of war. The incredibly swift advancement of the airplane was more far-reaching and vital to life throughout the world. The first gun to be fired from one was a rifle, but before long a German invented an interrupter gear so a machine gun could fire through a propeller, and soon the word "dogfight" was applied to aerial war. By the end of WWI, one Allied fighter, the British SAE-5, could reach a speed of 140 mph! It's hard to conceive just how close to being flying kites those WWI aircraft actually were, just as it's difficult to imagine the life of the pilots in combat. New replacements had little flying time. In open cockpits with no heat, often flying above a safe oxygen level without parachutes, with guns that jammed easily, and temperamental engines, against a foe in a deadly Fokker who was inspired by the heritage of the Red Baron, it's truly amazing how many American pilots survived the war.

A second lieutenant by the name of Frank Luke Jr. from Phoenix, Arizona, made a name for himself shooting down German observation balloons, those tethered lighter-than-air craft that got their start in the Civil War. Shooting down a balloon doesn't sound like too dangerous a feat, but this type was normally surrounded by scores of machine guns and antiaircraft weapons putting up heavy fire. Luke was a lone-wolf flier, in a day of more extensive formation flying, whose solo attacks soon earned him the sobriquet "the balloon buster."

He shot down thirteen of them in just five days in September 1918. In one day, he got two of them and three aircraft kills. Ten days later he was badly wounded and forced down. But before he landed, he strafed a German infantry column. As he climbed from the cockpit, he was surrounded by enemy riflemen. He ignored their surrender request, drew his pistol, started firing, and was killed by a hail of bullets.

Frank Luke, just twenty-one, was the ranking American ace at the time of his death, with four aircraft and fourteen balloons. He was the first aviator to be awarded the Medal of Honor. Luke Air Force Base, just west of Phoenix, is named for him.

★★★★★

The only other WWI pilot to receive America's highest medal was the most famous one of the conflict. And he earned it in that famous 94th Aero Squadron, the Hat-in-the-Ring outfit that Captain Raul Lufberry had commanded earlier. Before the war, he became quite famous as a racing driver—which was how he became a GHQ chauffeur when he first went to France. But the jaunty twenty-seven-year-old Ohioan soon transferred to pilot training. His name, of course, was Eddie Rickenbacker. Once he got a pursuit plane under him, he began racking up kills, also as a lone wolf, and accumulated more combat flying time than any other American. His citation for the Distinguished Service Cross reads:

> For extraordinary heroism in action near Montsec, France, 29 April 1918. Lt. Rickenbacker attacked an enemy Albatros monoplane and after a vigorous fight, in which he followed his foe into German territory, he succeeded in shooting it down near Vigneulles-les-Hatten-Chatel.

The citation for his Medal of Honor reads:

> Edward V. Rickenbacker, Colonel, specialist reserve, then first lieutenant, 94th Aero Squadron, Air Service, American Expeditionary Forces. For conspicuous gallantry and intrepidity above and beyond the call of duty in action against the enemy near Billy, France, 25 September 1918. While on a voluntary patrol over the lines, Lieutenant Rickenbacker attacked seven enemy planes (five Fokkers protecting two Halberstadt photographic planes). Disregarding the odds against him, he dived on them and shot down one of the Fokkers out of control. He then attacked one of the Halberstadts and sent it down also....

During October 1918, Rickenbacker scored fourteen victories for what he and WWI historians have always claimed made a total of twenty-six. In the 1960s the US Air Force fractionalized his shared victories, reducing his total to 24.33, including four balloons. He flew a total of three hundred combat hours, more than any other American pilot, and survived 134 aerial encounters with the enemy. "So many close calls renewed my thankfulness to the Power above, which had seen fit to preserve me," he wrote in his memoirs.

But he did more than shoot down Germans. When he was promoted to commander of the 94th, he whipped it into shape as the outstanding squadron in the Air Service. Billy Mitchell doted on him.

After the war Rickenbacker bought and operated the Indianapolis Speedway, and later was president of Eastern Airlines for many years. During WWII, he was on a secret mission as a civilian aboard a B-17 that had to ditch in the Pacific. He and six companions survived twenty-two days on life rafts before being rescued. Then he went on to meet MacArthur in New Guinea. He died in 1973 at the age of eighty-three.

★★★★★

There's another famous flier who deserves mention—a *real* flier with real feathers. "Cher Ami" was a registered Black Check Cock carrier pigeon, one of six hundred birds owned and flown by the US Army Signal Corps in France during WWI.

He delivered twelve important messages within the American sector at Verdun, France. On his last mission, Cher Ami, shot through the breast by enemy fire, managed to return to his loft. A message capsule was found dangling from the ligaments of one of his legs that had been shattered by enemy fire. The message he carried was from Major Whittlesey's "Lost Battalion" of the 77th Infantry Division that had been isolated from other American forces. Just a few hours after the message was received, 194 survivors of the battalion were safe behind American lines. Cher Ami lived for over a year, standing on his one good leg, not knowing (we think) that the French had awarded him the Croix de Guerre with palm, or that he had become the most famous soldier/pigeon in the world.

★★★★★

Again, there is no way to touch on the thousands of heroic acts in that war that was to end all wars. World War I was so quickly pushed into the shadows by the conflict that came along a quarter of a century later that it became, quite literally, "the first forgotten war."

Black Jack Pershing returned to the States as the great hero he was. His iron will, his brilliance in command and logistics, his stern insistence that American soldiers fight in their own units, and his overall management of the AEF, justified his fame. He never did marry Nita Patton, nor anyone else in his later years. In 1919 he was promoted to general of the armies, a five-star rank. He became army chief of staff after the war, and retired in 1924. His memoir, *My Experience in the World War,* won the Pulitzer Prize in 1931. He died at the age of eighty-eight in Walter Reed Army Hospital in 1948, and was buried in Arlington Cemetery near his WWI soldiers—at his direction. He also directed that his headstone be the simple issue type that they received. His grandson, who was killed as a second lieutenant in Vietnam, is buried beside him. Black Jack Pershing ranks as one of the greatest American military leaders.

CHAPTER NINE

IN BETWEEN WARS

The years that followed brought rapid development in automobiles and many other thingamajigs. The military was cut back drastically as is always the case after a war because the peacemongers always think disarmament is the solution to everything. It seems there is never a halfway point. But as the twenties rolled in and on, and President Wilson's ill-fated League of Nations stumbled along, broken Germany was not so broken. Secretly, the "nonexistent" General Staff set up a tank school at Kazan, Russia, and the so-called Black Luftwaffe was equipped and trained elsewhere in the Soviet state.

In Wisconsin a tall, lanky young man had become interested in aviation and had tried his hand at wing walking, parachuting, and all other elements of barnstorming. He piled up many hours of flying time as a pilot. In 1924 he went through the Army Air Corps cadet program and was rated as a pursuit pilot, but he opted for a commission in the National Guard and began the hazardous civilian job of flying the mail. About the time he was promoted to captain (he was undoubtedly the most experienced pilot in the Guard) he became interested in the Ortieg Prize of $25,000 for the first nonstop flight across the Atlantic. As he would show later, it wasn't the money that attracted him as much as the sheer challenge. Attempts had been made, some with tragic results. New ones were being readied, so he had to hurry. He had to find backers and get himself an airplane that might get him to Paris.

His name was Charles Lindbergh.

He found his backers in St. Louis. A small aircraft company named Ryan in San Diego agreed to build the aircraft to his rigid specifications. Time was their enemy, but by working night and day, with Lindbergh there to make changes, the people of Ryan produced the *Spirit of St. Louis* in record time.

On its first major test flight, Lindbergh broke the transcontinental speed record flying from California to New York. Then at Roosevelt Field, Long Island, he sweated out the weather until he decided to go for it. (Roosevelt Field was named for Quentin Roosevelt, the youngest of Teddy's offspring, who was shot down and killed behind enemy lines in WWI.) Lindbergh had had practically no sleep in the previous two days, but that didn't deter him. He measured everything he took on board against the precious gasoline he figured he needed. Four sandwiches, two canteens of water, and 451 gallons of gasoline constituted his essentials. Then it was go! The overloaded plane bounced down the muddy runway, gathering speed and finally lifted off a couple of feet, until at last it began to climb. Barely clearing the wires at the end of the field, Lindy headed northeast for Nova Scotia.

And America waited. People gathered in Times Square for bulletins. The *New York Times* received over six hundred telephone inquiries that day requesting information—and the next day it would run into the thousands. People throughout the country were glued to their radios.

Although his flight had been most carefully planned, he had only a few navigational tools: rudimentary maps, a magnetic compass, and an altimeter. Since the gas tanks were between the cockpit and the engine in the Ryan, forward vision was achieved through a tiny periscope or by sticking his head out the window. The method of navigation was called "dead reckoning," although Lindy took out the first word. Of all the many unknowns in this flight, the most serious were weather and wind. The "ifs" were huge. If his Wright Whirlwind engine remained faithful, if he could stay out of icing conditions, if he were not blown too far off course, if, if, if—he *might* make it. Lloyds of London quoted no odds because they "felt the risk was too great."

Perhaps the most important obstacle was Lindbergh himself. Starting with no rest, how much stamina did he have? The only way he could possibly handle other obstacles was to stay awake and alert. (I was an Army aviator for thirteen years, flying light airplanes and helicopters, and I fought sleep many times, but I cannot imagine how *anyone* could fly 33.5 hours, with the steady drone of an engine deadening one's senses, without falling completely asleep.)

His first real test, he said, was when he flew out over the ocean for 250 miles. But when he reached Nova Scotia at noon he was just six miles off course and readily adjusted. It took four hours and flying through some squalls to cross the province, then it was on to Newfoundland and finally to the open ocean. He tried to occupy his mind by keeping a log and continually switching the use of his fuel tanks, but after just eight hours, his eyes were "feeling dry and hard as stones." He would alternately force them wide open, then tightly shut them. And all the time, the water below was dangerously hypnotic.

He climbed to 10,000 feet above the fog and clouds into the most solitary world any single man had ever known, not aware, as Scott Berg wrote in his great biography *Lindbergh*, that "he was also ascending in public consciousness to Olympian heights," and that "modern man realized that nobody had ever subjected himself to so extreme a test of human courage and capability.... Not even Columbus sailed alone."

Humorist Will Rogers played it straight that day by writing, "A ... slim, tall, bashful American boy is somewhere over the middle of the Atlantic Ocean, where no lone human being has ever ventured before. He is being prayed for to every kind of a Supreme Being that had a following. If he is lost it will be the most universally regretted loss we ever had."

Fourteen hours out, at 10,000 feet, a cold Lindbergh was trying to get around some monstrous storm clouds when the *Spirit of St. Louis* began to ice up—an absolutely deadly occurrence. He quickly headed down to warmer air and miraculously found his way out of the storms. Now his troubles returned to the *inside* of the cockpit. His physical condition was deteriorating, and only the absolute necessity of flying the plane kept him even partially alert. He wrote, "It seems impossible to go on longer. All I want in life is to throw myself down down flat—stretch out, and sleep."

After the arrival of daylight, he descended to one hundred feet above the waves, then he hit fog and had to climb into the soup. He flew blind at 1,500 feet for two hours before breaking out. In his twenty-second hour he flew right above the waves so the spray of the whitecaps through the open window would help him stay awake. On and on he flew, fighting each new problem and wondering where he was. At last he saw a seagull, and then a fishing boat, which he circled just above its mast and hollered, *"Which way is Ireland?"* Of course he got no response from the startled fishermen, so he turned back on course and sped on. (They probably swore off alcohol for good!) Before long, he arrived at Dingle Bay on the southwest coast of Ireland. Incredibly, he was less than three miles off course!

Paris was just six hours away.

Lindy sped on, somewhat euphorically . . . five hours, four, three, two, one, and then a glow began to grow in the distance. It spread, getting brighter, taking shape, and soon the great capital of France was below his wings. But after circling the Eiffel Tower, he had trouble locating the airport, Le Bourjet. He had no way of knowing at first that the long stream of lights leading to the black space that should have been his destination were the headlamps of thousands of automobiles stuck in traffic on the road to the airport.

Finally the *Spirit of St. Louis* touched down and turned toward the floodlights on the other side of the field. What Lindy saw was incredible—a flood of humans, he would find out later, that was estimated at 150,000 was there to greet him. They swarmed over the *Spirit.* Also he would soon discover that he was the most popular hero the world had ever known! In America, people simply went nuts! The French loved him and didn't want him to leave. The British wanted him. Every country wanted him. In London, King George pinned the Air Force Cross, Britain's highest peacetime medal, on him. Finally, he and the airplane that had so faithfully carried him safely to fame arrived on the coast of the United States aboard the cruiser USS *Memphis.*

Now it was his countrymen's turn. The cruiser was greeted at Chesapeake Bay by four destroyers, two army dirigibles, and forty airplanes. The humble Army captain mused, "I wonder if I deserve all this?"

When the ship docked at the Navy Yard the next morning, under an escort of eighty-nine aircraft, it was greeted by a roar from the huge waiting crowd that included cabinet members and heads of the armed services, as well as one other person, the only one who had been close to him in his life, his mother, Evangeline Lindbergh.

The Lindberghs were escorted to the vicinity of the Washington Monument, where a crowd of *250,000* awaited. President Calvin Coolidge and his guests also waited. "Silent Cal" outdid himself in a speech, and pinned on Lindbergh's lapel the first Distinguished Flying Cross ever awarded. Then he promoted Lucky Lindy to colonel on the spot.

When the nation's capital finished feting him, Lindbergh went on to New York City where he was honored by the biggest ticker-tape parade ever. It literally snowed paper as hundreds of thousands paid tribute and dapper mayor Jimmy Walker pinned on a special medal that had been designed just for "The Lone Eagle." A tour of the rest of the country followed and in 1928 Congress bestowed on Colonel Charles Lindbergh the Medal of Honor.

Unauthorized to do so, as a civilian observer in WWII, Lindy flew some dozen combat missions with the Navy and Marines before catching a hop to the Fifth Air Force area in the southwest Pacific. There, he flew twenty-five combat missions in ninety hours in the twin-engined P-38, strafing, bombing, shooting down a Japanese plane, and, as one report stated, "being shot at by nearly every anti-aircraft gun in western New Guinea." His savvy in cruise control extended the range of the P-38 by nearly 50 percent, a considerable contribution to the flying effort in that part of the war for "an observer."

The Lone Eagle died in 1974 at the age of seventy-two, without a doubt one of the greatest men to ever climb inside the cockpit of an aircraft.

CHAPTER TEN

WORLD WAR II

My argument is that War makes rattling good history;
but Peace is poor reading.
— Thomas Hardy, *The Dynasts* (1903–1908)

WORLD WAR, THE SECOND TIME AROUND

In 1933 a man named Adolf Hitler assumed the office of chancellor in Germany. On his arm he wore a band with the swastika, the symbol of his party—the Nazis. His fiery oratory blared the words the power-hungry German people wanted to hear: that they were the super race and that they would rule the world in a thousand-year Third Reich. The general staff, which had never really been deactivated after World War I, now made plans for war, and those tanks and aircraft that had been tested in Russia became a reality. In a few years, the nation's powerful Luftwaffe and its panzer armies would be ready to terrorize Europe. Germany's able factories began churning out the tools of war as the rest of Europe (and America) tried to pretend it wasn't happening. A convenient civil war in Spain gave Hitler's storm troopers and pilots a chance to test their new and modern weapons as the clock on the time bomb ticked away.

And down in the boot of Italy, a jut-jawed Fascist named Benito Mussolini tried to emulate Germany's *führer* by busily building his own war machine.

To complete the third element of what would become known as the Axis Powers, on the far side of the world yet another imperialistic war machine was on the march. Japan, which had enriched its *Bushido* heritage by defeating Russia in 1905, had overrun Manchuria and was successfully waging war on China, and was preparing to fulfill Billy Mitchell's scoffed-at prophecy.

British leaders fell for Hitler's lies, and his panzers sped into Poland on September 1, 1939. Led by his dive-bombing Stukas, a new art of war was introduced to the world—*blitzkrieg!* Poland fell easily, and soon the Germans were in Paris. By June of 1940, all of Europe, except Britain and some minor Axis allies, belonged to Adolf. And England, hanging on by a stubborn thread, was open to invasion. Only miscalculation by the Germans kept them off the British Isles. Aid and fifty destroyers from the United States helped the British, as did the valiant effort of the Royal Air Force in fighting off the hordes of Luftwaffe planes in what became famous as "The Battle of Britain." One element of this heroic stand was the "Eagle Squadron," which was made up of Yank pilots. Fighting spread to North Africa, where a German military genius named Field Marshal Erwin Rommel reigned. Then Hitler made his biggest mistake—in June 1941, he broke his pact with Russian dictator Josef Stalin and invaded Mother Russia.

As much as US president Franklin Delano Roosevelt wanted to help valiant Winston Churchill's Britain, the American concept of isolationism kept him from declaring war on the Axis until December 7, 1941, when General Hideki Tojo's Japanese navy fulfilled Billy Mitchell's prediction. His pilots bombed Pearl Harbor that unforgettable early Sunday morning, sinking twenty-two warships and decimating Battleship Row. The *Arizona* went down with a thousand sailors. The next day before a joint session of Congress, Roosevelt referred to it as "a day which will live in infamy," and declared war on the Axis Powers.

Admiral Isoroku Yamamoto, the poker and bridge–playing admiral who planned and executed the sneak attack on Pearl Harbor, warned that the United States would have to be defeated within six months because Japan "would be awakening a sleeping giant."

Calls of *"Remember Pearl Harbor!"* flooded America, as thousands of young men and women overran recruiting offices. The sleeping giant was already beginning to twitch.

In the Philippines, Douglas MacArthur was wearing two hats. He had retired from active duty in 1936 to become the commander of the commonwealth's armed forces, but FDR had just recalled him to command US Army forces there. He would soon be promoted to the four-star rank he had held in the early thirties as army chief of staff. On December 8, his limited air forces were virtually wiped out, and the small naval elements around Manila had to depart in the face of a powerful Japanese task force. Woefully ill-equipped, the Filipino and American forces on the islands were unable to withstand the invasion of Japanese General Masaharu Homma's battle-hardened Fourteenth Army, troops that had bloodied their bayonets in China. MacArthur directed a brilliant move to get his main force into the peninsula of Bataan on the island of Luzon, where it held off the Japanese and waited for fresh provisions and reenforcements from the States. He set up his headquarters on "The Rock," the small, heavily fortified island of Corregidor at the mouth of Manila Bay.

COLIN KELLY

Back on December 10, torpedo bombers had sunk both the *Prince of Wales* and the *Repulse*, England's two major warships in the Pacific, off Malaya. It was also a bad day for one of the only six B-17 Flying Fortresses left on the island of Luzon in the Philippines. Sitting in the rain on a rough strip near San Marcelino, hungry crews of three of the bombers were ordered to Clark Field to refuel and have bombs loaded to raid Formosa. Clark was a mess. Burned and wrecked aircraft were everywhere, the result of the decimating Japanese raid on December 8 (December 7 at Pearl Harbor). Before the three B-17Cs could be fully rearmed and refueled, another air raid warning sounded. They quickly took off, heading for their targets without fighter escort. One, flown by Captain Colin P. Kelly Jr., was bound for destiny.

Kelly was a 1937 graduate of West Point, a handsome, dark-haired twenty-six-year-old who had been a B-17 instructor. His ship held only three six-hundred-pound bombs, but in the desperation that clouded everything American at that time, he was about to do something very positive. Spotting a landing force at Appara on the northern coast of Luzon, Kelly radioed Clark Field for permission to divert and attack what appeared to be a battleship in the flotilla supporting the invasion. Receiving no permission, Captain Kelly decided to attack anyway. He made two dry runs on the large ship, which was actually a heavy cruiser, at 20,000 feet, then gave bombardier Sergeant Meyer Levin the order to drop on the third run. Two of the big bombs straddled the ship, while the middle one hit at midship, the crew thought. No more accurate report could be made because smoke quickly obscured the target.

Kelly quickly wheeled the big aircraft and headed back to Clark. But trouble awaited him there in the form of a swarm of enemy fighters. Their first pass killed a crew member and smashed the instrument panel in the cockpit. The second pass set the left wing ablaze. Fire quickly spread to the fuselage. Fighting the controls, Kelly ordered the crew to bail out at once. The last to leave was the copilot, Second Lieutenant Donald Robins, but just as he was exiting the upper escape hatch, the lurching, blazing ship exploded, blowing him clear. The charred remains of the bomber were found five miles from Clark Field; Kelly's remains were in them.

Surviving crew members related what they knew of the story, and the word of the first major heroic act by an American serviceman flashed across America. The name Colin Kelly was on the lips of millions of Americans! Schoolkids heard it and remembered. (FDR promised to give his nearly two-year-old son, Colin P. Kelly III, an appointment to West Point.) As dazed Americans tried to grasp the reality of Pearl Harbor, they latched onto the heroic B-17 pilot's selfless deed. Kelly was also the first West Pointer killed in WWII. For his courageous act, he was awarded a posthumous Distinguished Service Cross. (Of interest is the fact that his son graduated from West Point in the class of 1963, and served as a chaplain for most of his twenty years of service. He retired as a lieutenant colonel and now is pastor of an Episcopal Church in Los Alamos, New Mexico.)

The Fall of the Philippines

As December moved along and 1942 arrived, disaster was rampant. Word came to Corregidor that Guam and Wake Island had fallen. Singapore was taken, and the rest of the major Allied holdings in the Southwest Pacific fell. The Japanese tide seemed invincible everywhere except in the Philippines.

Although the forces on Bataan fought gallantly, resupply from the States wasn't forthcoming. Reduced rations sapped their strength, and ammunition ran short. In mid-March, FDR ordered MacArthur to Australia to assume command of Allied operations in the Southwest Pacific. The general nearly resigned rather than leave his men in the Philippines, and his promise of "I shall return" became famous. As a sidebar, the marines remaining on The Rock parodied the statement when they went to the latrine, saying to their buddies, "I shall return." Command of the Philippines reverted to Major General "Skinny" Wainwright.

The trip to Melbourne, on sea, by air, and by train, was arduous. The PT boat journey that took MacArthur's party to Mindanao, the large southern Philippine island, was extremely hazardous, and the long flight to Australia in two jammed B-17s had to constantly evade alerted Japanese aircraft. When the general finally arrived at his destination he was shocked to find that he had no army. Most of the

Australian army troops were off in Africa fighting for the empire. MacArthur was furious and demanded the means to fight. Instead, Washington gave him the Medal of Honor he had long coveted. The long road back looked terribly bleak.

The conditions on Bataan continued to deteriorate, with the worsening diet leading to diseases such as malaria, dengue fever, beriberi, scurvy, and dysentery. Yet the brave men, Americans and Filipinos, hung on. One piece of doggerel, attributed to correspondent Frank Hewlett, became famous:

> *We're the battling bastards of Bataan:*
> *No momma, no poppa, no Uncle Sam,*
> *No aunts, no uncles, no nephews, no nieces,*
> *No rifles, or planes, or artillery pieces,*
> *... And nobody gives a damn.*

This group of paladins included the gutsy little Filipino Scouts, a regular outfit that never backed away from a fight. The 200th Coast Artillery Regiment of the New Mexico National Guard had arrived in time to get caught in the phalanx of Philippine defenders. Heroes too numerous to mention abounded in this tropical morass that had become, finally, a prison. A grisly note had also been sent to the White House: *"Dear Mr. President, Please send us a P-40* [Warhawk fighter plane]. *The one we have is all shot up."*

In early April 1943, Japanese general Homma's reenforced army bombarded the Bataan positions with a relentless, pulverizing artillery barrage, then attacked the weakened, crumbling Allied lines. On April 9 (coincidentally the date of Lee's surrender at Appomattox) Major General Edward King, commanding Bataan, held up the white flag and surrendered seventy thousand starving and ill Filipinos and Americans. Many on the peninsula fled to Corregidor, but less than a month later, Wainwright, overrun on The Rock, was forced to capitulate. But not before Wild Bill Massello had his say.

WILD BILL MASSELLO

Thirty-five-year-old Captain Massello graduated from West Point in the class of 1932 and was commissioned in the Coast Artillery Corps. When the war concentrated on Bataan, the searchlight battery he commanded was sent there from The Rock. Somewhat of a maverick, he disobeyed a few orders to get the maximum effect out of his big flashlights. Just before King surrendered on Bataan, Massello brought his men, minus their searchlights, back to jam-packed Corregidor. There he discovered some huge old mortars in a section called Battery Way. He had fired mortars as a new second lieutenant several years earlier, so he was no stranger to the big, squat guns.

While under fire, he quickly taught the brave men of his battery mortar firing. At the same time, ordinance artificers struggled to get the old weapons in shape to shoot. Since mortar rounds subscribed a high, long arc, Massello came up with a short-fuse solution for the armor-piercing shells that were still available. He was ready to start sending back some of the constant hell the Japanese were showering on the fortress. On Emperor Hirohito's birthday, April 29, Massello was ready. With sixteen men on each of the four mortars, the gun captains began to pull the lanyards. Firing one at a time, they heaved thousand-pound shells at the Japanese positions. Naturally Wild Bill's ancient guns drew all of the enemy guns' attention, so he had to get his men back under cover.

Following a massive bombardment on all of The Rock's gun positions that took out the powder magazine and left only two of Massello's mortars in working order, the Japanese invasion forces hit the beach on the evening of May 3. As Wild Bill's guns continued firing, one more was knocked out and his position took casualties. Massello personally handled and repaired the last huge gun as it began to malfunction. Each time it was rolled back to be reloaded it was necessary to sweep the tracks clear. Wild Bill insisted on doing this chore himself. Under heavy fire he shouted, *"If they ever get me, what a hell of a way for a soldier to go—with a goddamn broom in my hand!"*

Firing the mortar alone, after ordering his men to remain under cover, he was hit by a blast of jagged shrapnel that got him in the legs and severed an artery in his arm. Dragged back under cover by his men, he was given first aid, and from his stretcher he continued to conduct the firing until at last the mortar's breechblock froze, and the valiant saga of Battery Way was over. Somehow, after The Rock fell, Massello, his right hand paralyzed, made the six-mile Death March through Manila on his infected leg. He survived three years as a prisoner, stayed in the Army, retired as a colonel in 1960 with thirty-seven years of service, and became a public school teacher. For his actions on Bataan and Corregidor, William Massello was awarded the DSC, three Silver Stars, and four Purple Hearts.

WILLIAM DYESS

The infamous Bataan Death March, in which thousands of American and Filipino soldiers were subjected to unbelievable brutality and death, began shortly after the surrender. It lasted from April 12 to April 24, 1942. Just to survive, one had to have incredible fortitude and be very lucky. There was hardly any food and almost no water for the marchers. Most who fell out or sometimes just stumbled were bayoneted or shot. Then came the long ordeal of the prison camps, and for many prisoners, the hell ships that took them to Japan to perform forced labor. There were different kinds of bravery, different kinds of heroes and heroines. Sixty-five nurses became prisoners of war. Their stories are remarkable. The movie *Cry Havoc* (1943), starring Margaret Sullavan, came out after escapees brought back word of the camp atrocities.

Many Filipinos and a few Americans escaped and fought as guerrillas. Captain William E. Dyess was one of the most successful. A Texan from a long line of Dyesses that stretched back to South Carolina during the Revolution, he was a P-40 pilot who wound up on Bataan with nothing to fly. That didn't bother him—the twenty-five-year-old pilot formed his own little infantry command and fought fiercely with a rifle. After the fall of Bataan he tried to hold his group together but it was impossible in the chaos of the Death March. Surviving the march, three prison camps, and a prison ship, he escaped and joined up with some other Americans and some Filipinos in guerrilla operations on the Philippine island of Mindanao. Soon his exploits were so successful that he became known as "The One-Man Scourge." He finally made his way out and returned to the States for hospitalization and recovery, after which he requested retraining so he could get back into combat. Promoted to lieutenant colonel, he was flying in a P-38 over Burbank, California, when his aircraft caught fire. Rather than bail out over a populated area, Dyess rode it down in a field and was killed in the crash. His decorations included two DSCs, and two Silver Stars. Dyess Air Force Base, outside of Abilene, Texas, is named for him.

PATTON RESURFACES

Judgement comes from experience and experience comes from bad judgement.
—General Simon Bolivar Buckner

Although in his arrogance, former Corporal Shicklgruber—Adolf Hitler, to those who are unaware of his real name—would never admit to what Sam Grant's former friend and later adversary had to say, he would prove it over and over in WWII. In this case, on June 22, 1941, Hitler broke his nonaggression pact with Comrade/Marshal Stalin, and the German army poured into Soviet Russia. The blitzkrieg rolled almost unopposed along two major thrusts—one leading toward Moscow, the other to Stalingrad. The Luftwaffe knocked out most of the Russian air force, much of it on the ground, almost immediately. Hitler was elated, but only a few months ahead lay the enemy that Hitler forgot had defeated Napoleon. Not only would the Wehrmacht have to deal with the unrelenting heart of Mother Russia, but also a general (later marshal) named Georgy Zhukov and his greatest ally, the formidable Russian winter.

To explain America's entry into the European war we need to go back to Georgie Patton, the ultimate warrior. In the late thirties, he was frustrated that he would never get the war that he believed held his great destiny. One polo accident that created a slurring of speech could have ended his career, as a horse kick that almost crippled him for life could have done. But his iron will brought recovery and he was soon pulling general duty. With war clouds gathering in Europe in 1938 and Army purse strings loosening, Patton was promoted to colonel and given command of a regiment of the First Cavalry Division at Fort Clark, Texas. He was in his glory.

But the assignment was short-lived. In early 1939, he was summoned to Washington to take command of Fort Myer, the old show post by Arlington Cemetery that housed so many generals. His predecessor, Colonel Jonathon Wainwright, had nearly gone bankrupt trying to keep up with the social requirements. Patton had money, or at least his wealthy wife did. With tears streaming down his cheeks, he looked at Bea and said, "You and your money have ruined my career."

However, he got to know George Marshall, Pershing's Chaumont whiz kid from WWI, who was the new Army chief of staff. When an armored force was authorized in 1940, Patton was given command of a brigade in the 2nd Armored Division. He brilliantly trained it and soon got his long-yearned-for star. White-haired and back with his tanks at fifty-five, he decided that destiny had given him his chance. He later became the division commander and received his second star. Patton's penchant for learning the art of command over the years now came fully into play as he profanely and forcefully whipped the 2nd Armored into the most combat-ready division in the army. He bought an airplane and learned to fly it so he could cover its marches. His mechanical knowledge and tank experience from France in the last war came into play. He seemed to have a sixth sense for being wherever anything went wrong, and he knew how to fix it. His discipline was rigid as he preached offensive warfare. His men adored him. So did the media. He became known as "Old Blood and Guts." And the 2nd Armored adopted a name that was attached to the bottom of its patch: "*Hell on Wheels.*"

In 1939 Lieutenant Colonel Dwight "Ike" Eisenhower, MacArthur's chief of staff, had transferred to the States, and by 1941 had become Marshall's fair-haired boy. Now a general, Ike's personable ability to get along with nearly everyone had made him the logical choice for the ticklish political command with the British. But he wasn't all smiles and personality—he had proven himself to be an imaginative plans officer. Promoted to two stars, then three, he was placed in command of the joint British/American operation called *Torch* in 1942 to break Axis control of North Africa. Vichy (Occupied) France had agreed to a non-belligerency role with Germany, which meant it might defend its own (colonial North African) shores in the event of Allied invasion.

Ike was born in Denton, Texas, in 1890 and graduated in the West Point class of 1915 (called "the class the stars fell on" because of the many general officers it produced). A good athlete, he once aspired to be a major-league baseball player. He was inconspicuous—sixteen years as a major—until Marshall tapped him for the Mediterranean command. But he had served directly under Pershing and, because of a common interest in tanks, was a friend of Patton's. It was now time to call on his friend Georgie.

It was decided that Patton should take the first major American unit to go into ground combat in the war—the 2nd Armored Division—and invade Morocco from the Atlantic side. Patton was elated; he was finally going to get his chance in battle! But getting the division ready and prepared for a waterborne invasion across an unfriendly ocean was a logistical and planning nightmare. In spite of foul-ups, and because of his thorough preparedness, he managed to get the division ashore and quickly subdued the defending Vichy French forces. Then he was taken out of action and made to cool his heels and utilize his fluent French and continental manners as Eisenhower decided how best to further use him.

THE EAGLES

> *Never before have so many owed so much to so few.*
> —Winston Churchill, lauding the pilots
> of the Battle of Britain (August 20, 1940)

Well before Pearl Harbor there were the American Eagle Squadrons in the Royal Air Force (RAF), and before them, there was Billy Fiske. Billy was born into a wealthy banking family in Brooklyn in 1911. He went to school in Chicago and in France before matriculating to Cambridge University in Britain in 1928. He was an outstanding bobsledder, leading the American team in the 1928 Olympics at St. Moritz, Switzerland, and the 1932 Olympics at Lake Placid, New York. He was the youngest gold medal winner at age sixteen in the history of the sport. He liked fast cars, played a good game of golf, and learned to fly while living in England before the war. He even married a countess. He was in New York when war broke out in 1939, but he sailed back to London to become a member of the exclusive 601 Squadron and the first American to join the RAF in the war. (It wasn't a piece of cake to get in—he had to fabricate a story that he was Canadian and use his high connections to do so.)

He joined the squadron at Tangmere, learned to fly the RAF way, and on July 20, 1940, he flew his first Hurricane, the famous fighter that shared the Battle of Britain fame with the Spitfire. He shot down six enemy aircraft in the next three and a half weeks. But on August 16, after a sharp engagement with attacking German Stukas, Billy landed gear up and his Hurricane burst into flames. He died forty-eight hours later from shock, the first American in British service to die in WWII.

A tablet in his honor was placed in the crypt of St. Paul's Cathedral in London.

☆☆☆☆☆

If you were a young adventurer with at least three hundred hours of flying time and could pass a physical a bit less stringent than that of the US Army Air Force (USAAF), you could get in one of three RAF squadrons composed of Americans: 71, 113, and 121 (71 Squadron was formed first, in September 1940). All told, of the thousands who volunteered, 244 American pilots flew in the Eagle Squadrons. One, Leo Nomis wrote, "I think all of us, with very few exceptions, were simply adventurers and romanticists, and perhaps idealists." Howard Strickland said, "We were all motivated by the thought of high adventure, the excitement of combat flying, and a desire to help the British."

English pilots were assigned to the command positions, and by the time the Eagles disbanded in September 1942 to join the USAAF, five were dead. Seventy-seven Americans gave their lives. The Eagles flew both Hurricanes and Spitfires. Some of the terms for missions were explanatory: a "circus" was a combined fighter/bomber mission designed to draw out the Luftwaffe; "ramrods" were bomber escort missions; a "balboa" was a decoy mission; a fighter sweep was called a "rodeo"; and the most popular mission was the one in which they could shoot up troops, tanks, trains, anything that even suggested it might be an enemy military target—it was a "rhubarb."

Eight of the American pilots became aces as Eagles. Red McColpin had 5.5 kills with 71 Squadron and two with 133 Squadron; Gus Daymond had seven with 71 Squadron; Chesley Peterson had six kills, plus three probables with 71 Squadron. Don Gentile shot down two while in 133 Squadron, but became one of America's leading aces by shooting down another twenty while in an American flight suit.

When the Eagles transferred over to the 4th Fighter Wing they were automatically given USAAF pilot's wings. Integrated into the different squadrons, these combat-experienced fighter pilots provided invaluable assistance in the training of green Americans. They were the nucleus of the thousands who would follow to fly our Lightnings, Mustangs, and Thunderbolts.

Fighter pilots come from a different time zone; their brain is said to have a third element—the macho one—possibly the same one as some paratroopers, some Seals, some rangers, most Green Berets, and some Marines just out of boot camp. There's an old joke: How do you recognize a fighter pilot at a cocktail party?... he'll *tell* you!

Down to the Sea in Ships

They forgot the ingenuity of the American seaman.
—Admiral David D. Porter

Well before the Pacific fleet was battered at Pearl Harbor, the Merchant Marine was plying the waters of the world in freighters loaded with what was called Lend Lease. President Roosevelt had found a way around the vaunted neutrality to get the needs of war first to Britain, then to the Soviet Union. This is a good place to mention the reason for getting equipment and supplies to Russia. As long as the Soviets were able to fight, Hitler had to keep a sizable army on the Eastern Front, an army (actually armies), that could have been on the Western Front, where Allied planners wanted to deliver a knockout punch as soon as an invasion across the English Channel was possible. At first, this invasion was planned for the spring of 1943, but it quickly became apparent that the huge numbers of men and equipment required could not be in place by then. Thus, in spite of extensive danger from German submarines on the dangerous Murmansk run, Russia's aid was delivered throughout the early war years.

In 1940 the number of men in the Merchant Marine, correctly called Mariners, was 55,000. By getting older seamen out of retirement, accepting youngsters of sixteen, and taking disabled and others rated 4F (unfit) by their draft boards, the wartime level of 215,000 Mariners saw service on the freighters that were constantly threatened by submarines, mines, armed raiders, destroyers, enemy aircraft, and the elements. Even when traveling in convoys, they weren't safe from U-boats that sometimes lay in wait as the escort ships passed overhead, then ascended to periscope depth in the middle of the formation to launch their deadly torpedos.

When Admiral Isoroku Yamamoto said the Japanese could "awaken a sleeping giant," he knew what he was talking about. In 1940 and 1941, Allied shipbuilding could barely keep up with the sinkings. As the Germans produced more and more submarines, it became worse. In 1942 an estimated 1,664 ships were sunk, some 1,100 of them in the North Atlantic. But then the sleeping giant's shipyards kicked in, and convoy safety became better.

An added element of protection was the installation of Naval Armed Guard gun crews on the merchant ships. Each ship got a four- or five-inch stern gun, and various types of antiaircraft guns, with a gun crew of one officer and up to twenty-eight men. In the smaller crews, a petty officer was sometimes in command. The Navy put Armed Guards on 6,236 merchantmen during the war. A total of 569 of these ships were lost. The Armed Guards covered themselves with glory on all oceans: 8,033 of them were decorated or received commendations. Five Navy Crosses, seventy-five Silver Stars, and fifty-four Bronze Stars were awarded to them. One destroyer, five destroyer escorts, and one transport were named for Armed Guard heroes.

(Of interest, the transport USS *Walsh* was named for Lieutenant [Junior Grade] Patrick J. Walsh for heroism aboard the SS *Patrick J. Hurley.* Patrick J. Hurley was secretary of war 1929–33, then, as a general, was sent to be minister to New Zealand shortly before MacArthur was pulled out of Corregidor. His note to FDR, recommending that MacArthur be ordered out as the only way to get him to leave his men, was instrumental in that ticklish exchange. Hurley was ambassador to China 1944–45. His tall son, Wilson, who graduated from West Point in the class of 1945, was a rated fighter pilot who was recalled to active duty to fly in Vietnam, and retired from the Air Force reserve as a lieutenant colonel. Wilson is one of the finest landscape artists in the world. A number of his military paintings are in the permanent collection of the US Air Force Museum at Dayton, Ohio, and the frontispiece of this book was painted by him.)

Back to the Mariners—

The sea is our life. Without it, there would be no clouds, no rain, no atmosphere. Without rain, there would be no vegetation, no rivers, no fish—no food of any kind. It is utterly beautiful, yet staggeringly dangerous. Seven-tenths of the planet's surface is water, with a face that ripples, roils, and crashes with splendor and incredible power on its edges. Parts of it can be covered by a thick or thin coat of icy mail, impassable by seacraft until a seasonal change occurs or when an ice-breaking ship rams her sharp prow into its white armor. Storms with wrathful winds and waterspouts reaching to the heavens can rip a ship apart, or fling it like a toy upon a reef or into another ship.

Without the enemy's violent craft of war, the sea along the many routes taken by those freighters, merchantmen, liberty ships, or victory ships—whichever name one wishes to apply to those hastily constructed and vulnerable supply wagons—was sometimes mightily formidable. And when Mariners had to go into its often icy, frequently fire-covered, briny waters, it was not kind. And so many thousands went into it.

In 1942 thirty-three Allied ships were sunk each week. Yet, what became the greatest merchant fleet in history ploughed on—in the Mediterranean, the Pacific, the coastal areas, the English Channel, all reaches of the North Atlantic, through the deadly, sub-infested waters to Murmansk.

Mariners constituted what was called America's fourth line of defense. As long as they were on board ship they were exempt from the draft. But if they spent more than thirty days away from sea duty, they were eligible. One young seaman had two ships sunk from under him, got a "Dear John" letter from his girlfriend, then was drafted into the Army a few years after the surrender, and was sent to fight as an infantryman in Korea! Bravery was part of everyday life among the Mariners.

The top Merchant Marine medal is the Merchant Marine Distinguished Service Medal; next is the Merchant Marine Meritorious

Service Medal. The Mariner's Medal was the equivalent of the Purple Heart. In order of precedence, 160, 362, and 5,099 were awarded. Even though the award of US military medals wasn't authorized to Mariners, some commanders overstepped the regulation on a few occasions. One Navy Cross, one Silver Star, and thirteen Bronze Stars were awarded to these seamen.

The contribution of our Mariners can never be fully appreciated.

BUTCH O'HARE

Paul Harvey's famous radio feature introduced the wealthy Chicago attorney and businessman as a member of Al Capone's organization—in short, the mob. But somewhere along the line, Edward J. "Easy Eddie" O'Hare decided to remove his son from the dishonor of his connections, so he sent the boy away to military school. There, young Ed, nicknamed Butch, excelled in marksmanship and did well enough scholastically to qualify for the US Naval Academy. Graduating in 1937, he applied for aviation, but had to spend the mandatory two years on a surface vessel—in his case, the battleship *New Mexico.*

In the meantime, Easy Eddie was gunned down and killed by the mob, supposedly for giving inside information to the government. The gangland-style assassination made headlines and no doubt caused a great deal of embarrassment to his son.

After getting the coveted gold wings of a naval aviator, young Butch went on to complete fighter training. In July 1940 he made his first carrier landing, "just about the most exciting thing a pilot can do in peacetime," he wrote. The great Jimmy Thach, his squadron executive officer, used to knock the new pilots down a notch by outflying them. He would let a novice gain an altitude advantage, and then, while reading a newspaper or eating an apple, he would outmaneuver him and get on his tail. But when he tried this with O'Hare, he couldn't do it. Realizing he had a pilot with special abilities nearly equalling his own, Thach made him his protégé.

In February 1942, with Pearl Harbor still a fresh burr in the Navy's hide, O'Hare's squadron, VF-3, now commanded by Thach, was assigned to the carrier USS *Lexington* in the southwest Pacific. The *Lex* was assigned the dangerous mission of getting close enough to Rabaul in the Solomon Islands for her planes to attack Japanese shipping there. But the carrier was spotted by a huge Kawanishi flying boat that radioed her position before Commander Thach shot it down.

That afternoon, while Thach was leading a flight of Wildcat fighters against a formation of enemy bombers, another nine Japanese bombers were headed for the carrier. Lieutenant O'Hare and five other F4F Wildcat pilots climbed up to meet them. Butch was the first to spot the enemy formation, just as his wingman discovered that his guns were jammed and had to pull away. Since none of the other four Wildcats were close enough to stop the bombers, Butch alone stood between them and his carrier. Without a moment's hesitation, O'Hare flashed into the enemy formation, shooting down one bomber as a flood of bright red tracers converged in his direction. A second bomber burst into smoke and spun seaward, then another. Two more were downed. When Thach reached the fight, he saw three enemy aircraft going down in flames at one time. The other F4Fs arrived just in time because Butch was out of ammo. The *Lexington* was saved, and O'Hare, through his amazing flying skill, was given the credit. Butch was promoted to lieutenant commander and awarded the Medal of Honor.

In November 1943, while CAG (Commander Air Group) of the carrier *Enterprise,* Commander Butch O'Hare was leading a night flight against attacking Betty bombers when his F6F Hellcat went down for unknown reasons. The Navy lost one of its most famous heroes. His father would have been proud of him, for Chicago's major international airport, O'Hare, is named for him.

Jimmy Thach was the architect of "the Thach weave," a fighter tactic that enabled the heavier Hellcats to hold their own with the more maneuverable Japanese Zeroes. At the end of the first year of the Pacific war fighter squadrons commanded by Admiral Thach accounted for over half the enemy fighters shot down by US Navy pilots. Thach, whose decorations included two Navy Crosses, a Silver Star, and a Bronze Star, continued a brilliant career, attaining the rank of four-star admiral before retiring in 1956.

MIDWAY, THE ROAD BACK

Admiral Ernest King, Annapolis class of 1901, smarted continuously over the destruction of so much of his Pacific fleet in the months that followed the Pearl Harbor disaster. As fleet admiral and chief of naval operations, he was also a member of the joint chiefs. The bitter taste in his mouth could only be removed by lashing back at Japan, and it colored his thinking. The Lorain, Ohio, naval leader even sidestepped Roosevelt's desire to throw much of America's seagoing might into the North Atlantic campaign. The first major retaliation in the Pacific was the Battle of Coral Sea, east of New Guinea, on May 7–8. In it, the Navy traded carriers, losing the *Lexington* that Butch O'Hare had saved three months earlier, while the Japanese lost a small carrier and the use of two of their supercarriers for several months while they returned home for major repairs. The *Yorktown*, after speedy repairs in Pearl Harbor, lived to fight a month later at the crucial Battle of Midway.

The Battle of Midway, fought over and near the tiny US mid-Pacific base at Midway atoll, was the strategic high-water mark of Japan's Pacific war. Before this early June battle, the Japanese navy was calling the shots throughout the western Pacific. Following that slugfest, the two opposing fleets were essentially equal, and the United States was able to take the offensive.

Admiral Yamamoto, the brilliant, poker-playing Japanese commander, sought to draw out Admiral Chester Nimitz's weaker carrier force and destroy it, but American intelligence intercepted communications that gave Nimitz fair warning. Instead the admiral laid a trap and ambushed the ambushers. The bravery and skill of the naval aviators as well as that of all of the ships' crews proved too much for Yamamoto. He lost three irreplaceable fleet carriers, while only one of the three US carriers was sunk. It was, unfortunately, the *Yorktown.*

Midway Island was saved for the Allies and played a vital role as a supply base in operations to come. Almost as important, a victory-thirsty American public finally had something to cheer about. Years later, a brilliant film titled *Midway*, with an all-star cast, captured the command drama of that battle.

It Was More Than Thirty Seconds

Even before this uplift of American spirits, the Navy had a carrier involved in perhaps the biggest boost to morale in the early part of the war—the USS *Ranger*. And from its crowded flight deck, sixteen fuel-laden B-25B medium bombers staggered into the air on April 18, 1942. Destination: Japan!

James "Jimmy" Doolittle was born in Alameda, California, in 1896. He earned his air service wings and was an instructor pilot during WWI. In 1920 he was promoted to first lieutenant and granted a Regular Army commission and assigned to the air corps. A consummate pilot, he was soon setting flying records that brought him international fame. To add to his flying skill, he completed both a master's degree and a PhD in aeronautical science at the Massachusetts Institute of Technology. He also received the Harmon Trophy for his experiments in "blind flying."

He had won the international Schneider Race before he went into the Reserves as a major in 1930 and went to work for Shell Oil Company. He won the 1931 Burbank to Cleveland Bendix Trophy Race. The next year he won the famed Thompson Trophy Race of unlimiteds in Cleveland in the stubby little Gee Bee racer that was so hard to fly that only the best pilots could handle it.

Doolittle went back on active duty in 1940 and was promoted to lieutenant colonel. Assigned to lead an audacious raid on Japan's homeland in January 1942, he rounded up volunteers for each of the five crew positions in a B-25B twin-engined "Mitchell" bomber. Those positions were: pilot, copilot, navigator, bombardier, and engineer/gunner. All these men knew was that they would serve on a dangerous mission. Training in short field takeoffs began at once. With final selections made, aircraft and crews were loaded aboard the new carrier USS *Hornet*, which headed west across the Pacific. Met by Admiral William "Bull" Halsey and his carrier the USS *Enterprise*, which would provide air cover, the *Hornet* proceeded toward its designated launch point four hundred miles east of Tokyo in a task force that also included three heavy cruisers, one light cruiser, and eight destroyers.

All machine guns, except for those in the top ball turret, were removed from the aircraft to save weight for added fuel tanks. Wooden dowels, painted black, were added to the tail ports to simulate guns, in an effort to keep any enemy fighters from attacking those blind spots.

On one bomb Doolittle fastened a medal that naval lieutenant Stephen Juricka had received from the Japanese while in Tokyo performing attaché duty prior to the war. One other element of interest was the presence of Lieutenant "Doc" White. A medical doctor, White had volunteered for the mission—whatever it might be—and had wrangled permission to train as a gunner and go along. He would prove quite valuable.

Finally, the eighty crew members and their backups were told where they were going, and they burst into a rousing cheer! It was true—*Tokyo* and environs, a dagger into the heart of the Japanese homeland!

Unfortunately, Japanese picket boats spotted the task force some six hundred miles east of the mainland and, assuming their position had been radioed, the mission was immediately set up for a same-day takeoff. It was April 18, 1942, a day earlier than planned. The B-25s were already loaded with four five-hundred-pound bombs each and as much fuel as they could carry, as the *Hornet* turned into the wind.

The first bombers had less deck for takeoff roll than those further back, but the system had been worked out so they would reach the end of their takeoff roll just as the flight deck surged to its highest point against the waves. Jimmy Doolittle was, naturally, piloting the first plane. Behind him all engines were idling. Holding the brakes, he eased the throttles forward. His eyes were glued on the deck officer. This was the biggest moment of his adventurous life. Nothing that had happened before meant an iota now. Had he done everything? Could they pull it off? The chips were stacked high, and they had to roll a natural or at least make a ten the hard way. *Then it was time!* The flag snapped back and forth as he pushed the throttles all the way forward, held the surging ship for a moment, then released the brakes. The B-25 lurched forward, quickly gaining speed as the bow rose. Then back on the control column. The bomber staggered into the air on the feather edge of stalling, and dipped over the front tip of the flight deck, grabbed airspeed, and climbed out. Then the second aircraft crawled into the air, and the third and fourth. Jimmy and his naval engineer who had planned everything had known what they were doing, for all sixteen bombers made it off the carrier, destined for Tokyo, Nagoya, and Yokohama. Heroic? In every way. The value of such a mission far outweighed the danger, but those eager crew members weren't thinking about such highfalutin concepts; they were off on the very biggest, most daring mission of their young lives!

At 1:30 PM undetected and unchallenged by enemy fighters, Doolittle led thirteen of the Mitchells roaring in low over Tokyo, dodging flak, and dropping their bombs on preassigned targets. Incendiaries and high-explosive bombs hit an unsuspecting, incredulous Japanese population. *How could it be?* Who had lied to them? Never again in this war would they feel complacent. Then it was on for the American raiders, on toward China, or as close to it as their limited fuel would take them. The extra two hundred miles would make it if not an impossible task, at least a tricky one of leaned-out fuel mixture control for those Wright R-2600 engines. The other three B-25s hit alternate targets and also sped west across the vast China Sea—haven for all: Chongjin.

Jimmy and his crew had to make a night bailout close to the Chinese shore. Others hit the silk when their props gasped to a halt. Still others crash-landed. One plane landed at Vladivostok, the Russian warm-weather port; its crew was detained for the duration because Russia was not at war with Japan. Chinese farmers hid some of the ones finding the mainland. Two crews suffered bad luck; of the ten members, two died in landing, and the other eight were captured. Of these, three were executed by the Japanese. Lieutenant Ted Lawson was the pilot of aircraft #7. He tried to crash-land on a beach and was seriously injured. When teamed up with aircraft #15's crew, Doc White amputated his leg and saved his life. Lawson survived to write the famous book *Thirty Seconds over Tokyo,* which became an immensely popular movie starring Spencer Tracy, Van Johnson, and Robert Walker.

Some sixty crew members reached safety with the Chinese and made it back to the States, and most of them continued to serve with distinction throughout the rest of the war. While the raid did little actual damage, its desired effect on American morale was remarkably successful. The crewmen were awarded Distinguished Flying Crosses, but the man who made it all happen, the jaunty little forty-five-year-old pilot who made the *Gee Bee* famous, was immediately promoted to brigadier general and awarded the Medal of Honor. Jimmy Doolittle would finish the war as a lieutenant general and receive the Silver Star, two DFCs, a Bronze Star, and four Air Medals. He lived to the ripe old age of ninety-six, and is probably up there somewhere looking for some angels to race.

GUADALCANAL

There's nothing I wouldn't do for this country.

—Joe Foss

Now a look at the naval boss in the Pacific, CINCPAC—Admiral Chester Nimitz. Born in Fredericksburg, Texas, in 1885, he entered Annapolis at age fifteen, and graduated seventh in the class of 1905. After service in surface ships, he fell in love with submarines and spent WWI in undersea craft. Between wars, he commanded two cruisers and the battleship *South Carolina,* as well as the Pearl Harbor submarine base. He was promoted to rear admiral in 1938 (the one-star rank of commodore having been suspended) and was Roosevelt's choice to take over the Pacific fleet after Pearl Harbor. Promoted directly to full admiral over twenty-eight flag officers who outranked him, he broke even at the Battle of Coral Sea, then brilliantly gambled on his intelligence to win at Midway, one of the greatest victories in the history of American sea warfare.

In the island-hopping campaigns that followed, Nimitz commanded all US military forces in the Central Pacific, while MacArthur continued to command those in the Southwest Pacific. Each commander had Army, Navy, and Marine elements under his jurisdiction. Nimitz fully understood senior command, leaving tactical control to admirals such as Raymond Spruance and William "Bull" Halsey.

Halsey, the descendant of a seafaring clan, was a couple of years older than Nimitz and had graduated from the Naval Academy a year ahead of him in 1904. He commanded escort-type vessels in WWI, and served in battleships during the following years. But he saw the handwriting on the wall concerning the role of aviation, and at age fifty-two he was the oldest officer to go through pilot training and get his gold wings. He was promoted to rear admiral in 1938 and vice admiral in 1940. He commanded the South Pacific area in early 1942, but missed the Midway battle because he was hospitalized with a skin infection. He recommended Spruance to handle his command in his absence.

Back at sea, Halsey was promoted to full admiral in November 1942, when the Solomon Islands, mainly Guadalcanal, became a strategic factor of the war. The 1st Marine Division landed on Guadalcanal on August 7, and met vigorous opposition from the Japanese, who had decided the island was critical. Before victory could be achieved, the 2nd Marine Division, the Twenty-fifth and Americal Army divisions, and a separate Army regiment had to be thrown in. Air and surface naval losses were staggering. The Marine ground troops had it rough, but Guadalcanal's Henderson Field, more cow pasture than airstrip, stayed in American hands.

As the campaign raged on, the airfield continued to be the number-one Japanese target. At night, Japanese warships would come down from the Solomons under the cover of darkness to the stretch of water between the north side of Guadalcanal and Tulagi islands to rain naval gunfire on Henderson. It became the dangerous mission of the limited number of US Navy ships to combat them. Battle after battle raged on that water. So many ships were sunk there, that it became known as "Ironbottom Sound." But its most popular nickname was "The Slot," and it was hell at night.

Enter "the Cactus Air Force, " so called because "Cactus" was the Allied call sign of Henderson Field. The most famous of the early Marine pilots to fly Hellcats out of Cactus was Captain Marion Carl, USMC, who earned his first Navy Cross at the Battle of Midway. He became the first Marine ace of the war, and his final score was 18.5 enemy planes downed. When he was shot down in September and spent five days hiding out with the natives, Major John Smith, his closest competitor, gained four kills on him. Just after his return, the Marine air commander asked him what he was going to do about it, and he replied, "Goddammit, General, ground him for five days!" Carl went on to retire as a major general, and tragically, when he was eighty-three years old, he was killed by an intruder in his Oregon home.

John Lucien Smith edged Marion Carl out in those early Guadalcanal days, flaming nineteen enemy aircraft while leading his VMF-223 squadron through vicious aerial warfare that sent them up against waves of Japanese Betty bombers escorted by swarms of Zeroes almost daily. When he departed Guadalcanal, he was promoted to lieutenant colonel and had earned both the Medal of Honor and a Navy Cross.

I have refrained from relating many of my personal experiences, even though I've had many connections, but now I think it appropriate to interrupt with an anecdote. In early summer 1958, I had just been assigned as the aviation advisor to the South Dakota Army National Guard. In those days, Army aviators flew light, fixed-wing airplanes and helicopters, and were assigned to nonaviation units authorized aviation sections. Headquarters of the national guard artillery group was stationed in Pierre, the state capital in the middle of the state. I was twenty-eight and full of vim, ready to develop an outstanding level of pilots in the state. After a few days in Rapid City, my home station, I flew over to Pierre to meet the two group pilots. One was an ex-WWII Marine pilot named Sam Skotvold, who had flown dive bombers in the Aleutians. He liked to claim that the only thing he ever hit was a seal—but it was an *enemy* seal! The other pilot was Curt Cameron, who had been a Navy dive-bomber pilot in WWII. He had been a lieutenant-commander who earned a Navy Cross by knocking out a Japanese cruiser.

I joined them over drinks after going to a drill. Eventually, we got around to the fact that there weren't enough aircraft for the pilots scattered around the state to get much flying time. They wanted to know if I was going to get them some more birds. I told them I couldn't do so, but they had a governor who was not only a reserve Air Force brigadier and a famous pilot, but was also a friend of the head of the Guard Bureau. *He* could get them some aircraft. After a couple more drinks, they asked me if I would tell him so the next day. "Sure!" I replied, confidently.

Curt Cameron, who was also the assistant state aviation director and had more flying hours than the Wright brothers, called me the next morning and said, "The governor will see us at nine-thirty."

I agreed to meet both guard pilots at the capitol, then shook my head. Here I was, a captain, brand new in the job, working for a full colonel in Rapid City, who knew nothing of what I was doing—about to go tell the governor of a sovereign state what to do!

He was tall, dark-haired, with a craggy face. He came around his desk with a smile, shook my hand, and said, "I understand you're going to get us some airplanes!"

I mumbled something like, "Not exactly, sir," and then told him how I thought he could get them. After some discussion about flying and fly fishing, the other pilots and I left and I called my boss. The colonel wasn't displeased.

The governor got us, quite incredibly, seven L-19 Birddogs, and six Hiller H-23 choppers! He left office several months later after two terms, but I ran into him periodically in the next three years as we each flew around the state.

In early 2002, I read that this same ex-governor, now eighty-six years old, had been stopped at security in Phoenix International Airport as he was heading toward a departure gate. Security had found an instrument in his jacket pocket with five points, and had decided it was a dangerous weapon. It was mounted on a light blue ribbon with little white stars. He tried to explain that it was the Medal of Honor, and that he was on his way to West Point to speak, but security *didn't know what the medal was* and detained him for further searches for nearly a half hour! He was finally allowed to get to his flight, but only after a certain amount of exasperation.

When I heard about this incident, I called him in Scottsdale and he confirmed the whole story. He told me he was still shaking his head.

Now back to the battle for Guadalcanal in 1942...

Joe Foss, executive officer of VMF-121, flew into Cactus with his F4-F squadron on October 9. After working his way through college, Joe had enlisted in the Marine Corps in 1940, and, already possessing a private pilot's license, had been accepted into naval cadets. Following graduation, he served as an instructor pilot in Pensacola until he talked his way into fighters and got shipped out to the South Pacific. Now twenty-seven, he was older than most fighter pilots but had the keen shooter's instincts of a midwestern farm boy who had grown up bringing down pheasants and doves. In just nine days, Foss was an ace, and before long the flight he commanded had become known as "Foss's Flying Circus." His victories mounted. On October 25, in two missions he had five kills, becoming the Marine Corps' first "ace in a day." But his enemy hunting in the cockpit was sometimes not enough, so now and then he'd grab an M-1 rifle and go off into the jungle on foot—until he was ordered to stop.

On November 7, while leading seven Hellcats up the Slot to shoot up a Japanese cruiser and several destroyers, Joe's plane got hit and he had to ditch in shark-infested waters. But he made it back to the cow pasture, and wracked up some more victories before malaria laid him low. His score now stood at 23. Evacuated to Australia, he recuperated and returned to Henderson Field on New Year's Day 1943. Three more kills brought him up to twenty-six, the same number as Rickenbacker had in WWI. Captain Foss was sent back to the States to sell war bonds, and in May of 1943 FDR pinned the Medal of Honor on his chest.

Now, for the story tie-in—if you haven't guessed: Joe went back to South Dakota and helped form the state's Air National Guard, and eventually was elected to the governor's seat. When he left the state government, he became commissioner of the American Football League. In 1988–90 Joe was president of the National Rifle Association, an organization whose mission he never quit promoting. Shortly after his trip to speak at West Point when he was harassed in the Phoenix International Airport for carrying his "dangerous" Medal of Honor, he was stricken with cancer. He died in January 2003, an eighty-seven-year-old hero's hero.

The Sullivans

No one is so foolish as to prefer war to peace, in which, instead of sons burying their fathers, fathers bury their sons.
—King Croesus, 430 BCE (Herodotus, *The Histories*)

Before we get back to Guadalcanal, we must go to Waterloo, Iowa. On December 7, 1941, five brothers in that town lost a good friend at Pearl Harbor. They decided they should all enlist in the navy and do what they could for their country. George, the eldest at twenty-six, and Frank, the second older brother, had both served an honorable four-year hitch in the navy and had been discharged a few months earlier. The other three brothers—Red, Matt, and Al—agreed they would join up if they could all stick together. Al, at nineteen, was the youngest and the only one who was married. He could have been deferred from the draft, but there was no way he was going to miss going with his brothers. His young wife, Katherine Mary, and their ten-month-old son, Jimmy, moved in with his parents. The Sullivans' motto was *We Stick Together.*

At first the naval recruiting office in Des Moines balked at their demand that they all serve together, but an agreement was reached and they all enlisted on January 3, 1942. After going through boot camp at Great Lakes Naval Training Station, they were assigned to the new light cruiser USS *Juneau* that had just been commissioned. The ship headed for the South Pacific, joining a cruiser task force under Rear Admiral Dan Callaghan. On November 12, having heard that a strong Japanese naval force was steaming toward Guadalcanal, the task force of five cruisers and eight destroyers took up its station in Ironbottom Sound. The Japanese flotilla of two battleships, a cruiser and eleven destroyers crashed into Callaghan's group at 1:45 AM the next day. Firing at point-blank range in the eerie blue-white searchlight beams and gun flashes, several ships on both sides were mortally wounded in just minutes by shells, torpedoes, and bombs from aircraft. The Japanese battleship *Hiei* was hit and soon sank. The fires of burning ships added to the wild nighttime sea-scape as the thunder of hundreds of guns rocked the night air. The heavy cruiser *San Francisco*, Callaghan's flagship, took heavy damage, killing him and the ship's captain.

With ships steaming furiously and weaving in and out of the car-nage, it was suddenly *Juneau*'s turn. Just a few minutes into the battle, the *Juneau* was hit by a Japanese torpedo on the port side near the forward fire room. The shock wave from the explosion buckled the deck, shattered the fire-control computers, and knocked out power. The cruiser limped away from the battle, down by the bow, strug-gling to maintain eighteen knots. She rejoined the surviving Amer-ican warships at dawn on November 13 and zigzagged to the south-east along with two other cruisers and three destroyers.

It seemed the *Juneau* would easily be able to reach a repair site and be patched up, but about an hour before noon, the task force encountered Japanese submarine I-26. At 11:01, the submarine fired three torpedoes at the *San Francisco*. None hit the cruiser, but one passed beyond it and struck the *Juneau* at her first wound location on the port side, hitting her magazine. One report said she "vaporized!" Actually, the huge explosion tore the cruiser in half, killing most of the crew instantly. She went down in two pieces almost immediately. Four of the Sullivan brothers died with her. It was reported that George, the eldest, survived, badly wounded on a raft for five days. Before he succumbed, he continually called out to his brothers, *"Frank, Matt, Red, Al!"*

Americans were thunderstruck at the loss of five sons on one ship.

A destroyer, the USS *The Sullivans*, commissioned in September 1943, was named for them. She was known as "the lucky ship" because of the shamrock painted on her hull and the fact that she was never seriously hit in WWII or the Korean War. The destroyer was decommissioned in 1965. The second USS *The Sullivans*, a guided missile destroyer, was christened in April 1997. She, too, wears the shamrock, and her motto is also "We Stick Together."

THE COAST GUARD

Before we end our discussion of the heroes of Guadalcanal, a Coast Guard story must be told. During the war, the US Coast Guard became a part of the Navy, with guardsmen manning transports and sometimes destroyers. Having small boat experience, these men also operated landing craft during invasions. Enter Signalman First Class Douglas Munro from Cle Elum, Washington. Dividing his time as a signalman and operator of assault craft, he was called on in late September 1942 to land some marines behind enemy lines on a beach called Point Cruz. Lieutenant Colonel Lewis B. "Chesty" Puller sent a battalion from his Seventh Marines to encircle a difficult Japanese strong point. Under supporting fire from the five-inch guns of the destroyer USS *Monssen*, the landing was made successfully and the five hundred marines hurried to their objective. But the Japanese got behind them and they had to fight their way to the beach to be evacuated, or they were doomed. In the meantime, Japanese bombers had chased the destroyer out to sea, so that support wasn't as accurate.

Hearing that the Marines needed to be withdrawn, Munro volunteered to lead assault boats back to the same beach where he had earlier dropped them off. The Marines arrived on the beach to board the landing craft while the Japanese kept up a murderous fire from the ridges about five hundred yards away. Munro, seeing the dangerous situation, maneuvered his boat between the enemy and those withdrawing to protect the remnants of the battalion. With Munro successfully providing cover, all the Marines, including twenty-five wounded, managed to escape.

But as they were heading out to safety, Munro saw that another boatload of Marines had gotten stuck on a sandbar. The signalman directed the recovery of the beached boat and saw it off to safety before he was struck at the base of the skull by an enemy machine-gun bullet. He died a short time later. Douglas Munro was awarded the Medal of Honor posthumously, the *only* Coast Guardsman ever to receive one.

Surely, though, in its many years of service, the Coast Guard has had numerous unheralded acts of heroism. Its motto, *Semper Paratus*—"Always Ready"—says it all.

"WE BUILD, WE FIGHT"

This motto is inscribed on the great memorial to the Seabees along the inspiring drive to Arlington National Cemetery. The Seabees are so named for CBs, construction battalions, the Navy's answer to construction and maintenance, that were created in early 1942. A Department of the Navy history states,

> The first recruits were the men who had helped to build Boulder Dam, the national highways, and New York's skyscrapers; who had worked in the mines and quarries and dug the subway tunnels; who had worked in shipyards and built docks and wharfs and even ocean liners and aircraft carriers. By the end of the war, 325,000 such men had enlisted in the Seabees. They knew more than 60 skilled trades, not to mention the unofficial ones of souvenir making and "moonlight procurement." Nearly 11,400 officers joined the Civil Engineer Corps during the war, and nearly 8,000 of them served with the Seabees.

They were rough and tough, and could enlist up to age fifty, although many at least a decade older managed to get in. After a quick period of basic training that taught them the rudiments of military courtesy and how to use small arms, they were off to exotic places like Henderson Field on Guadalcanal, where PSP (pierced steel plank) runways had to be laid, or to Tarawa, where Hawkins Field needed the same. They could install fuel tanks and operate them, drive steam shovels, build almost anything, and blow up almost anything. They were everywhere before the end of the war. Their pontoons were the breaches of difficult landings. Actually this tool of war wasn't new. The Persian king Xerxes had used such devices to cross the Hellespont when he invaded Greece in the fifth century BCE. But the Seabees made them work for modern amphibious warfare. They used them at Sicily and in the landings at the Italian shore. They built offshore docking, and they operated huge ferries called "Rhinos" that brought men and supplies onto beaches from offshore shipping. On the coast of France after Normandy they rebuilt harbors (another chapter the French have forgotten). They built whole military bases. There wasn't much the Seabees couldn't do.

And when they had to they could fight. And that was often in the battle areas. They landed with the Marines on the beaches of Saipan, Guam, and Tinian. At the latter, they built the runways that the huge B-29s used to bomb Japan. In spite of the fighting they did, they received woefully few decorations: five Navy Crosses, thirty-three Silver Stars.

The movie *The Fighting Seabees* was released in 1944. Starring John Wayne and Susan Hayward, the popular film made the Seabees famous.

PATTON AGAIN, AND THE NATIONAL GUARD'S BOB MOORE

> *But whoso is heroic will always find crises to try his edge.*
> —Ralph Waldo Emerson, "Heroism," *Essays: First Series* (1841)

When we left George Patton in Morocco, he was languishing in Casablanca, doing his senior American officer thing well, managing the political side with the French and the Arabs, but eager to get back into action. In the meantime, Mark Clark, a favorite of Eisenhower's and some eight years Patton's junior at West Point, was given his third star and command of the newly organized Fifth Army. This was salt in the wound of the man who *knew* his destiny lay in high command. Patton anguished—*would the chance pass him by again?*

And it almost did.

Eisenhower called Patton on March 4, while George was planning with his staff for a major role in the invasion of Sicily. The II US Army Corps had not fought well at the Battle of Kasserine Pass, and Georgie was to go to Tunisia and somehow shape it up in less than two weeks. With Major General Omar Bradley as his second in command, Patton roared into II Corps and brilliantly got the job done. He jacked up discipline as he seemed to be everywhere getting his stringent policies enforced. Eight days after Ike's call, George got his coveted third star. II Corps fought well and Patton returned to his reenforced 1st Armored Corps to get ready to go to Sicily.

But before we leave North Africa, a National Guard regiment and some of its members deserve some mention.

The town of Villisca, in the southwestern part of Iowa, had a hair over two thousand inhabitants when a census taker was being liberal in his count back in 1940. Remarkably, the small town's major claim to fame was the unsolved axe murders of six of its citizens, including four children, back in 1912. The local drugstore was owned by an Irish family named Moore. Their son Robert enlisted in Company F, Second Battalion, 168th Infantry Regiment when he was seventeen. That was in 1922. In 1928 Bob Moore took command of that company and became known as "the Boy Captain." Some of the older members of the company called him "Captain Bob." Convinced that his boys, mostly from Villisca, would have to fight in a war, he was a dedicated commander who took training seriously.

In 1941 Bob Moore marched F Company's young men away from their families for what was supposed to be a year's training, but Pearl Harbor changed all of that. In the fall of 1942, as the executive officer of the Second Battalion, Major Bob Moore went to North Africa with the regiment—now part of the 34th Infantry Division. The patch of the 34th featured the red head of a bull; thus its nickname: the Red Bull Division. Before the war was over, it would own one of the most heroic combat records of any American division. And it had good company: in North Africa, the famous 100th Nisei Battalion was attached to it and later, in Italy, the whole "Go for Broke" Nisei Regimental Combat Team fought alongside Moore's men.

The 168th had some illustrious blood lines. Born in 1861 as the Fourth Iowa Volunteer Infantry Regiment, it saw service throughout the Civil War, again on the Mexican border in 1916, and was assigned to the Rainbow Division in WWI. And now one of its leaders was the druggist from Villisca.

When Moore's battalion landed in Algeria, the navy put its soldiers on the wrong beach, eight miles from where they were supposed to be. Moore sent out a patrol, then struck out with his part of the command. Hours later, his weary troops ran into a French machine-gun nest that killed two of his men and wounded two others. (The good old French!) French snipers were well located in a house overlooking his position, and caused more havoc before Moore tried to personally flank them. One sniper must have had him in his scope because he was suddenly knocked flat. When he glanced at his steel helmet, he found a deep groove where a bullet had just missed ruining his day. Moore's men captured the position. Bob Moore was later awarded a Silver Star for his heroism that day.

At the Battle of Kasserine Pass, Moore, now a lieutenant colonel commanding the Second Battalion, found himself and nine hundred of his men surrounded by German armor and infantry on a hill called Djebl Lessouda. At this time, handsome Lieutenant Colonel John Waters, a class of 1931 West Pointer who was commanding an adjacent armored unit, was down the slope, but he was unable to communicate with Moore. Waters was captured, and quite a catch he was, being George Patton's beloved son-in-law.

Moore had to break out. He didn't know just how, but he couldn't stay on Djebl Lessouda, or come morning half the German Afrika Korps would descend on him. It was February 15, 1942, at 10:30 PM, when the druggist briefed his men. No heavy weapons, travel as light as possible with *nothing* that would make a hint of noise. They were going to sneak right through the Germans! They would travel in two columns, thirty yards apart, and move as fast as possible. The full moon would both help and hinder. Company F, Moore's pride of Villisca, would take the lead with him. And down the hill they went, silently trusting in the colonel. Once they slipped by a German 88's gun crew so close they could hear them snoring. They moved on, slowly eating up the nine miles they had to go. Twice they were challenged; the second time, enemy machine-gun fire broke the silence of the now dark night. *"Scatter!"* Moore yelled. *"Run like hell!"*

As the command broke and ran in several directions, German artillery and mortars opened up, their shells bursting in the suddenly uncalm desert. Those who weren't hit crawled out of the death scene. At 5:00 in the morning, Moore led his bloodied survivors into a friendly outpost. All told, 432 members of the Second Battalion out of the 904 Moore had led off Djebl Lessouda survived. The one-time boy captain became an instant Associated Press hero.

On April 9 (what a fateful day—Lee surrendered at Appomattox, and seventy-seven years later Bataan fell) Bob Moore was nearly killed by a German bomb. Temporarily deaf and blind, he was evacuated. After he recovered, he went home on leave, arriving July 15, 1943—but let Rick Atkinson tell it, because I could never capture the scene as movingly as he did in his superb *An Army at Dawn*:

> Moore stepped from the Burlington No. 6 in Villisca at 9:30 AM, clutching the camel-hide briefcase his men had given him as a farewell gift. Into his arms leaped his seven-year-old daughter, Nancy; a newspaper photographer captured the moment in a picture that would win the Pulitzer Prize. Fire bells rang to announce the homecoming and American flags lined Third Avenue in front of the family drugstore.

Bob Moore would rise to the rank of brigadier general in the Guard, a testimonial, like the proud 168th and the famed Red Bulls, to the civilian components of the American military. He lived nearly nine decades and when he died, the signboard in front of Villisca's Presbyterian church bore the simple tribute that another great American named MacArthur had made famous, "Old soldiers never die."

☆☆☆☆☆

One more anecdote that Atkinson mentions in his book made the rounds in North Africa, providing much-needed laughter. General Eisenhower had selected an attractive former London model name Kay Summersby as his driver. Thirty-four and a good bridge player like the general, she was engaged to an American staff officer. But Ike was the four-star, and he knew a well-turned ankle when he saw one. Rumors flew. The story went that Ike's sedan stalled on a backroad, and Kay lifted the hood to see if she could get it going. The general promptly got into the trunk and brought her the tool kit. "Screwdriver?" he asked. "Might as well," the lovely Kay replied. "I can't get the goddamn motor fixed."

THE MOST RESOUNDING SLAP IN HISTORY

Redesignated the Seventh Army while aboard ship, Patton's command would distinguish itself on Sicily. One of its divisions was the 1st Infantry, the "Big Red One" of WWI fame, commanded by Terry de la Mesa Allen, whose assistant division commander was Brigadier General Ted Roosevelt Jr., the hard-fighting son of Rough Rider Teddy.

Despite a rough landing on Sicily, Patton drove his army to Messina, beating the vain British Field Marshal Bernard Montgomery to that prize, and adding more fame and recognition for the American fighting man. Georgie was awarded his second DSC and it seemed his destiny had arrived. But trouble lay ahead.

While visiting hospital wards and passing out both congratulations and Purple Hearts to wounded soldiers, he encountered two who were in their wards for what was called "combat fatigue." When a soldier told him it was his nerves, Patton exploded and slapped him with his gloves. A similar incident occurred a short time later. Patton simply did not understand a soldier who couldn't fight. Ike relieved him of command and got the press to keep the incidents quiet for morale purposes. But a muckraker journalist named Drew Pearson pulled the plug, printed the story, and the wrath of America came down on Patton's head.

Still, Ike couldn't afford to lose him, so Patton was brought to England to both mislead the Germans by seeming to command what was actually a ghost army, and prepare for a major role in the forth-coming cross-channel invasion. But Italy still had to be dealt with—even though the dictator Mussolini had been deposed and the country had surrendered. The German armies still had to be removed. The British under Montgomery landed at the toe, while General Mark Clark's Fifth Army hit the beaches at Salerno, just south of Naples.

One of the elements of that army was the 442nd Regimental Combat Team (RCT).

Go for Broke

> *The patriot volunteer, fighting for his country and his rights,*
> *makes the most reliable soldier on earth.*
>
> —Stonewall Jackson

Following the Japanese attack on Pearl Harbor, a certain amount of hysteria gripped the West Coast and particularly California. During the previous half century, many thousands of Japanese had emi-grated there. Most of them were farmhands but the usual shop-keepers and other tradesmen were included in their communities. Like the distinct Chinatowns, there were distinct Japantowns. The Japanese men were not permitted to marry Anglo women or own land, because of the Oriental Exclusion policy brought on by the flood of Chinese immigrants before them. They brought "picture brides," young women, usually from villages in Japan, whom they knew only from letters and photos, to marry. And when their children were born, the kids were American citizens. The immigrants, the *Isei*, were diligent and required their children, the *Nisei*, to go to both American schools and the Japanese schools they operated. After the children were born, some of the Japanese got smart and bought land in their offspring's names. But discrimination was strong, particularly in California. In Hawaii the situation was slightly different in that many of the immigrants worked for the huge sugar plantations. Nearly all Japanese immigrants proclaimed themselves Americans, particularly the proud Nisei.

Shortly after Pearl Harbor, the Japanese and their families on the West Coast were rounded up with few belongings and, in one of the worst breaches of democracy ever carried out in the United States, they were thrown into what were called "relocation camps." There Japanese immigrants and their children lived in tarpaper barracks with paper-thin partitions and common bathrooms, surrounded by barbed wire and guarded by towers occupied by armed soldiers. But they made a life, had schools for their children, and coped. What they didn't have was freedom. The majority of their businesses and farms were illegally confiscated. In short, they were considered enemy aliens and they were in concentration camps.

Yet the Army soon came to know the worth of their young men, both on the mainland and in Hawaii. A high percentage resented what the Japanese government had done at Pearl Harbor, and wanted to prove they were good Americans. A few were already in the Army as intelligence specialists and translators. But in Hawaii, the two National Guard regiments were forced to discharge the hundreds of young Nisei in their ranks. Then the 100th Infantry Battalion was formed in Hawaii—all Japanese Americans—and sent to the mainland to train before going to North Africa. Their motto was emblazoned on their unit colors: *Remember Pearl Harbor.* Next came word that a regiment would be formed on the mainland, the 442nd Infantry—again, young Japanese Americans rushed to the colors by the thousands.

The common slogan among the new soldiers in both the 100th and the 442nd was "Go for Broke," which meant risk everything.

Slang was prevalent. Hawaiian Japanese Americans were called "Buddhaheads," while mainlanders were "Kotonks." Later, in combat, Buddhaheads were great radio operators because they communicated in their special pidgin English and drove the Germans nuts.

The average Nisei soldier was far from being a John Wayne. He was about five feet four inches tall and weighed 125 pounds, often with his M-1 rifle. They gave the uniform people at quartermaster fits. One private was so small he wore size 2.5EEE footwear. But the esprit de corps in the Nisei outfits was unequaled anywhere in the Army. Their patch in the 442nd was the torch of the Statue of Liberty on a blue background. They would never have so much as a single incident of a soldier going AWOL in a war zone.

After further training and some fighting in North Africa, the 100th Battalion went into combat at Salerno attached to the 34th Infantry Division, which was ably commanded by Major General Charles Ryder. The 100th soon began amassing an outstanding combat record, sustaining heavy losses in the attacks to take infamous Monte Cassino Abbey and other objectives. So many of its members were wounded that it became known as "the Purple Heart Battalion." It was in heavy combat for nine months before the 442nd caught up with it. Arriving in Italy, the RCT had left its 1st Battalion behind in the States to train replacements and the 100th, retaining its "One Puka Puka" designation, became part of the combat team. The 522nd Field Artillery Battalion, Cannon Company, the 232nd Combat Engineer Company, and the 206th US Army Band were the other major elements of the 442nd. When in action the band worked the supply trains and served as litter bearers.

Four of the Masaoka brothers—Tad, Ike, Ben, and Mike—served with the RCT; their brother Henry served with the 101st Airborne. One soldier, Kobe Shoji, broke his arm just before departure for Europe, but insisted on staying with his company. The whole package married up with the 100th north of Rome on June 10, 1944. Of the thirteen hundred men who had gone into combat with the One Puka Puka, over nine hundred were casualties. Its Nisei replacements had come from the 442nd in the States. And now what would become the most decorated unit of its type in the history of the army had arrived to fight the Germans with a motivation unknown to normal *hakujin* (white) commands. It was time for them to prove every bigot in America wrong.

The 442nd slugged its way up to Pisa and the Arno River. Heroics became commonplace, an accepted part of the responsibility of the Americans with the "different eyes." And then it was off to the south of France, where the Go for Broke boys had a date with a bunch of hard-fighting Texans—the 36th Division. Facing the American command were Wehrmacht units with their backs to the wall, for behind the Germans was the Fatherland, and they were ready to defend it to the death with every tool of war at their disposal. One day back in Camp Shelby, a second lieutenant had reported into the 100th. He had the eyes and skin of an Asian, but he was Korean. Knowing Koreans had suffered strong discrimination from the Japanese for many years, the colonel offered to transfer him, but the young officer told him, "I don't want to be transferred. I'm an American and all the soldiers are American."

"Very well," the colonel replied. "But on probation. If you get along with the men, you can stay."

At first Kim *didn't* get along with the men. He was hard-nosed and demanding, "chicken," as the term went. But soon the men saw that he didn't ask them to do anything he wouldn't do, and they began to respect him. In combat with so many officers becoming casualties, he once briefly commanded the battalion as a first lieutenant! As a captain, he commanded E Company and served as battalion executive officer for a time. He earned the DSC, a Silver Star, and four Purple Hearts. After the war, he stayed in the Army and retired as a colonel with a chest full of ribbons.

The fighting was savage in the French Vosges Mountains, and finally one of the most amazing events of the war took place. On October 24, 1944, the First Battalion of the Texan's 141st Infantry Regiment ran into overpowering opposition and after a fierce battle its 275 survivors were cut off from the regiment. Their small hilltop perimeter was surrounded by seven hundred Germans who had tanks and artillery and were being reenforced by the hour. The senior of the three US officers remaining was the artillery observer, First Lieutenant Erwin Blonder. On the only working radio in the command he had scratchy radio contact with regimental headquarters. Therefore, the division commander, Major General John Dahlquist, was well aware of the battalion's precarious position: no food, no water, mounting casualties, and ammunition running short. And the 36th couldn't get through to rescue its beleaguered men. Even an air drop failed to get supplies to them. The "lost battalion" was brought to the attention of the army commander, and the two commanding generals called on the 442nd's Colonel Charles Pence to handle the rescue mission.

Battle weary from a solid week of tough fighting, the Nisei dragged themselves back into combat on October 30. The fighting was brutal, and at times General Dahlquist joined them. On one occasion his aide, Lieutenant Wells Lewis, son of Nobel Prize–winning author Sinclair Lewis, was killed at his side. Little did anyone know that Hitler personally had ordered the lost battalion captured or destroyed! After five days of bitter combat, I Company, 442nd, which had started the mission with 205 men, was down to two platoons—one had six men left out of forty, the other, two. It broke through to the lost battalion. The point man was Private First Class Matt Sakumoto. When he met the first of the now 211 surviving T-Patchers, he looked into a filthy, haggard face with disbelieving eyes, smiled, and said, "Want a smoke?"

The 442nd had opened the breach through which the lost battalion could get back to its division and recover from its ordeal. But it had been costly—the regiment had traded 800 Nisei to save the 211. To this day, Texas honors the Nisei of the 442nd.

Go for Broke was the most decorated unit of its size in the history of the army. Authorized forty-five hundred men, over eighteen thousand Americans served under its colors. It had a casualty rate of

300 percent, received seven Presidential Unit Citations, earned seven major campaign streamers, and received thirty-six Army Commendations and eighty-seven Divisional Commendations. Its men were awarded one Medal of Honor, 52 Distinguished Service Crosses, 560 Silver Stars (22 with Oak Leaf Clusters for a multiple award), some 4,000 Bronze Stars, and approximately 9,500 Purple Hearts. In the year 2000 twenty-one of its heroes were upgraded to the Medal of Honor, including Senator Dan Inyoue.

There were heroic Nisei elsewhere in the armed forces, particularly as interpreters and analysts in Military Intelligence positions. Most of these served in the Pacific and in China/Burma, so they never received as much recognition as those in the 442nd. But never before and probably never again will a group of ethnic Americans give as much for their country, in such a heroic manner, as the Go for Broke soldiers.

☆☆☆☆☆

We can't leave the 36th Division without mentioning Commando Kelly. An infantryman in Company L, 143rd Infantry, then private Chuck Kelly, who was a former gang member from Pittsburgh, went on a long one-man reconnaissance under heavy enemy fire on September 13, 1943, in Italy. That same day he led three men to the town of Altavilla, where he wiped out a machine-gun nest and was credited with personally killing forty Germans.

Early the next morning the enemy counterattacked and Kelly spent most of the day in a one-man war from the second story of a house. His weapons included an M1 rifle, a carbine, an old .03 Springfield rifle, and a bazooka. Later in the day, he found some 60 mm mortar shells and figured out how to arm them so they would detonate on impact. With them, he blunted a German attack, and the enemy withdrew.

Commando Kelly returned to a huge welcome in Pittsburgh wearing the Medal of Honor and two Silver Stars.

THE MIGHTY EIGHTH

> *A great country can have no such thing as a little war.*
> —Duke of Wellington (1815)

The Eighth Air Force's headquarters arrived in England in February 1942, soon followed by operational elements. The Eighth flew its first mission on July 4, 1942, in DB-7 Boston (A-20) medium bombers borrowed from the British. Imagine, America's first bombing raid in Europe was in an American bomber *borrowed* from the RAF! Six weeks later, on August 17, 1942, the Eighth flew its first all-American heavy bomber raid from England, using B-17 Flying Fortresses, against German installation at Rouen, France.

General Ira Eaker was in command, but a doughty little pilot who could fly almost anything well, be it the Gee Bee or the lead B-25 from a bouncing carrier deck, stopped by with a bomber wing. Of course it was Jimmy Doolittle. But he didn't stay long; he was ordered to North Africa to command the Twelfth Air Force. Promoted to major general, he moved on to command the Fifteenth Air Force in the Mediterranean, then in January of 1944 he was sent back to England to be the boss of the by then massive Eighth Air Force as a three-star.

In 1943 it was decided that it would take both daylight and nighttime bombing to destroy Germany's industrial and tactical capacity to make war. The British didn't believe in daylight bombing, due to the problems presented by enemy fighters and antiaircraft fire, so they chose darkness for their forays deep into the Third Reich. The B-17s and B-24 Liberators of the Eighth Air Force took on the hazardous daytime missions. The raids were always dangerous, particularly so before the long-range P-51 Mustang fighter arrived in sufficient numbers for escort duty all the way to and from the targets. The P-38 Lightnings and the heavily armed P-47 Thunderbolts, also known as "Jugs" were good fighters, but they simply didn't have the range required for the deeper raids. The B-17s, known affectionately as "the big-assed birds," got the most media attention. Of course there were medium bomber units flying the unforgiving Martin B-26s, the B-25s, and some A-20s. Fighters flew tactical recon and ground support missions, while numerous other types of aircraft flew the photographic and other support missions that kept the behemoth Eighth operational.

Heavy bomber crews took serious losses, in spite of the formation tactics that provided formidable fields of fire from their machine guns. Until the later-model B-17s were armed with twin .50 nose guns, those formations were vulnerable to head-on attacks by fighters. For a long time, twenty-five was the magic number of missions that permitted crew rotation to the States. Many, many crew members didn't make it. The crew of the *Memphis Belle* was one that did, and a movie was made of her last mission. One of the finest war movies ever made was the stirring *Twelve O'Clock High* (1949), starring Gregory Peck. Remarkably authentic, it is a good look at the rigors of command in a B-17 group.

It is difficult to imagine the problems these crews faced, aside from enemy fighters and antiaircraft fire (flak). On occasion, the temperature at higher altitudes hovered around −50 degrees Fahrenheit, creating frost inside the aircraft and ice up to two inches thick on the windows. Oxygen masks iced, making breathing difficult; frigid wind broke into the waist gun positions; and frostbite struck in a matter of seconds if gloves were removed. There was simply no heat in most of the crew locations, and the warmest of flight clothing wasn't enough to ward off the cold of high-altitude flying.

The Eighth Air Force became the greatest air armada in history. By mid-1944 it had reached a total strength of more than 200,000 people, and it is estimated that more than 350,000 Americans served in the Eighth Air Force during the war in Europe. Its aircraft operated out of 112 bases in England. At peak strength the Eighth Air Force could dispatch more than two thousand four-engine bombers and more than one thousand fighters on a single mission. For these reasons, it became known as the "Mighty Eighth."

Aircraft nose art became highly popular, with nudes getting the most favor. When such art was censored, it was said that crews "skirted the regulations, rather than the ladies." But for those artists attempting to appease, it didn't take much ingenuity to add a tight swimsuit or a revealing negligee. (In my novel *Renegade Lightning*, which was based on a true story in which a marauding Italian pilot in a captured P-38 was shooting down Allied bombers, nose art depicting the enemy ace's wife was actually painted on a heavily armored bomber [the YB-40] to draw him into close contact.)

Many stories of individual heroism are the legacy of the Eighth Air Force.

On May 1, 1943, a 423rd Squadron Flying Fort piloted by First Lieutenant Lewis Johnson received several hits returning from a raid on Saint-Nazaire, at the mouth of the Loire River. Fires had started in the tail wheel housing and radio compartment. The ball turret gunner, Staff Sergeant Maynard "Snuffy" Smith, on his first mission, climbed down from his guns as the two waist gunners and the radio operator bailed out. But instead of following the veterans, he elected to stay with the apparently doomed plane. The raging fire in the radio department isolated him from the officers up front, so he had no way of knowing if and when they might jump.

Wrapping a sweater around his face for protection against the thickening smoke, he battled the fire with a hand extinguisher. Since the Fortress was still in formation, he guessed his pilots were still at the controls and turned his attention to the minor fire in the rear. There he discovered that the tail gunner had not jumped and was lying outside his compartment badly wounded. Smith rendered first aid, then went back to fight the other fire. German fighters were now attacking, so Smith split his time firing waist guns, tending to the wounded crewman, and battling the flames that escaping oxygen had turned into intense heat. Ammunition boxes began to explode, so Smith heaved them through a huge hole the fire had burned in the side of the fuselage. He fought the flames for ninety minutes, finally urinating on the wreckage. As the badly damaged Fortress approached the English coast, Snuffy tossed overboard every item he could to lessen the strain on the weakened rear of the aircraft. A short time later, Lieutenant Johnson landed "the big-assed bird" safely at Predannack Aerodrome near Britain's Land's End.

Staff Sergeant Snuffy Smith, the skinny little son of a Michigan judge, was the first living member of the Fighting Eighth to receive the Medal of Honor.

★ ★ ★ ★ ★

On November 16, a B-24 Liberator piloted by First Lieutenant R. C. Griffith came home from a Norway raid on three uncertain engines. Arriving over Shipdham Aerodrome, Griffith found he could get only one main landing gear down. Aware that the bomber was low on fuel, the tower instructed the pilot to put the aircraft on a seaward heading and have all crew members bail out. But after ordering everyone out, Griffith discovered that a gunner was too badly wounded to jump, so he decided that a crash landing was the only way he could possibly save the man. Making the attempt even more hazardous was the fact that the starboard rudder and flaps weren't working. This is the kind of a situation that pilots like to refer to as "hairy."

Griffith set up a good approach and touched down on the runway on the one main gear, and by sheer strength managed to hold the Liberator level for some 1,200 feet. Finally, the left wing fell and spun the big aircraft around to a screeching halt. No fire started, and Griffith quickly got the wounded gunner out and into an ambulance. Later a mechanic discovered an unexploded 20 mm shell in the one good engine.

Hairy!

★ ★ ★ ★ ★

There were 261 fighter aces in the Eighth Air Force in World War II; 31 aces had fifteen or more aircraft kills apiece. The only Medal of

Honor awarded to a fighter pilot engaged in aerial combat over Europe was pinned on Major James Howard, commanding officer of the 356th Fighter Squadron. While escorting a bombing raid over Oschersleben, a city in central Germany, on January 11, 1944, he became separated from his command and spotted a large formation of enemy fighters heading for the bombers. Without hesitating he banked straight for them. Roaring into the middle of the formation in his Thunderbolt, Howard began a turkey shoot, in which he claimed six kills. He fought what was estimated to be thirty enemy planes for thirty minutes. He was credited with three kills, and broke off his one-man air war only when three of his guns went out. So disruptive was his attack that the shattered enemy formation broke off its attack, and stayed away from the bombers. Major Howard retired as a brigadier general in Bellair Bluffs, Florida.

☆☆☆☆☆

The most well-known ace of the European theater was Francis "Gabby" Grabeski, the son of Polish immigrants who had emigrated to Oil City, Pennsylvania. Born in 1919, Gabby was a new pilot at Wheeler Field, Hawaii, when Pearl Harbor was attacked. He arrived in Britain in January 1943 and flew thirteen missions in Spitfire Mark Vs with the Polish pilots in 315 Squadron, RAF. Returning to the 56th Fighter Group, he commanded a squadron and allowed some of his new Polish friends to fly some missions as "lodgers." His final score was twenty-eight air victories in 153 combat missions, but it could have been higher had he not been forced to crash-land his Thunderbolt in Germany on July 20th, 1944. A lieutenant colonel at the time, he eluded capture for five days, but wound up in Stalag Luft 1 until the end of the war. He stayed in the Air Force where he accumulated six and a half kills in the Korean War, retiring as a colonel in 1967.

☆☆☆☆☆

Major George Preddy, born in February 1919 in Greensboro, North Carolina, started the war flying P-40s against the Japanese in defense of northern Australia. Joining the Eighth Fighter Command in the summer of 1943, he didn't get his first victory until December 1. Handsome and sporting a thin black mustache, the Carolinian piled up multiple kills on several days, getting two three times, three one time, and *six* on July 18, 1944. Preddy was awarded the DSC, two Silver Stars, nine Distinguished Flying Crosses, eight Air Medals, and a Purple Heart. He was killed when he was shot down by flak over the Belgian border on Christmas Day 1944. He was credited with twenty-seven victories.

☆☆☆☆☆

Don Gentile learned to fly while in high school in Piqua, Ohio. The son of Italian immigrants, he wound up in the Eagle Squadron, where he got two kills before joining the US Fourth Fighter Group in September 1942. Another handsome fighter pilot with a thin black mustache, he ran up a score of twenty-two before returning to the States in April 1944 to be a test pilot at Wright-Patterson AFB at Dayton. Gentile was killed in an aircraft accident in January 1951. His decorations included a DSC, a Silver Star, some DFCs, Air Medals, a British DFC, and several foreign decorations.

☆☆☆☆☆

The list is long. Colonel Hubert Zemke was considered by many to be the most brilliant fighter leader in the Eighth. The Missoula, Montana, native was lost when his P-51 broke up in a storm on October 30, 1944. Surviving, he was the senior Allied officer at Stalag Luft 1 until the end of the war. He had eighteen kills and his medals included the DSC. He retired from the Air Force in 1967.

Others who were high-ranking aces in fighter cockpits were: Major "Bud" Mahurin of Fort Wayne, Indiana; Major Duanee Beeson of Boise, Idaho; Lieutenant Colonel Glenn Duncan of Houston, Texas, who was shot down and fought with the Dutch underground from July 7, 1944, until Allied armies arrived in the spring of 1945. There was also Major John Godfrey, from Woonsocket, Rhode Island, who was Preddy's wingman for a time and ran up eighteen victories. His P-47 and his P-51s were dubbed *Reggie's Reply*, named for his brother who was lost at sea in combat.

PLOESTI

Without a doubt, the most famous bombing raid in WWII was on the Ploesti, Romania, oilfields, the source of one-third of Germany's oil. While three of the five bomb groups that participated on August 1, 1943, were from the Eighth Air Force, the mission was planned and controlled by Headquarters, Ninth Air Force, in Libya. Ploesti was defended by the heaviest concentration of guns ever assembled— some two hundred of the vicious 88mms and thousands of smaller caliber guns. Additionally, some three hundred enemy fighters awaited the call to burst into the air and intercept incoming allied bombers. This was what the mission given the code name Operation Tidal Wave had to face when its aircraft broke into Ploesti airspace.

It was a B-24 mission all the way, even though the Liberator was a high-altitude bomber. Regardless of any other negatives, the B-24s were to head for the targets low, like fighters, below radar range. This meant around 200 feet, meaning many of them would get down to 35 to 50 feet. Lots of *stuff* can get in the air in front of a big Liberator at those altitudes, particularly after preceding bombers have blown things like huge storage tanks to smithereens and ignited massive fires. Additionally, since they'd be in formation, the bombers would be unable to maneuver or take evasive action in the target area; they would, in effect, be nice big fat targets as they lumbered through.

But as William Tecumseh Sherman said, "War is hell," and Ploesti had to be destroyed or at least crippled.

The Ploesti Raid consisted of 177 bombers that departed from airfields around Benghazi, Libya. They carried 316 tons of five-hundred- and one-thousand-pound American bombs, and some 1,775 American crew members. The round-trip flight was twenty-four hundred miles. Brigadier General Uzal Ent commanded and led the raid.

After the initial wave passed through the target areas, the air space was every bit the hell it was expected to be. In several cases, aircraft commanders had to make quick decisions that placed them more in harm's way than expected. One such was Second Lieutenant Lloyd Hughes, who was leading his formation and was hit prior to reaching the target. A bad leak of gasoline had fuel streaming along the fuselage. But for him to alter his course would have meant his whole element would have missed their specific target. Without a moment's hesitation, he plunged his B-24 into the inferno. It didn't come out.

Commanders of other groups also had to take their aircraft into the towering blazes. A total of 163 Liberators made it over their targets. Forty-one went down, eight were forced to land in Turkey, and five were lost for other reasons. Many of those who made it back were badly shot up. The Medal of Honor was awarded to:

Colonel Leon Johnson
Colonel John Kane
Lieutenant Colonel Addison Baker (posthumously)
Major John Jerstad (posthumously)
Second Lieutenant Lloyd Hughes (posthumously)

Four of the five medals went to Eighth Air Force pilots. No other mission before or since has produced as many Medal of Honor feats; only thirty-five were awarded to the entire Air Force in WWII. Did the raid destroy the oil fields? No, but the Fifteenth Air Force banged away during the following summer until Ploesti went out of business.

There were several other numbered Air Forces in the war, and all not only did a superb job, but also had many heroic actions by their members—in fact, too numerous to make this limited space.

The Tuskegee Guys

Who were the only two black officers serving in a combat arm in the late 1930s? Both were named Benjamin O. Davis. They were father and son. Benjamin Sr. was the first black man to become a general. Who was the first black man to solo a military aircraft? Benjamin Jr., a 1936 graduate of West Point, at Tuskegee Institute Airfield in July 1941. He and other members of that first twelve-man cadet class of blacks had their pilot's wings pinned on the following March. They were not only the forerunners of the nearly one thousand black "Tuskegee Airmen" but they were the core pilots of the 99th Pursuit Squadron that would earn an enviable combat record in the war.

Benjamin Jr. was a lieutenant colonel commanding the 99th when it went to North Africa in 1943. After a combat stint that took the squadron to Italy, he returned to the States to form the 332nd Fighter Group, an all-black outfit that would merge the 99th with the 100th, 301st, and 302nd Fighter Squadrons. Promoted to full colonel, Davis led the group until the end of the war. They moved from their original P-40s in North Africa to Thunderbolts, then to P-51s. They painted their nose spinners and tail sections a bright red, earning them the nickname "The Red Tails." Soon they were given the mission of long-range bomber escort. One B-24 pilot remembered, "The P-38s always stayed too far out. Some of the Mustang group stayed in too close.... Other groups, we got the feeling that they just wanted to go and shoot down 109s.... The Red Tails were always out there where we wanted them to be.... We had no idea they were Black; it was the Army's best kept secret."

Counting the six thousand combat sorties the 99th flew before joining the group, the 332nd flew some fifteen thousand combat sorties, some of them extremely long-range. They destroyed 111 enemy aircraft in the air, and 150 on the ground. But most important, *not one single bomber escorted by the Red Tails was ever shot down.*

Benjamin Davis Jr. went through an illustrious career in the Air Force, retiring as a lieutenant general. He formed the sky marshal program and served as assistant secretary of transportation. Promoted to full general on the retired list in 1998, he died at the age of 89 in Walter Reed Army Hospital on the Fourth of July 2002.

NORMANDY AND TEDDY ROOSEVELT JR.

> *I would rather explain why I went to the war than why I did not.*
> —Teddy Roosevelt as quoted by his son
> Brigadier General Ted Roosevelt in his book
> *Average Americans in Olive Drab*

Finally, after over two years of planning and preparing, the cross-channel invasion of Fortress Europe was put into effect in June 1944. After using all sorts of subterfuge to keep the Germans from discovering just where the Allied forces would land, Operation Overlord hit the Continent on the early morning of June 6. Although there have been D-Days in numerous operations before and since, that great event will always be remembered as "D-Day." It was further made famous by the stirring movie *Saving Private Ryan* (1998).

Allied air forces had virtually cleared the sky of the Luftwaffe and had pummeled German defenses prior to the landings, but the enemy's well-built emplacements couldn't be destroyed. They would prove formidable barriers. Naval underwater demolition teams, the forerunners of the SEALs, cleared many of the obstacles in the water, and Navy Seabees played a major role. Additionally, the French underground performed sabotage in the German rear area.

The gigantic invasion armada consisted of some five thousand seacraft carrying 132,000 troops across the choppy channel. Airborne troops numbering 23,500 were dropped just inland of the beaches, and ten thousand aircraft moved in close to support the landing.

The invasion's scope was vast. Ike was the supreme commander, while the field command went to Sir Bernard Montgomery (whose ego hadn't been offended when King George VI knighted him). The British command on the eastern portion of the French coast consisted of the British Second Army, the Canadian First Army, and the British 6th Airborne Division. Their landing sites were named Gold, Juno, and Sword beaches. The American force under Lieutenant General Omar Bradley went in on the western beaches named Omaha and Utah. The US 82nd and 101st Airborne Divisions made their drops and glider landings behind the defenses.

But we must stop here to meet Ted Roosevelt Jr. He was President Theodore Roosevelt's oldest son, who was mentioned earlier. Major General Bruce Jacobs did a good job on Ted Jr. in his fine 1956 book, *Heroes of the Army*. He quoted a friend as saying, "Old Teddy was a dilettante soldier and a first-class politician; young Teddy was a dilettante politician and a first-class soldier." A small, slender man, Ted (he later dropped the Junior) was a thirty-one-year-old colonel commanding the Twenty-sixth Infantry Regiment of the 1st Division at the end of WWI. Because he was unafraid of anything, Ted's men loved him, although at times his superiors weren't so enamored. He was gassed, wounded, and eventually awarded both the DSC and the Silver Star.

Ted never won any of the elections in which he ran for public office. He and his cousin Franklin Delano differed both in party and political philosophy, and the rift wasn't healed until Ted went to see the president at the outbreak of WWII and mended fences. Ted was appointed assistant secretary of the Navy in 1921, then was defeated by Al Smith for governor of New York. President Coolidge appointed Ted governor of Puerto Rico, then governor general of the Philippines—but when FDR became president, that assignment ended. The capable author of eight books, Ted was vice president of the publishing firm of Doubleday, Doran & Company during the rest of the 1930s.

Following Pearl Harbor, Ted once again became commanding officer of the Twenty-sixth Infantry. He was soon promoted to brigadier and moved up to assistant division commander of the 1st Division under Major General Terry de la Mesa Allen. Together, they were terrors, believing the Big Red One was God's gift to the Army. Another general once bitterly said, "Allen and Roosevelt seem to think the United States Army consists of the 1st Infantry Division and eleven million replacements."

In North Africa Ted could always be found near the front with his men and with his trademark swagger stick in hand. Utterly fearless, and sloppier in uniform than any general in the Army, he was unabashedly loved by the troops. He could roar with them in laughter, and was reported to have said while in Algeria, "Beat hell out of the Germans and Italians and we'll go back to Oran and beat up every MP in town."

Unfortunately, the soldiers took him at his word and when the North African campaign was over, they made life quite miserable for the military police in Oran. But when they hit the beach at Sicily, they were unstoppable. Moving inland, Ted formed a special task force centered around the division's cavalry recon troop. Naturally, it was named "The Rough Riders." It slashed through German positions with great effect and was often the division's lead element. The Big Red One captured eighteen cities in less than a month, then was relieved by the 9th Infantry Division.

But the word was out to break up the unholy pair of generals. Omar Bradley, their commander, called them in and told them, "...the 1st Division has become increasingly temperamental, and has thought itself exempt from discipline by virtue of its months on line." Then he relieved both of them. Terry Allen was sent back to the States to command another division that would do an excellent job after the Normandy invasion, while Ted was assigned as liaison to French general Henri Girard. Roosevelt, unable to stay out of the line of fire, went in with the first waves with Girard's command at Corsica. Later, knowing that Operation Overlord was brewing, he wrote to Eisenhower to be included. But he heard nothing in response. He was just too old. He wrote a second letter, then a third, begging.

Finally, orders came through sending him to England. He would be an extra brigadier in the 4th Infantry Division, an untried command, and he would go in with the first wave as a steadying influence for the green troops. It was a wise decision because there was a foul-up and the first landing team hit the beach over a mile south of its planned landing site. Disaster? No, Ted recognized the error and made a reconnaissance behind the German defenses, where he found the causeway on which the division was to drive inland. He then brilliantly altered the assault plan and coordinated attacks on enemy positions leading to the roadway.

Ted was everywhere, waving his famous swagger stick, ordering, encouraging the tired troops to keep fighting and moving. When darkness fell, the whole division was in France and its forward elements had linked up with the 101st Airborne Division. A month later, Eisenhower and Bradley were considering available generals to take over the 90th Infantry Division. On July 13 they decided to give the command to Ted Roosevelt.

But on that very day, Ted Roosevelt died of a heart attack. He was fifty-six.

On September 28 he was awarded the Medal of Honor for his D-Day heroics. He was considered one of the Army's bravest and capable combat generals, even though he was a reserve officer. After the war, the remains of Ted and his fun-loving younger brother, Quentin, who had been shot down in a fighter in WWI, found their final resting place side by side in the Normandy American Cemetery in France.

It was said that although he dearly loved his firstborn, Old Teddy never got over Quentin's death. The former Rough Rider died six months afterward in 1919. If he was looking down from somewhere on D-Day, he would have been immensely proud of his namesake.

PATTON, THE THIRD ARMY, AND "NUTS"

Following the invasion of France, more divisions were sent in and General George S. Patton was pulled out of limbo to command the Third Army. Like all of his previous commands, that army was quickly whipped into shape and became possibly the most dynamic

GEORGE S. PATTON

American army in Europe. And with his penchant for publicity, it was certainly the most well known. In December the Germans kicked off their huge counteroffensive, which became known as the Battle of the Bulge. Its major goal was to break through the Belgian Ardennes and reach the port of Antwerp, where most of the Allies's resupply was entering the Continent. One obstacle in the way was the American 101st Airborne, commanded by Brigadier General Tony McAuliffe. After the superior number of Germans surrounded the town and the Americans, and bombed it heavily, the enemy commander ordered McAuliffe to surrender. His answer was one of the most famous statements in the history of the American military: *"Nuts!"*

The paratroopers of the 101st fought valiantly and held off the huge enemy force until Patton, knowing their plight, finally broke through to relieve them. This action broke the back of the German offensive and was the beginning of the end for the Germans. Patton would dash on to the Rhine River, where he made true his promise to urinate in that mighty stream. Copies of the photo, while considered crude by many, were distributed throughout the Third Army and were quite a humorous morale booster.

The Kid from Texas

In the meantime, a legend had been born. He was a poor farm boy from Texas who came from a sharecropping family of twelve children, only nine of which survived. His father bailed out when the future hero was fairly young, and when the boy was sixteen his mother died, leaving him to care for his younger siblings. When war hit, he was so scrawny at five feet five and 110 pounds that he couldn't get in the Marines or the paratroops. At seventeen he enlisted in the infantry, and after completing training, sewed on the square patch with diagonal blue-and-white stripes of the 3rd Infantry Division. It was early 1943; he was assigned to Company B of the Fifteenth Infantry.

His company commander tried to talk him into a transfer because of his baby face and small frame, but the young private refused. The captain made him a runner, figuring that would keep him out of heavy combat, but the kid slipped off on patrols whenever he could after the Sicily invasion. He was a dead shot and cool under fire, so the captain gave up, promoted him to corporal, and made him a squad leader.

After the Allies landed at Salerno on the mainland, he distinguished himself and was promoted to buck sergeant. The Anzio stalemate was months of heavy fighting in which the kid volunteered for many patrols. One day the captain offered him a direct commission, but he turned it down so he could stay with his buddies in the platoon. Ordered to take and hold a house on a prominent hill that could be used for an artillery observation post, the kid sergeant mined the road leading to the hill. When a column of German Tiger tanks approached, the lead vehicle was badly damaged, and since the surrounding fields were wet, this temporarily blocked the column. But a repair party came out under the cover of darkness to fix the tank. The young sergeant led a patrol down the road and, crawling forward alone, he fired rifle grenades into the tank's treads, rendering it once more immovable. He was awarded the Bronze Star.

On August 15, 1944, the division landed in southern France. A short time later, with his unit blocked by heavy machine guns high up on a ridge, the kid took a light machine gun and managed to suppress part of the enemy fire. When he ran out of ammo, he and one of his soldiers charged. But the other man, a close friend, was killed and the enraged kid grabbed an enemy machine gun and charged the other German positions. By the time his violent charge was over, he had killed all of the enemy soldiers within them. He was awarded the DSC.

In his next exploit, the kid saved a patrol he led from an ambush and received the Silver Star. A few days later, his platoon was ambushed again; he crawled to where he could observe the enemy position and, while under heavy fire, directed artillery fire on the German force. This action brought him his second Silver Star.

Given permission to remain with his platoon as an officer, he then accepted a battlefield commission. He'd come a long way from that poor sharecropper's farm, but he still had a way to go. After recovering from a wound, the kid returned to his company and headed an attack on a German stronghold. Soon, as the only surviving officer, he took command of the company. Facing six tanks and waves of enemy infantrymen, he ordered his men to withdraw while he remained forward to direct artillery fire. A nearby tank destroyer received a direct hit and began to burn. The young officer climbed aboard and quickly manned its .50 caliber machine gun. Exposed to German infantry on three sides, he continued to mow them down. The German tanks, losing infantry support, pulled back as he continued to hold his position until he ran out of ammunition. Wounded in the leg, he finally made his way back to the company, refusing medical attention and reorganizing the command for a counterattack.

On February 22, 1945, the commander of the Seventh Army awarded him the Legion of Merit and hung the blue-and-white ribbon of the Medal of Honor around his neck. He joined the Texas Guard after the war and was eventually promoted to major. He starred in forty-four movies, including *To Hell and Back,* from his book by the same title. America's most highly decorated hero of World War II, he was killed in a civilian plane crash at the age of forty-nine. After John F. Kennedy's grave, his is the second most visited in Arlington Cemetery.

He was, of course, Audie Murphy.

The Polks

And now for another family story, perhaps the most illustrious family in American military history. It all began when a Scot named Robert Pollock, who was a Cromwell officer, decided to flee Ireland. He purchased a small sailing ship—a bark—outfitted it, recruited a crew and passengers, and began the arduous voyage across the Atlantic to the New World. Reaching Chesapeake Bay in early 1680, Captain Pollock and his little band of immigrants settled on swampy land in northeast Maryland. By then the family name had evolved into Polk.

One of his sons, William, begat a dynasty that would produce a US president and many other eminent Americans, including governors of Delaware, Tennessee, and Missouri, and a daughter who was married to a governor of Maryland. His son, William II, begat Thomas, who was the father of another William. But let's pause here in the midst of all this begetting and begatting. By now, this branch of the family was residing in North Carolina. Thomas became a colonel in the Revolutionary War, but his son, William, became more famous. Will was a lieutenant at sixteen, and was the first soldier wounded south of Lexington. He finished the war as a lieutenant colonel with honors from several battles.

William's son, Ezekial, was the grandfather of James Knox Polk, a politician since his school days. After graduating with honors from the University of North Carolina, James wound up in Tennessee, where he later became governor. He was twice Speaker of the House of Representatives before being elected the eleventh president of the United States in 1844. War with Mexico—often referred to as "Polk's War"—followed.

James K. Polk didn't wear a uniform, but he commanded all of those who did while he was in office. Referred to as an "expansionist," he brought more new territory into the Union than any other president: Texas, California, and the vast New Mexico and Oregon territories. Leaving office in bad health from hard work, James died in 1849.

Leodinas Polk, a cousin, graduated from West Point in the class of 1827. While he was still a cadet, he underwent a powerful conversion to the Episcopal Church. Immediately after graduation, he got out of the Army and eventually became the Episcopal bishop of the Southeast. He founded the University of the South in Sewanee,

Tennessee. When the Civil War erupted, his old classmate Jefferson Davis commissioned him a major general, and he took part in many battles before being killed by a Union artillery shell on Pine Mountain during the Atlanta campaign. He was then a lieutenant general commanding a Confederate corps.

A nephew was a captain in the Tennessee cavalry during that same conflict. In 1910 Harding Polk graduated from West Point and at one time was the commandant of Virginia Military Institute, where he had been a roommate of Georgie Patton before going to the Military Academy. He retired as a colonel, but on the way, he sired three sons—John, who would retire as an Army colonel; Thomas, who would retire as a Navy captain; and James, or Jimmy, as he was known by his friends.

Jimmy scraped through West Point and was commissioned a second lieutenant of cavalry in 1936. A talented horseman, he was a member of the world-famous Army Equestrian Team and was a leading Army polo player. In 1939 Jimmy won the Military and Police Jumping championship at the National Horse Show in New York's Madison Square Garden. Movie actress Rita Hayworth presented the trophy to him, which didn't actually please his beautiful young El Paso wife, Joey.

The year 1943 found him in the 106th Mechanized Cavalry Group, first as a squadron commander, then as regimental executive officer. He went into Normandy at Utah Beach shortly after D-Day, where the 106th was involved in heavy fighting. After short stints as temporary commanding officer of two cavalry groups, he was given the reins of the Third Cavalry Group, the famous "Brave Rifles" from the Mexican War. The Third soon became known as "Task Force Polk," and was one of Patton's pet units. Jimmy led his often fast-moving light tanks from the front, spearheading the fast Third Army dashes. He led the way for the Ardennes counterattack in 1945, and plunged on into Germany with the Third Army. Promoted to full colonel at thirty-two, Jimmy had one of his Silver Stars for personal heroism pinned on by Patton himself.

After serving on Douglas MacArthur's staff through part of the Korean War, Polk finally was promoted to brigadier general in 1956, at which time Mrs. Patton gave him a pair of Georgie's silver-plated stars. The tall, dark-browed Polk commanded the hot spot of Berlin in the early 1960s and then the 4th Armored Division near Nuremberg. Seemingly glued to Western Europe, he rose to the command of the Seventh Army and Headquarters, USAEUR (United States Army Europe), as well as Central Army Group, NATO, as a four-star general. He went on to many other honors, including chairman of the board of the US Horse Cavalry Association, before he died in 1992.

Throughout the years since Captain Robert Pollock landed his small group of battered immigrants at Chesapeake Bay, Polks have been in the forefront of our wars.

ADIOS ADOLF

As the war in Europe was winding down, Hitler killed himself by taking poison in a bunker in the shattered capital of Berlin. He had proved that even the remarkable wartime industrial capability of Germany and the brilliance of his flag officers could not make up for the grievous meddling and mistakes of a despot who had never risen above the rank of corporal. As Patton crossed the Rhine, victorious Soviet armies led by Marshal Georgy Zhukov roared into Berlin from the east. Patton wanted to keep going, and history bore him out. He received his fourth star, but was cheated of the glorious death in combat that he would have preferred. Instead, he died in an auto accident. Generals Dwight Eisenhower, Omar Bradley, and the Army Air Corps' Hap Arnold all received their fifth stars. George Catlett Marshall was also promoted to general of the Army; he later served as secretary of state, and also as secretary of defense. His "Marshal Plan" helped feed Europe after the war.

The official surrender of Germany took place in a little schoolhouse in Reims, France, on May 8, 1945.

It was VE-Day...Victory in Europe.

Another famous photo of the war was taken in Times Square, where a sailor kisses a nurse he holds in his arms. America breathed its first big sigh of relief, but more fighting lay ahead.

BACK TO THE PACIFIC

Only destruction of the enemy can be called victory.
—Admiral Stepan O. Makarov, at Port Arthur (1904)

While much of the world celebrated the great victory in Europe, the job wasn't finished with the nation that had so violently attacked Pearl Harbor. We left MacArthur two years earlier in Australia. When he finally assembled an adequate fighting force in 1943, he put his masterful planning acuity to work. Marching up the island of New Guinea in "leap-frog" moves, his men progressed one thousand miles. Admiral Chester Nimitz headed the Central Pacific campaign that hopped westward from island chain to island chain. Starting in the Solomon Islands his naval amphibious forces had driven the Japanese about two thousand miles west of Guadalcanal. Closing like a pincer, both advances were aimed straight toward the Philippines. One more series of conquests and Douglas MacArthur would be able to fulfill his promise to return and liberate the Philippines.

But let's leave the strategic aspect and go down to where the troops are. Nearly everyone who remembers WWII will recall the "Ballad of Private Rodger Young." Both the music and the lyrics were stirring and catchy. Let's meet the young man who inspired it.

It happened on a basketball court in a small town in Ohio. He was short and thin, but an excellent athlete. The town was Green Springs, near Tiffin, and he was playing as a freshman, a reserve on the high-school basketball team. He was also a scrub on the football team and was a cinch to make the baseball team in the spring when the Buckeye snows were gone and the new buds were opening. Being small, he played guard on the basketball team and was a good passer. He also dove recklessly for any loose ball and was perhaps the most spirited player on the team. His name was Rodger Young and he would become the most famous private of World War II.

In fact, it was his zealous, devil-may-care approach to the game that caused the trouble. One night, with his team behind, the coach put him in the game. Rodger shot from the top of the key, missing but following in to get the rebound. But just as he jumped, the big right arm of the opposing center whacked him across the forehead, knocking him backward to the floor. Rodger landed on his head, and when he awoke in the local hospital, he had trouble hearing and seeing. His hearing improved, but he needed glasses. He was crushed, because his days in sports were over. Oh, he could tape the glasses on and get in pickup games, but he wasn't able to compete again in any of the three sports. Finally, he dropped out of school and went to work in a factory. Then he heard about the National Guard and how joining it would give him a few extra bucks. The idea was appealing, so he enlisted in the 37th Infantry Division, the famous "Fried Egg" Buckeye Division. That was in 1939. After Pearl Harbor, the division shipped out to the Pacific. By then, Young was an infantry squad leader, a sergeant proud of his rank and skills.

Young was enthusiastic and dedicated. In spite of his bad eyesight, he became an expert rifleman. He put his squad through extra hoops of training, making his charges better riflemen and forging them into a finely honed fighting team. But his hearing was deteriorating and one day he went to his company commander to ask permission to turn in his stripes. "I don't want anyone to get hurt because I can't hear," he stated. "But I want to stay with my squad."

His request was granted, and he went just as proudly about his duties as a bare-sleeved private as he had as a sergeant. Then his outfit went up against a strong Japanese command on a neighboring island to Guadalcanal—New Georgia—and the 37th had a fight on its hands. Near Munda, an airfield vital to the Japanese, Young's company ran into an enemy machine-gun emplacement that blocked its progress. Young was struck in the shoulder by a round that hit a vital artery. He looked at the blood gushing from the wound and, checking his M1 rifle, began to crawl toward the enemy gun.

The Ohioan fired as he continued to move forward, oblivious to or unhearing the shouts of his buddies to stop. Fifty yards... stop, shoot, crawl. A Japanese soldier shouted a warning to his gunner! Young got to his knees and fired, then crept forward. Twenty-five yards. The machine gun swung around and flashed at him. Bullets tore into him, but he still continued forward. Fifteen yards, he stumbled to his knees, pulling a grenade from its harness. He threw it into the nest, tossed another as more enemy rounds hit him, then somehow—another.

The Japanese position was wiped out, but when his squad reached him, Private Rodger Young was already dead of his numerous wounds.

> *But in every soldier's heart in all the Infantry*
> *Shines the name, shines the name of Rodger Young.*

Rodger Young's parents were given his Medal of Honor, and Private First Class Frank Loesser, who would become one of America's foremost songwriters, wrote the "Ballad of Rodger Young," one of the most famous and moving songs of World War II. It became the unofficial ballad of the infantry. Even the ship in Robert Heinlein's *Starship Troopers* is named the *Rodger Young.*

His Name Was Tommy

Frank Nichols and I were friends. When I had cancer of the larynx a dozen years ago, he told me with his little electronic throat resonator, "I'll be there for whatever you have to do." It wasn't lip service.

Frank had experienced cancer of the larynx five years earlier, and since we were both retired military pilots, we belonged to an organization called the "Daedalians." Honoring World War I pilots, it was so named because, in Greek mythology, Daedalus was the father of Icarus. According to the story, Daedalus admonished his son not to fly too close to the sun with his wings of feathers and wax. But the brash young man, full of himself and not heeding the old man, like so many other youngsters down through the millennia, soared higher and higher until his wings melted and he promptly crashed into the waiting sea. (Today there are some fourteen thousand Daedalians, all rated military pilots, active or retired, and the ranks have recently been opened to military pilots who no longer fit either category.)

Frank Nichols was a fighter pilot, in fact, he was a fighter pilot's fighter pilot. A graduate of Washington and Lee College, the school where Robert E. Lee was president after the Civil War, Frank was a second lieutenant at Pearl Harbor—stationed at Wheeler Field. But on that fateful December 7 Sunday morning, he was at home about to leave for the golf course when the armada of Japanese aircraft struck battleship row. He didn't get near his plane in time to do anything about the raid that devastated America's Pacific fleet.

However, precisely one year to the day later, Frank had his personal revenge. As a captain leading a flight of four P-40 Tomahawks at 18,000 feet over New Guinea, he spotted a formation of an estimated eighteen Japanese bombers escorted by a dozen Zero fighters. The enemy formation was some 6,000 feet below and headed toward Buna, a major American-held shipping port on Papua's north coast. Signaling to his flight to follow, he dove without hesitation at the lead bomber. He held his fire until the last second, then hit the trigger to his six machine guns and blew the enemy aircraft out of the sky. For some reason, the enemy formation then made a sweeping turn and headed back toward Rabaul on New Britain Island from whence they had apparently come. Frank never did figure out why losing its leader would cause the whole enemy mission to abort. All he knew was that it did, and it was his personal revenge for Pearl Harbor.

But that isn't the end of Frank Nichols's story.

In New Guinea on October 17, 1943, Nichols was a major commanding the 431st Fighter Squadron—part of General George C. Kenney's proud new all-P-38 fighter group. (The twin-engined Lockheed Lightning was America's answer to the successful Zero, and its pilots loved it.) Frank had a strict rule that *nobody* flew his private P-38. On this particular day, Frank had gone over to headquarters in Port Moresby by Gooney Bird—a C-47, the military adaptation of the old DC-3 airliner. In his absence, Japanese Zeroes had been spotted heading for his field, so one of his pilots, a skinny first lieutenant with one of those thin fighter pilot mustaches, jumped into the last combat-ready plane left and roared off into the fray. He sustained severe damage during the dogfight, and had to bail out of the crippled P-38 over water.

Rescued, the lieutenant got back before Frank returned. As the Gooney Bird shut down its engines, the worried lieutenant met Frank climbing down the transport's ladder. Tossing off a sloppy salute, he said, "I'm sorry, sir."

Frank, who was a diminutive five feet six inches tall, looked at the troubled lieutenant quizzically. "For what, Tommy?"

"I got shot down in your airplane, sir. It's in the drink."

Frank looked at him incredulously, his anger quickly rising to the surface. "You know better than to fly my bird!"

"It was the only one—"

"I don't give a damn if it was the last one in the *Pacific!*"

At that moment, Frank's operations officer walked up. "Don't get too upset, Major. Before Tommy bailed out, he shot down three Zeroes."

Frank looked at the captain, then back to Tommy, and shook his head. *"Three?"*

Tommy nodded. "Yes, sir, and I sure am sorry about your airplane."

The major put his arm around Tommy's shoulder and said softly, "That's okay, Tommy, I can get a new one."

The lieutenant was the remarkable Tommy McGuire, who had

shot down *five* Japanese planes in his first two missions—the equivalent of a rookie pitching a no-hitter and a one-hitter in his first two games. He already had the Silver Star and the Distinguished Flying Cross, and he was the Fifth Air Force's instant hero, following in the wake of the famous Dick Bong.

Born in Ridgewood, New Jersey, on August 1, 1920, McGuire spent most of his childhood in Sebring, Florida, where he played clarinet in his high school's famed marching band while establishing himself as a potential fighter pilot by often racing his car through the little town. Tommy graduated from the Army Air Force cadets in February 1942 and married Marilynn, a lovely young woman nicknamed "Pudgy"—the name he would give a succession of aircraft he would fly in combat.

He eventually checked out in the Lightning, and as a superb pilot wound up in Frank Nichols's 431st Squadron in August of 1943. Later, when Nichols moved up, McGuire became the squadron commander. He was promoted to major in May of 1944, at which time, following a long drought in the air, he had accumulated sixteen kills. At this time, Charles Lindbergh visited as a civilian consultant, and they shared a tent. Then McGuire got hot and shot down seventeen enemy planes in the last part of the year. On December 25 and 26 alone he had seven kills.

On January 7, 1945, McGuire was leading a low-level, early-morning fighter sweep when something malfunctioned in his aircraft and he snap-rolled to his death. That quickly, one of the brightest lights in military history went out. He had thirty-eight confirmed victories, two short of Bong's record, and the Medal of Honor was bestowed posthumously. McGuire Air Force Base in New Jersey is named for him, and outside its gate stands a P-38 emblazoned with the name *Pudgy V.*

Major General Frank Nichols had an illustrious career. He died in 2002 at the age of eighty-four. The El Paso flight of Daedalians was renamed for him.

THE HAWK

In 1917 a boy of three was severely burned when a neighbor woman accidentally spilled a pan of boiling water on him. His mother, the daughter of a doctor, refused to let surgery be performed on her deformed child—instead she massaged his crippled limbs daily for over a year. Then, miraculously, the boy, whose name was William Dean Hawkins, learned to walk again. A few years later, he began swimming, though the other kids cruelly made fun of his hideous scars. When he was eight years old, his father died. His mother, Jane, a teacher, raised him alone, encouraging whatever interests he acquired. (A woman who had studied under her told me Jane Hawkins was the finest teacher she had ever known.)

Dean, or Hawk, as he was called, decided he wanted to attend the US Naval Academy at Annapolis. But he was turned down because of his scars. Disappointed, he accepted a scholarship to the Texas School of Mines in his hometown of El Paso. When Pearl Harbor threw the country into WWII, he tried to enlist in the Army Air Corps cadet program. But he was once more rejected because of his scars, even though he was by now a top athlete. He turned to the Marines, who accepted him as an infantry private.

Hawk found his calling and was soon a sergeant on Guadalcanal. His exploits on long-range reconnaissance patrols there and on the island of Tulagi earned him a battlefield commission, and before long, he was a first lieutenant leading an elite "scout and sniper" platoon. Under his leadership, the thirty-four-man platoon became so proficient Hawkins said they could lick any two-hundred-man unit in the world. Then it was time for Tarawa.

Betio was the tiny main island of the Tarawa Atoll. In MacArthur's island-hopping plan, its airfield was a vital link in the Gilbert Islands. It was held by a strong, heavily fortified Japanese army command when the Marine invasion force prepared to strike on the morning of November 20, 1943. The Second Marines was the assault regiment, and twenty-nine-year-old Lieutenant Hawkins and his elite scout and sniper platoon were its spearhead. Their mission: to neu-tralize a six-hundred-yard-long Burns-Phillips pier jutting out from the shore. Numerous enemy machine-gun nests, protected by sand-bags, were slung beneath the pier. Protected Japanese rifle positions were located among the shacks near the seaplane ramp at the end of the pier, and unknown numbers of booby traps and mines awaited the invaders. The pier had to be taken because raking enfilade fire from its enemy positions could make the beaches to each side impossible to hold. Additionally, it was thought that the Japanese had rigged explo-sives to the drums of gasoline stacked at the head of the pier.

There was a mix-up in the timing of the naval barrage, so the Hawk and his men in their landing craft arrived without covering fire. As they approached their objective, heavy Japanese slugs crashed into their boats, but the Hawk leaped onto the pier and the frantic fight was on. With the major assault force still some fifteen hundred yards offshore, Hawk and some engineers with flame-throwers hurled themselves down the objective. The Texan used his handheld machine gun with ferocity, going some thirty yards along the pier, clearing the way for his men.

No one knew what drove the Hawk—was it all the slights he'd received because of his scars, or was it just a fierce heroic strain that even he didn't understand or wish to? One sergeant recalled, "You see, Hawk loved trouble. If there was a tough job to do, he'd ask for it."

When the initial fighting died down, the pier was aflame. It had taken all of six minutes. But after the breather, the battle raged on. By the end of the day Hawk had lost nearly a third of his men, and he had taken shrapnel from a mortar in his shoulder. But he bound it up and readied his men for "day two" of the heavy fighting. In the morning he was again wounded, but continued leading the platoon as they destroyed enemy pillboxes and bunkers. In one attack on a pillbox, he charged it with grenades by himself and took a machine-gun slug in the middle of his chest. Still, he refused to quit fighting. Approaching yet another pillbox, he ordered his men to stay under cover, and charged the enemy position. While lobbing grenades, he was practically torn apart by another Japanese machine gun. An important artery in his intact shoulder began gushing blood as his men knocked out the bunker and got him to a nearby field hospital.

But over twenty pints of blood couldn't save him. During the night the Hawk slipped away to wherever "the bravest of the brave" go. The Betio airfield was quickly named for him. His regimental commander, Colonel David Shoup (later a four-star commandant of the Marine Corps), stated, "It isn't often you can credit a first lieutenant with winning a battle, but Hawkins came as near to it as any many could."

On a later day, with another Marine general looking on, Jane Hawkins received the Medal of Honor posthumously for her hero son from President Franklin D. Roosevelt in the White House. Her moist eyes must have gone back to the hundreds of hours in which she massaged her tiny son's terrible burn wounds, or perhaps to the days when he came home crying because the other kids had ridiculed him for having the scars. The five-pointed star medal on a light blue ribbon with tiny white stars wouldn't bring him back or still the pain that must have nearly consumed her, but knowing of his great contribution would help.

A middle school in his hometown is named for him, and at the Marine School for Company Grade Officers in Quantico, Virginia, where all new officers today go through a twenty-six-week course, there is a room known throughout the Corps as "The Hawk."

MacArthur Returns

For gold the merchant ploughs the main,
The farmer ploughs the manor;
But glory is the sodger's prize;
The sodger's wealth is honour....

—From an 1812 Army song

General Douglas MacArthur kept his promise to the Filipinos. It was decided that for strategic reasons, the island of Leyte in the central

Philippines would be best for the Allied invasion. The Japanese knew if they lost the archipelago, they were doomed, so they threw everything they could into what became known as the Second Battle of the Philippine Sea (it would later be called the biggest battle in naval history). It was the beginning of the end for the once powerful Japanese navy; it would never again be a factor in the war. The victory on Saipan provided a base for American bombers to operate against the Japanese home islands, and the occupation of Tinian Island brought Tokyo well within reach of the new Boeing Super Forts, the B-29s.

On October 20, 1944, MacArthur waded ashore, knee-deep, behind his invasion force on the beach at Leyte. The photo is one of the most famous of the war. One can only imagine what must have been going through his head, coming back to the people he loved, to those who believed in him.

The fighting was bitter on Luzon, the main island. The 11th Airborne Division did a lot of it and its 511th Parachute Infantry Regiment made a combat jump to free the prisoners at Loso Banos Prison Camp. Over twenty-one hundred military and civilian internees were liberated, with only light casualties. The 503rd Parachute Infantry Regiment jumped on Corregidor as part of a joint airborne/amphibious operation. The 503rd still has "The Rock" in its personal patch. Instead of Manila being treated as an "Open City," as it had been when the Japanese invaded, the enemy navy and marines fought to the bitter end there—raping and brutalizing the local Filipinos before killing them: one hundred thousand died with the city reduced to rubble before the carnage was over. It was senseless butchery, orchestrated by the Japanese navy commanders there, not General Yamashita, who had withdrawn his army to the mountains.

As William Manchester wrote in *American Caesar*, "GIs fought them hand by hand, room by room, closet by closet." The Japanese retreated to the old walled city of Intramuros, and MacArthur's air commander, General George Kenney, wanted to attack it from the air, but MacArthur said no, not wanting any more civilians than necessary to suffer. As the bloody fighting went on, MacArthur went to the liberated prison camps: first Bilibid, then Santo Tomas. There he was surrounded by sobbing, emaciated men wearing the filthy rags that were all they had left. Those who could, attempted to stand at attention. The general wrote, "They remained silent, as though at inspection. I looked down the lines of men, bearded and soiled… with toes sticking out of such shoes as remained, with suffering and torture written on their gaunt faces. Here was all that was left of my men of Bataan and Corregidor.… As I passed slowly down the scrawny, suffering column, a murmur accompanied me as each man barely speaking above a whisper, said, 'You're back,' or 'You made it.' …I could only reply, 'I'm a little late, but we finally came.'"

Once more, according to Manchester, after Manila was finally retaken, the general made a short speech to the senior Filipino officials. At its conclusion, his voice trembled, he buried his face in his hands, and he wept. Gathering himself, he wiped his eyes on his sleeve, and concluded brokenly, "In humble and devout manifestation of gratitude to almighty God for bringing this decisive victory to our arms, I ask that all present rise and join me in reciting the Lord's Prayer."

DOWN THE STRETCH—THE *ENOLA GAY*

Iwo Jima and Okinawa were taken in more bloody fighting, and preparations began for the final invasion of the homeland islands of Japan, which was already tasting the steady bombing of American airpower. On just one night in April 1945 it was estimated that there were seventy thousand casualties in Tokyo. And just as the Allies were readying for the invasion, the youth and any other men of Japan who could fight were preparing to meet the intruders. It was estimated that some two million of them would be thrown into battle defending their homeland. And the veteran forces in China would never surrender. Projected American losses could have reached one million.

But on July 16 a mushroom cloud arose from a bomb test in the New Mexico desert near White Sands and a whole new era was brought to the world. Secretly, a small, special bombing unit quickly trained at nearby Wendover Field. On August 6 Colonel Paul Tibbets Jr., at the controls of the *Enola Gay*, led two other B-29s toward the center of Hiroshima's bright green delta at a speed of 287 miles per hour. The bomb run had begun four minutes out, and now most of the crew members were covering their eyes with the dark glasses they had been issued. Inside the bomb bay was the strange black weapon that was ten feet in length and twenty-eight inches in diameter.

Below Tibbets, in the nose compartment, Major Thomas Ferebee peered intently through the Norden bombsight and began to pick up the familiar landmarks that he had studied so intently prior to the mission. Sliding up fast were the six islands, the hills, the docks. He spotted Aioi Bridge—his aiming point—just as he pressed the intercom button and announced, "I've got it." They were one minute and fifteen seconds from drop.

One can not help but wonder in that minute and fifteen seconds how many of that crew thought of Pearl Harbor, and the Bataan Death March, and perhaps what they may have seen in newspaper photos of the emaciated prisoners freed from prison camps. It was estimated that the fireball of that first bomb contained for a fraction of a second a temperature of nearly one million degrees. Its piercing heat instantly incinerated everything within several hundred yards of its hypocenter, and almost as quickly ignited all that would burn within two kilometers. The shock of the titanic explosion flattened much of the city as if its buildings were fragile matchsticks.

The next day, a second such bomb was dropped on Nagasaki.

The following day the Japanese government sued for peace.

One million Americans would not lose their lives in a protracted battle on the home islands or in China.

On September 2, aboard Bull Halsey's flagship, the battleship USS *Missouri*, in Tokyo Bay, a large number of Allied officers assembled to meet with senior officers and statesmen from Japan. The quarterdeck was a hot stove, but the task at hand was so monumental that a little heat didn't matter. The two five-stars, MacArthur and Nimitz (Halsey would get his later), were there to sign the papers. MacArthur, as Supreme Commander for the Allied Powers, gave a short but eloquent speech that highly impressed even the vanquished who were present. It was then time for signing the instrument of surrender. As the eighteen-minute ritual of signing came to an end, the man whose father had earned the Medal of Honor as a youthful adjutant leading a charge up Missionary Hill, quietly sat down and affixed his signature to both copies.

It was V-J Day.

World War II, with its hundreds of thousands of heroes, was over.

CHAPTER ELEVEN

THE KOREAN WAR

THE INTERIM

I t is normal to disarm after a war. But sometimes that disarmament is too severe, leaving a nation's armed forces a shell of what they should be. However, President Harry Truman and his administration were a little circumspect in the dismantling of the nation's mammoth war machine. On June 30, 1947, the Army was a volunteer force of 684,000 ground troops and 306,000 airmen (a year later those airmen would become a separate branch). At the same time, the Navy was 484,000 strong and the Marine Corps 92,000. A large portion of these forces were assigned overseas in the occupation of Europe and Japan along with the naval support such an operation involved.

Perhaps the wisest decision was to make General of the Army Douglas MacArthur Supreme Commander, Allied Powers. He, in effect, became the American potentate of Japan. Oh, he suffered the emperor, but in the years he ruled, MacArthur left little doubt about who was the boss. And he did it superbly; his majesty, his aloofness, and yet his fairness were just what the defeated Japanese needed to reconstruct their shattered country and psyche in such a way that they would one day become a valued ally and a power in international trade. The Japanese people, a paternal society, loved or at least admired him.

But brighter and darker days lay ahead for the man William Manchester called "The American Caesar" in his great biography of MacArthur.

DOUGLAS MACARTHUR

In the meantime, George Patton's theory that the Russians were also an enemy proved more than prescient. Immediately after the war, the Soviets took over Eastern Europe and, as Winston Churchill warned, were lowering an "iron curtain" across that continent. Stalin's intransigence included Korea, where he insisted that unification could be established only under a Communist government. Thus two countries came into being: the Democratic People's Republic of Korea and the Republic of South Korea. The latter, according to Manchester, "hangs like a lumpy phallus between the sprawling thighs of Manchuria and the Sea of Japan."

WAR AND RETREAT!

On June 25, 1950, North Korea struck, rolling into the south.

The South Korean (ROK) military was a weak sister, poorly equipped and poorly trained, whereas the North Korean army and air force had modern Soviet tanks, artillery, and aircraft. Many members of the People's Army were veterans of WWII, having fought with China and the Soviet Union. The Communists easily smashed through the southern capital, Seoul, as the new United Nations told the aggressors to stop and return to their borders—the first feeble effort by that body of world governments. In the meantime, President Truman ordered General MacArthur to send support to the beleaguered ROK forces. He also placed the Seventh Fleet in position to block a Red China move on Formosa (Taiwan).

The first combat element arriving to fight in Korea was an undersized two-company battalion supported by mortars and a 105 mm howitzer battery out of the 24th Infantry Division in Japan. Dubbed "Task Force Smith" for its commander, Lieutenant Colonel Brad Smith, it had been flown in on short notice with minimal rations and ammunition, and went into position astride the main highway ten miles below Suwon, an hour south of Seoul. Cruising along that road toward the 540-man band of Americans was a North Korean division of some 6,000 men, supported by thirty-three heavily armored T-34 tanks. A night of heavy rain soaked the 24th Infantry Division soldiers right after they arrived, ruining their radios and their sleep. The North Koreans crashed into their position at eight the next morning—July 5. It was hardly a contest, but with insufficient weaponry the brave "task force" managed to knock out four tanks, kill forty-two of the enemy, and wound nearly ninety more. Before the Americans were routed, they had held out against this superior force for seven hours.

In the next few days, the rest of the 24th Division arrived, as did the 25th and 1st Cavalry divisions. On July 20 the North Koreans won the Battle of Taejon by pushing the 24th Division back to the south. But that's too impersonal a fact.

Its commander, Major General William Dean, had himself a rather quick and furious war. He was born in Carlyle, Illinois, in 1899, graduating from the University of California, Berkeley in 1922. He was commissioned in the California Guard in 1921 and granted a Regular Army commission in 1923. He was promoted to major general and given command of the 44th Infantry Division in WWII. His troops captured some thirty thousand Germans in 1944 and helped force the surrender of their Nineteenth Army. He was awarded the DSC for bravery during that period.

After commanding the 7th Infantry Division in Japan in the late 1940s, and a stint as Eighth Army chief of staff, he became commanding general of the 24th Infantry Division in Japan. He came to Korea on the heels of Task Force Smith's brief little war and set up his headquarters in Taejon, shortly over a hundred miles south of Seoul. His orders were to hold there, if possible, until July 20. With his regiments getting decimated, General Dean personally led tank-killer teams, gaining fame from exploits such as single-handedly charging and knocking out a T-34 tank with only a grenade and a pistol. On July 20 he became separated from the division and after evading capture for a month was finally caught by the North Koreans. As a general officer, he was a prize prisoner. He was held for three years, during which time he was awarded the Medal of Honor for his actions at Taejon. Bill Dean modestly insisted after his release that he should have done a better job as a general in combat. "I wouldn't," he said, "have awarded myself a wooden star for what I did as a commander." He died in 1981 and is buried in the Presidio of San Francisco.

Those were bad days at Taejon. In the midst of its carnage, First Lieutenant Ernest P. Terrell of Battery A, 11th Field Artillery Battalion had its six 155 mm howitzers in place north of the city when they came under continuing enemy attack. Even though several of his men were killed or wounded, he kept his guns firing. Withdrawing into the city, he soon faced enemy tanks that broke through the infantry lines. Terrell personally placed direct fire from two of his howitzers right into their gun barrels, knocking out one and driving the rest away. Soon enemy infantry was moving into the city and Terrell was ordered to evacuate his position, saving as much of his equipment as possible. Retaining twelve men to help him retrieve his five surviving howitzers, he ordered the rest of his battery personnel out. He managed to get all of the guns out of the city and into the withdrawing division convoy in spite of heavy enemy fire.

Ernie Terrell was in a three-quarter-ton truck that took a direct hit, but he survived and got the shattered vehicle off the road to keep from blocking the convoy. Climbing on one of his M5 tractors, he was three miles out of the flaming city before hitting an enemy roadblock and crashing into a telephone pole. He jumped on another tractor and proceeded five more miles before finding the road clogged with damaged vehicles. Dismounting, he supervised the removal of dead and wounded soldiers from the stalled vehicles, then had his tractor clear the road. But his luck was running thin; it was there that he got hit by mortar fire. However, this twenty-year-old Officers Candidate School graduate wasn't about to be captured. Joining a small foot party, Terrell managed to make his way south through the mountains. On the evening of July 24, dressed in native clothing and weak from hunger and exposure, he stumbled into the Eighth Cavalry Regiment area.

He received the DSC, became a regular army officer, and retired as a colonel. He is, as of this writing, the Honorary Colonel of the Twenty-first Artillery Regiment.

THE WAY BACK

"The Forgotten War" is an appropriate term for what also became known as the "Police Action" in Korea. With the taste of WWII victory still on American lips, the actuality of what was happening in Korea was hard to grasp. Hadn't we just fought and won a great war in Europe, then nearly blasted Japan off the map with the most powerful weapon the world had ever known? With a sigh of weariness, Americans wondered how some little Asian country most of them had never heard of could possibly be fighting them, let alone be knocking their army around, shoving them toward the sea.

And that's what was happening. The Army had stacked arms in Japan, and wasn't well equipped. The Air Force wasn't in much better shape with a few operational F-80 jets. Some P-51s in storage in Japan were quickly readied for much-needed ground support, while other WWII aircraft in the States were rushed to Korea. The Eighth Army command was continually pushed toward the southeast corner of the peninsula, to what became known as the Pusan Perimeter. MacArthur's command was redesignated the United Nations Command, for whatever that meant, and the 2nd and 7th divisions arrived, as well as the 29th Regimental Combat Team (RCT) from Okinawa, and then the 5th RCT from Hawaii. The Marines also landed their 1st Brigade. The 187th Airborne RCT was soon on its way from Fort Campbell, Kentucky; it would be the only parachute outfit in the war.

The Eighth Army CG was Lieutenant General Walton Walker, a native of Texas who graduated from West Point in 1912. In WWI he was a battalion commander at St. Mihiel and at Meuse-Argonne. He led the XXth Corps in Patton's Third Army from Normandy till the end of WWII. In fact, the XXth often moved so fast it was called the "Ghost Corps." He was promoted to lieutenant general by having the very same stars pinned on his collar that Eisenhower used to promote Patton. He was stocky, often called "Bulldog," and was a tough, no-nonsense commander. At the Pusan Perimeter, he moved his limited troops around brilliantly, filling holes in the wide line, maintaining the battle integrity that permitted survival against far superior numbers. His chest was filled with ribbons. Heading his decorations for valor were two DSCs and three Silver Stars.

MacArthur Hits!

Now the big boss in Tokyo took one look at his situation map and saw what the victorious march had done to the North Koreans—they had stretched their supply capability extremely thin and were wide open on the flanks. MacArthur looked at Inchon, some twenty-five miles west of Seoul, and decided that was the place to invade with the Xth Corps. However, the tricky tides and shallow water off the limited beaches made such a landing highly precarious. But the general used his strong persuasive skills to convince his subordinates that it could be done, and then, through brilliant planning and timing, pulled it off in mid-September. (Since I was a baby second lieutenant forward observer with the 187th Airborne RCT, and I came in air-landed without our guns, then proceeded to have quite an adventure directing fire for everything from amtracks with 75mm howitzers to two cruisers and the battleship *Missouri*, I just *had* to mention it.)

The Xth Corps consisted of the 7th Infantry Division, which had pulled out of the Pusan Perimeter, the 1st Marine Division, and numerous South Korean units. After heavy naval bombardment, the corps moved inland. But Seoul wasn't easy to recapture; it took days of heavy street fighting. Then the American troops headed south. The reenforced units in the Pusan Perimeter broke out and started north at the same time. They victoriously joined up on September 27. North Korea's picnic in the south was over. It was, in the opinion of many, MacArthur's greatest moment, at least his most ingenious.

CHINESE INTERVENTION

The Allies (in reality, numerous units of the British and Common-wealth military fought in the Korean War... not so much a result of UN command, but of mutual support for the US stance. America still provided some 90 percent of the effort), without major opposi-tion, moved into North Korea and took its capital, Pyongyang, in mid-October 1950. Elements moved on northwest toward the Yalu River, the border between North Korea and Red China. The word was out that many American soldiers would be home by Christmas. But at the end of November, the honeymoon ended abruptly when a massive Communist Chinese force crashed, unpredicted, into the Allies, forcing a major retreat in bitter winter conditions.

Surrounded, the soldiers and Marines had a fierce fight on their hands just to get out. They retreated to Seoul, and en route there were heroes aplenty. On December 23, General Walker was killed in a jeep accident. (Isn't it strange that Patton died from a vehicle acci-dent, and only five years later one of his favorite corps commanders would die from the same cause?) He was replaced by the brilliant Lieutenant General Matthew Ridgway.

RIDGWAY

Ridgway was an Army brat who graduated 56th out of his class of 139 from West Point in 1917. Yet, in spite of that mediocrity at the Academy, he was quite promising in the peacetime army and served on the War Department General Staff in the early part of WWII. In June of 1942 he became the CG of the 82nd Airborne Division, taking it to Sicily, then Italy, where it made its second combat jump. By D-Day, Ridgway was in command of the XVIII Airborne Corps. Its 82nd and 101st Airborne divisions parachuted and landed by glider behind the beachhead in France. After being awarded two DSCs, two Silver Stars, two Bronze Stars, and a Purple Heart, Ridgway was promoted to lieutenant general at the end of the war in Europe.

MiG Alley

By the time of the demoralizing retreat from North Korea, the Far Eastern Air Force (FEAF) had gained and lost air supremacy over Korea. However, just prior to the Chinese entry into the war the Soviet MiG-15 jet fighter showed its face. With the appearance of this new and very dangerous adversary, the air war entered a new phase. On November 8, 1950, First Lieutenant Russell Brown, flying an F-80, shot down a MiG-15 in the first all-jet dogfight in history. It was apparent, however, that the MiG-15 was superior to any aircraft then in FEAF's inventory. The MiG's pilots were also very good, being mostly veteran Russian fliers. But FEAF soon had a worthy opponent for the MiG-15—the superb F-86 Sabre. Many of the Sabre pilots were veterans of World War II and their expertise soon became obvious: before long, the Sabres and MiGs were mixing it up over northwest Korea, an area that became known as "MiG Alley."

But not all fighter pilots were Air Force—here is an interesting citation for the Medal of Honor for a naval aviator:

HUDNER, THOMAS JEROME, JR. Rank and organization: Lieutenant (J.G. [Junior Grade]) US Navy, pilot in Fighter Squadron 32, attached to USS *Leyte*. Place and date: Chosin Reservoir area of Korea, 4 December 1950. Entered service at: Fall River, Mass. Born: 31 August 1924, Fall River, Mass. Citation. For conspicuous gallantry and intrepidity at the risk of his life above and beyond the call of duty as a pilot in Fighter Squadron 32, while attempting to rescue a squadron mate whose plane struck by anti-aircraft fire and trailing smoke, was forced down behind enemy lines. Quickly maneuvering to circle the downed pilot and protect him from enemy troops infesting the area, Lt. (J.G.) Hudner risked his life to save the injured flier who was trapped alive in the burning wreckage. Fully aware of the extreme danger in landing on the rough mountainous terrain and the scant hope of escape or survival in subzero temperature, he put his plane down skillfully in a deliberate wheels-up landing in the presence of enemy troops. With his bare hands, he packed the fuselage with snow to keep the flames away from the pilot and struggled to pull him free. Unsuccessful in this, he returned to his crashed aircraft and radioed other airborne planes, requesting that a helicopter be dispatched with an ax and fire extinguisher. He then remained on the spot despite the continuing danger from enemy action and, with the assistance of the rescue pilot, renewed a desperate but unavailing battle against time, cold, and flames. Lt. (J.G.) Hudner's exceptionally valiant action and selfless devotion to a shipmate sustain and enhance the highest traditions of the US Naval Service.

What the citation misses is the fact that Hudner's squadron mate who was shot down was Ensign Jesse Brown, the Navy's first black pilot. He was part of the flight of four F4U Corsairs that had been searching for targets of opportunity. Brown, unfortunately, died before the rescue chopper arrived. His squadron mates returned a few days later and dropped napalm on the crash site to cremate his body, rather than leave it to the mercy of the elements or any predatory animals—two-legged or otherwise.

Hudner commented, "Jesse looked shaken and drifted in and out of consciousness. Seeing him die there in that frigid area after we tried so hard to save him was one of the most terrible frustrations I've ever experienced.... If I hadn't gone down to check on Jesse, someone else would have because we all shared a common bond—a brotherhood. It didn't matter what color you were, you were part of the family."

OLD SOLDIERS NEVER DIE

Back to the Korean ground war. General Ridgway reorganized the disheartened soldiers and Marines on a line forty miles below Seoul. He told his commanders, "We must wage a war of maneuver—slashing at the enemy when he withdraws and fighting delaying actions when he attacks."

He believed he could achieve these goals, but MacArthur in Tokyo wasn't so sure. The Boss had grander ideas; he wanted major reenforcement, and wanted to go after the Red Chinese in conjunction with Chinese Nationalist forces. He wanted to bomb north of the Yalu and, in one word, *win!* But Washington thought the whole Korean scenario was part of a Soviet master plan for global conflict, and they didn't want to ignite it. The joint chiefs turned him down, ordering him to hold in Korea with what he had, and if he couldn't do that he was to pull everything back to Japan and toss Korea to the wolves. (This Washington decision of "beware of the Russians" by President Truman and his cabinet was behind the Joint Chiefs of Staff's decision.) Army chief of staff General J. Lawton Collins flew to Korea, saw how Ridgway had jacked up the Eighth Army's fighting spirit, and announced, "We are going to stay and fight."

And fight they did! Moving north cautiously from ridge line to ridge line, there was no "haul ass and by-pass." In February, one regiment, the Twenty-third of the 2nd Infantry Division, symbolized the fighting will of the command by holding off a much larger Chinese force at Chipyong-ni. Seoul was recaptured in mid-March, and in a few days American forces were just below the thirty-eighth parallel. Ridgway went beyond that demarcation in early April, but by then MacArthur was at fully crossed swords with Truman. They had met for a talk on Wake Island in mid-October, in what is now generally considered a political ploy by the president. But in late March, MacArthur had sent a message to the Republican leader in the House without clearing it with the Joint Chiefs of Staff. Truman was furious. He fired the American Caesar on April 11 and named Ridgway his successor.

MacArthur returned to the States, receiving the plaudits of his shocked countrymen. He addressed Congress in joint session, drawing upon his remarkable oratorical ability and brilliant rhetoric to mesmerize that body. Over thirty million Americans were watching on TV or listening on the radio when he said in his closing remarks, "Old soldiers never die. They just fade away. And like the soldier of the ballad, I now close my military career and just fade away—an old soldier who tried to do his duty as God gave him the light to see that duty." He paused and added softly, "Good-bye."

The applause shook the roof of the Capitol.

The ticker-tape parade in New York was four times what it had been for Eisenhower when he returned from WWII. An avalanche of congratulatory mail greeted the general there. The seventy-one-year-old Douglas MacArthur, who had served in the Army for some fifty-two years, was referred to by powerful Democratic Senator Richard Russell of Georgia as "one of the great captains of history."

He died at the age of eighty-four in 1964, certainly the most remarkable of our heroes.

CHESTY

Lieutenant General James A. Van Fleet took over the Eighth Army when Ridgway moved to Tokyo. After some more heavy fighting, the Americans settled down along a line that was geared to good defensive positions. Long talks regarding an armistice lay ahead, as did some sporadically severe fighting in hot spots with names such as the Punchbowl, Bloody Ridge, Heartbreak Ridge, and Pork Chop Hill. MiG Alley remained busy over North Korea, where the Air Force picked up four Medals of Honor. The great baseball player Ted Williams was one of those recalled as a Marine pilot. And speaking of Marines—

"He was ramrod straight with a stubby pipe in his mouth all the time. He was approachable. He'd often say 'Hello son, how are you doing?' when he came across a Marine." A historian described him in 1942 as

... not very tall, he stood with a kind of stiffness with his chest thrown out, hence his nickname 'Chesty.' His face was yellow-brown from the sun and atabrine, the anti-malaria drug that was used then. His face looked, as someone has said, as though it were carved out of teakwood. There was a lantern jaw, a mouth like the proverbial steel trap, and small, piercing eyes that drilled right through you and never seemed to blink.

CHESTY PULLER

Lewis "Chesty" Puller at forty-four was already a legend in the Corps. After a year at Virginia Military Institute, he enlisted in the Marines, but he was too late to get over to Europe in World War I. He received a reserve commission and was discharged, but he'd found a home, so he reenlisted. While serving in Haiti, he led patrols against the Caco rebels in more than forty engagements. His leadership proven, he pinned on the bars of a second john (lieutenant) and went into combat in Nicaragua in 1930, this time against rebels led by the notorious Augustus Sandino. He was awarded the Navy Cross for his heroic actions. Returning two years later, he was greeted by newspaper headlines heralding his arrival. Sandino put a five-thousand-peso price on his head. But it was never collected; instead Chesty won his second Navy Cross.

The year 1933 found him with the China marines at Peiping (modern Beijing), where he had an opportunity to observe the occupying Japanese infantry in training. A few years later, he saw them in action. As a lieutenant colonel commanding 1st Battalion, Seventh Marines, on Guadalcanal. There in one battle with his battalion spread thin on a one-mile front, Chesty led from the front in killing nearly fourteen hundred of the enemy, while keeping his own losses low. He was awarded his third Navy Cross.

As executive officer of the Seventh Marine Regiment on New Britain in 1944, he reorganized two battalions whose commanders had been hit and led them under heavy enemy fire against a fortified position. The campaign led to a *fourth* Navy Cross being pinned on Chesty's protruding chest.

At the Frozen Chosin Reservoir December 5–10, 1950, Colonel Puller was commanding the First Marines when ten Chinese divisions smashed into the regiment. Facing attack from all sides, his Marines broke out, and during two massive enemy attacks on the rear guard, Puller's direct leadership ensured all casualties were evacuated, and all salvageable equipment was brought out. He was awarded an unprecedented fifth Navy Cross, *plus* the army added a DSC! Never, ever, had anyone been awarded the nation's second-highest award for valor in one action from two branches of the service.

Chesty was promoted to brigadier general, then to major general to command a division in the States. He retired due to illness in 1955. Promoted to lieutenant general, he had a sergeant major who had served under him pin on the three stars. In 1966 he volunteered for Vietnam, but the Marine Corps felt he was a bit old for another bout of combat. The man who once stated "We're surrounded—that simplifies our problem" died at the age of seventy-three in 1971.

OUR HISPANICS

Several Hispanics have earned the Medal of Honor in America's wars. One of the first was Corporal Joseph De Castro of Company I, Nineteenth Massachusetts Infantry at the Battle of Gettysburg in the Civil War. Pickett's Charge on the third day has been glorified, and rightfully so, but De Castro was charging downhill to meet the ill-fated rebels. Quite strangely, the colors he captured were those of the 19th Virginia! He later married Rosalia Rodriguez, a name that recurs with that honor eighty-eight years later.

Private First Class Joseph C. Rodriguez, a skinny kid from San Bernadino, California, was a draftee who picked up his soldiering skills like an old soldier. His leadership qualities had been noticed by his superiors early on, but like the rest of his buddies, he had been relatively untested. However, as an assistant squad leader in Company F, 17th Regiment, Seventh Infantry Division, he had his big moment, one that would create a life few young Hispanics of the time would ever dream possible. On May 21, 1951, near Munye-ri, Korea, "Chuck" Rodriguez was participating in an attack against a fanatical hostile force occupying well-fortified positions on rugged commanding terrain, when his squad's advance was halted within approximately sixty yards of the enemy position by a withering barrage of automatic weapons and small-arms fire from five emplacements directly to the front and right and left flanks, together with grenades that the enemy rolled down the hill toward the advancing troops. Fully aware of the odds against him, Rodriguez leaped to his feet, dashed up the fire-swept slope, and, after lobbing grenades into the first foxhole with deadly accuracy, ran around the left flank, silenced an automatic weapon with two grenades, and continued his

JOSEPH C. RODRIGUEZ

whirlwind assault to the top of the peak, wiping out two more fox-holes. Reaching the right flank, he tossed grenades into the remaining emplacement, destroying the gun and annihilating its crew. PFC Rodriguez's intrepid actions exacted a toll of fifteen enemy dead. As a result of his incredible display of valor, the defense of the opposition was broken, the enemy was routed, and the strategic strongpoint secured. He finished the Korean War as a sergeant.

Chuck stayed in the Army and later received a Regular Army commission. He retired in 1980 as the post engineer at Fort Bliss, Texas. He was a full colonel. For the next several years he held essentially the same job for the University of Texas at El Paso. He and his wife, Rose, a realtor, reside in that city as of this writing.

PRESIDENT EISENHOWER

In May of 1952 General Ridgway relieved General Eisenhower as supreme commander of Supreme Headquarters Allied Powers in Europe when Ike retired to successfully run for and become the thirty-fourth president of the United States. A little over a year later, Ridgway came back to Washington to become chief of staff of the Army. He held this position for two years of Ike's presidency, retiring in 1955 with his lovely young wife to Pittsburgh, where he served as chairman of the board of trustees of the Mellon Institute for Industrial Research. He lived to the ripe old age of ninety-eight.

The Korean War dragged on with armistice negotiations stalled at Panmunjom. It seemed that North Korea would continue its unreasonable stance indefinitely. The Red Chinese launched a vicious attack that made an eight-mile penetration of the Eighth Army line in early July. But General Mark Clark, who followed Ridgway in command, finally worked out an agreement, and all fighting ceased on July 27, 1953.

On the Korean War Memorial in Washington is the inscription *Freedom Is Not Free.*

American Indian Medal of Honor Recipients

Five American Indians have been award the Medal of Honor while serving in the US Army during the twentieth century. Two gave the ultimate sacrifice, their lives, during the Korean conflict:

Corporal Mitchell Red Cloud Jr., a Winnebago from Wisconsin in Company E, Nineteenth Infantry Regiment, 24th Infantry Division, on November 5, 1950, against Chinese Communist forces.

Private First Class Charles George, a Cherokee from North Carolina, in Company C, 179th Infantry Regiment, 45th Infantry Division, on November 30, 1952, against enemy forces.

In World War II:

Second Lieutenant Ernest Childers, a Creek from Oklahoma, in Company C, 180th Infantry Regiment, 45th Infantry Division, on September 22, 1943, against German army forces. Lieutenant Childers was the first American Indian to receive the Medal of Honor. He retired as a lieutenant colonel from the US Army.

First Lieutenant Jack Montgomery, a Cherokee from Oklahoma, in the 45th Infantry Division, on February 22, 1944, in Italy against German forces. Lieutenant Montgomery was also the recipient of the Silver Star and the Bronze Star. He is deceased.

Technical Sergeant Van Barfoot, a Choctaw from Mississippi, in Company L, 157th Infantry Regiment, 45th Infantry Division. Let's look at the official citation:

> For conspicuous gallantry and intrepidity at the risk of life above and beyond the call of duty on 23 May 1944, near Carano, Italy. With his platoon heavily engaged during an assault against forces well entrenched on commanding ground, 2d Lt. Barfoot (then Tech. Sgt.) moved off alone upon the enemy left flank. He crawled to the proximity of 1 machinegun nest and made a direct hit on it with a hand grenade, killing 2 and wounding 3 Germans. He continued along the German defense line to another machinegun emplacement, and with his tommygun killed 2 and captured 3 soldiers. Members of another enemy machinegun crew then aban-

doned their position and gave themselves up to Sgt. Barfoot. Leaving the prisoners for his support squad to pick up, he proceeded to mop up positions in the immediate area, capturing more prisoners and bringing his total count to 17. Later that day, after he had reorganized his men and consolidated the newly captured ground, the enemy launched a fierce armored counterattack directly at his platoon positions. Securing a bazooka, Sgt. Barfoot took up an exposed position directly in front of 3 advancing Mark VI tanks. From a distance of 75 yards his first shot destroyed the track of the leading tank, effectively disabling it, while the other 2 changed direction toward the flank. As the crew of the disabled tank dismounted, Sgt. Barfoot killed 3 of them with his tommygun. He continued onward into enemy terrain and destroyed a recently abandoned German fieldpiece with a demolition charge placed in the breech. While returning to his platoon position, Sgt. Barfoot, though greatly fatigued by his Herculean efforts, assisted 2 of his seriously wounded men 1,700 yards to a position of safety. Sgt. Barfoot's extraordinary heroism, demonstration of magnificent valor, and aggressive determination in the face of pointblank fire are a perpetual inspiration to his fellow soldiers.

I wanted to know more about Van Barfoot, so I finally tracked him down near Richmond, Virginia, and reached him on the phone. Like Ernest Childers, he had a full career in the Army, but when he was forty-two, as a lieutenant colonel, he went to flight school and became an Army aviator. This gave us a lot of common ground, so our telephone conversation became livelier. Colonel Barfoot was a vital cog in the tactical development of army aviation before his retirement. He served thirty-four years, but that's not his only contribution; his son, Van Jr., was a helicopter pilot in Vietnam, took a regular army commission, and retired as a lieutenant colonel. Now Van Sr. has a fish farm and at age eighty-five, as of this writing, is quite energetic.

Interesting, isn't it, that four of the five recipients, including one in a different war, were in the 45th Thunderbird Division?

CHAPTER TWELVE

VIETNAM

Whence are we, and why are we?

—Percy Bysshe Shelley, "Adonais" (1821)

INVOLVED

Shelley could well have written that question in the 1960s and early 1970s. Then the servicemen who were fighting in and around Vietnam knew *whence* they were, and most of them knew *why* they were there. It was simple: they were fighting Communists because their country was fighting Communists. But as the war drew on, a vocal minority of the American public grew increasingly louder and more disruptive in its protests about *why* we were there. But we are ahead of the story.

Here's the short version: in order to prevent French Indochina from falling under the Communist boot in the 1950s, the United Sates began to provide military assistance to the French forces stationed there, including those in Vietnam. It was the same story as Korea—Red China and Soviet Russia saw Vietnam as one more country to serve in their bid for Communist world domination. A veteran Communist leader, Ho Chi Minh, led Red forces called the Viet Minh in the north of the elongated country. A conference in Switzerland produced the Geneva Accords, which provided for a division of the country at the sevententh parallel, but Ho didn't accept this decision because his goal was to rule all of Vietnam. He called on Communist insurgents, known as the Viet Cong, to conduct assassinations, terrorism, abductions, sabotage, and other attacks in the south.

The South Vietnamese army (ARVN) was woefully incapable of subduing the Viet Cong assault, so American support was increased to over eleven thousand advisers and support elements by President John F. Kennedy in 1962. More Army Special Forces teams were soon brought in to train and organize the Montagnard tribesmen in the Central Highlands and other Vietnamese forces. Trails and roads were built by the North Vietnamese in Laos along the Vietnam border. Named the Ho Chi Minh Trail, these supply routes contained bases and relay stations capable of supporting major military units.

THE GREEN BERETS

But first, let's talk about Army Special Forces. Born in 1952 at Fort Bragg, the 10th Special Forces Group (Airborne) was sent to Bad Tölz, Germany, a little over a year later. An offshoot of Wild Bill Donovan's OSS (Office of Strategic Services), the 10th Group was also the baby of Colonel Aaron Bank. The basic unit, called an "A team," usually had about a dozen members, including its two officers. They were trained in light weapons, heavy weapons, communications, medical treatment, and demolitions, as well as the language of the country in which they were to operate. Many were cross-trained, and all were parachutists. Their mission was to jump into a location and train guerrillas, quite often for an extended period. (I was with the 10th in Bad Tölz as an aviator when the first green beret was designed. Never before had a beret been worn in the US military. I remember flying to Stuttgart shortly after we first put them on. As I walked into airfield operations, I was greeted by another captain with, "Well, hello, Sweetie. Ain't you pretty?")

BUILDUP

In a country where dense jungle often prohibited anything but road travel, which was vulnerable to ambush, a new vehicle of war began to make its presence known: the helicopter. Originally the H-21 "Flying Banana" was the workhorse, then the faster and more capable UH-1 "Huey" began to arrive in large numbers. Chopper pilots in this jet-powered aircraft could transport nearly anything, and provide medical evacuation, and gunship support.

After Kennedy's assassination in November 1963, Lyndon Johnson became president and, following reported attacks on US destroyers in the South Vietnamese Bay of Tonkin, stepped up US involvement and authorized bombing of North Vietnam by US Navy planes. Marines occupied Da Nang, a deepwater port to the north, and the 173rd Airborne Brigade arrived in country. The US Air Force also began a major buildup and an aerial offensive. In the midst of all this increase in American participation, a stable government seemed to emerge in Saigon. With Nguyen Van Thieu as head of state, and handsome Air Marshal Nguyen Cao Ky as his premier, promise of stable representative rule seemed assured. Time would prove it wasn't.

South Vietnam was barely in the twentieth century. Saigon's harbor was jammed with shipping. Tan Son Nhut, the city's airport, was the only field that could handle jet traffic, and the only major railroad was inoperative. Logistics were a nightmare. Medical care was extremely limited. The country was a mess. The engineer construction program began a remarkable plan that built the ports of Cam Ranh Bay, Nha Trang, Qui Nhon, Vung Tau, Vung Ro, and vastly improved the one at Saigon. Half a million cubic feet of refrigerated storage, seventeen hundred miles of roads, four million square yards of airfields and heliports, vast numbers of base camps, and millions of feet of storage facilities were constructed. And American military personnel arrived by the thousands.

One facility that Uncle Sam didn't build, but provided occupants for, was the Hanoi Hilton and its counterparts.

Prisoners of What?

We've discussed prisoners of war a bit, but not in any detail or at any length. The Civil War had its Andersonville scandal, and we know the Japanese horribly treated prisoners in the Philippines. The Germans were more humane, although the *stalags* were certainly not rec areas; but at least the Nazis observed the Geneva Convention rules relative to prisoners of war to a certain extent. The North Koreans were the first to institute "brainwashing," the system of trying to convert prisoners to their side, mostly through sensory deprivation and continual haranguing. Their camps, too, were hardly Club Med.

But the North Vietnamese and their Chinese mentors were from a different cut of cloth. They considered Americans foreign invaders and colonists, similar to the French, and as such, no-holds-barred was their approach. They refused the "prisoner of war" label, instead branding the captured men "criminals" of one ilk or another. They inflicted intolerable pain and injury upon these young men, and many POWs died. Brutish, bestial, sadistic, criminal, barbaric, savage, inhuman—none of these descriptive words quite describes the grotesque treatment that was visited upon these prisoners. When they weren't being brutalized physically and mentally, they were kept in cages, barely large enough to sit or lie in, often in their own waste. They were generally afflicted by malnutrition, forced to eat rotten food, sometimes covered by mosquitoes and other insects, and they were usually bankrupt of hope.

The very courage to survive, let alone resist, boggles the civilized mind. (I went through numerous training programs, some pretty tough, in my twenty years of service, but I am in absolute awe of their fortitude, and I wonder if I would have had the guts to survive not just days or weeks, but the *years* that many of these remarkably heroic men managed.)

The Geneva Convention, which the leaders of North Vietnam signed, requires that a prisoner give only his name, rank, and serial number to any captor. The Vietnamese Communists decided early on to make prisoners provide incriminating statements, that in their captors' twisted thinking would be of propaganda value to the North.

The question has arisen as to whether the POWs were heroic, or just trying to survive. Can their survival in most cases not be heroic if they, in one manner or another, *resisted for years* in the face of physical brutality and starvation, inadequate medical treatment, innocuous bribes, mental anguish, and lies about their families and the American government? These are some of their stories.

The Early POWs

The East Room
July 8, 2002
3:07 PM EDT

PRESIDENT GEORGE W. BUSH: Good afternoon, and welcome to the White House. It's a—this is a special occasion. I am honored to be a part of the gathering as we pay tribute to a true American patriot, and a hero, Captain Humbert "Rocky" Versace. Nearly four decades ago, his courage and defiance while being held captive in Vietnam cost him his life. Today it is my great privilege to recognize his extraordinary sacrifices by awarding him the Medal of Honor.... I thank the classmates and friends and supporters of Rocky for coming. I also want to thank the previous Medal of Honor recipients who are here with us today. That would be Harvey Barnum and Brian Thacker and Roger Donlon. Thank you all for coming.

Rocky was a soldier's soldier—a West Point graduate, a Green Beret, who lived and breathed the code of duty and honor and country. One of Rocky's superiors said that the term "gung-ho" fit him perfectly. Others remember his strong sense of moral purpose and unbending belief in his principles.... When Rocky completed his one-year tour of duty, he volunteered for another tour. And two weeks before his time was up, on October the 29th, 1963, he set out with several companies of South Vietnamese troops, planning to take out a Viet Cong command post. It was a daring mission, and an unusually dangerous one for someone so close to going home to volunteer for. After some initial successes, a vastly larger Viet Cong force ambushed and overran Rocky's unit. Under siege and suffering from multiple bullet wounds, Rocky kept providing covering fire so that friendly forces could withdraw from the killing zone. Eventually, he and two other Americans, Lieutenant Nick Rowe and Sergeant Dan Pitzer, were captured, bound and forced to walk barefoot to a prison camp deep within the jungle.

For much of the next two years, their home would be bamboo cages, six feet long, two feet wide, and three feet high. They were given little to eat, and little protection against the elements. On nights when their netting was taken away, so many mosquitoes would swarm their shackled feet it looked like they were wearing black socks. The point was not merely to physically torture the prisoners, but also to persuade them to confess to phony crimes and use their confessions for propaganda. But Rocky's captors clearly had no idea who they were dealing with. Four times he tried to escape, the first time crawling on his stomach because his leg injuries prevented him from walking. He insisted on giving no more information than required by the Geneva Convention; and cited the treaty, chapter and verse, over and over again.

He was fluent in English, French and Vietnamese, and would tell his guards to go to hell in all three. Eventually the Viet Cong stopped using French and Vietnamese in their indoctrination sessions, because they didn't want the sentries or the villagers to listen to Rocky's effective rebuttals to their propaganda. Rocky knew precisely what he was doing. By focusing his captors' anger on him, he made life a measure more tolerable for his fellow prisoners, who looked to him as a role model of principled resistance. Eventually the Viet Cong separated Rocky from the other prisoners. Yet even in separation, he continued to inspire them. The last time they heard his voice, he was singing "God Bless America" at the top of his lungs.

On September the 26th, 1965, Rocky's struggle ended in his execution. In his too short life, he traveled to a distant land to bring the hope of freedom to the people he never met. In his defiance and later his death, he set an example of extraordinary dedication that changed the lives of his fellow soldiers who saw it firsthand. His story echoes across the years, reminding us of liberty's high price, and of the noble passion that caused one good man to pay that price in full.

Last Tuesday would have been Rocky's 65th birthday. So today, we award Rocky—Rocky Versace—the first Medal of Honor given to an Army POW for actions taken during captivity in Southeast Asia. We thank his family for so great a sacrifice. And we commit our country to always remember what Rocky gave—to his fellow prisoners, to the people of Vietnam, and to the cause of freedom.

★★★★★

Forty years earlier, Army Captain Humbert Roque "Rocky" Versace wanted to become a priest and work with Vietnamese orphans. He'd been accepted into a seminary, but his dream was not to be fulfilled.

Two weeks before he was due to return home, Versace, twenty-seven, a class of 1959 Academy graduate and the son of an Army colonel, was captured on October 29, 1963, by Viet Cong guerrillas who spent the next two years torturing and trying to brainwash him. In return, he mounted four escape attempts, ridiculed his interrogators, swore at them in three languages, and confounded them as best he could, according to two US soldiers captured with him.

The Viet Cong (VC) could not afford to let him live longer. What is puzzling is that they let him remain alive that long.

★★★★★

Lieutenant Nick Rowe, who was captured with Rocky, gives us more insight. Writing in his diary, on January 6, 1968, at the No-K (Corral) prison camp: *"Loss of sleep affecting strength, disposition, morale. Now working on mental buck-up before trouble sets in. Can't fight on multiple fronts—political is enough; add fatigue, strong homesickness, extreme tiredness of POW life plus the chance of health breakdown and the picture is not bright. Tonite the buck-up begins, tomorrow a new day, a new, brighter outlook."*

This was *four-and-a half years* after they were captured.

The following New Year's Eve, Nick Rowe grabbed an opportunity and made good his escape. Hauled out of a clearing amidst heavy VC gunfire a short time later, the black-clad West Pointer found that the pilot of the air cavalry chopper had thought he was bringing out a VC captive. When he saw he had picked up an American, he grinned and shouted over the whine of the Huey's jet, *"Happy New Year!"*

Twenty minutes later at Ca Mau, Rowe was handed a drink and a fatigue jacket with new major's leaves on the collar. Next came socks and shoes, something he hadn't worn in over five years. He wound up back at Fort Bragg and stayed in the Army until 1974, when he got out to try his hand in politics and on the lecture circuit. But in 1980, he went back into uniform, and nine years later, while wearing colonel's eagles, he was in charge of counterinsurgency training with the Joint Military Advisory Group in the Philippines. Incredibly, after all he'd been through as a prisoner, he was ambushed and killed by a probable terrorist force.

He was always quick to state that Rocky Versace was the bravest man he ever knew. But Nick Rowe's own courage and his means of subtly defeating his brutal captors for all those years is still part of today's prisoner survival thinking.

The Later POWs

As the war intensified, and American aircraft began to get shot down over heavily defended targets in the North, new camps were established other than those run by the Viet Cong. The most well known of these was really much more than a camp, it was a formidable prison. The French built it at the turn of the century, a huge compound with thick walls fifteen to twenty feet high. It was divided into four areas, named by the pilots "Heartbreak Hotel," "New Guy Village," "Little Vegas," and "Camp Unity." Guard towers dotted the exterior walls, which were topped with barbed wire and jagged shards of glass, believed to be from broken French champagne bottles. Even if a prisoner somehow managed an unbelievable escape, he would find himself—a Caucasian—in inhospitable downtown Hanoi. There were no escapes.

With the grim irony that always seems to accompany American POWs, this sinister slammer was finally dubbed the "Hanoi Hilton."

The Hilton's first inhabitant was Navy Lieutenant (Junior Grade) Everett Alvarez Jr. From Salinas, California, Alvarez had completed a degree in electrical engineering from the University of California at Santa Clara before entering the Navy for flight training in 1960. He was shot down on August 5, 1964, a major prize for Hanoi. The interrogators tried everything to get him to acknowledge that he was a war criminal, including continued persuasion that he write a contrite confessional letter to Ho Chi Minh, which they would circulate throughout the Communist world. He fed them clever misinformation, but refused to write the letter. His confinement conditions, even though he lived in a room instead of a cage, were horrible. Rats, up to a foot long, visited him night and day. The food was literally sickening—rotten fish, chicken heads, spoiled vegetables, and other slimy remains of once-edible victuals.

The Navy pilot lost forty pounds and suffered terribly from bloody diarrhea until his jailers realized they might lose him if they didn't feed him a little better.

He had thrown away his wedding ring, knowing his captors would capitalize on his being married, but they quickly discovered from American press releases that he had a wife. They tantalized him with newspaper photos of her, but it backfired—he kept the pictures as reenforcement during his entire period as a prisoner, and brought their tattered remains home with him in 1973.

When they couldn't get him to write to Ho, they brought Robert

F. Williams to see him and try to convince him otherwise. Williams was an American fugitive who rotated among China, North Vietnam, and Cuba. He and his wife, Mabel, had been on tour making pro-Communist speeches. Alvarez enjoyed the refreshments he was fed during their visit, then went back to his steady resistance to his captors.

Everett Alvarez Jr., one of the bravest of America's Hispanic paladins, was one of the last POWs to come home, having been in custody for some eight and a half years. He retired from the Navy as a commander and later served as deputy director for the Peace Corps and as deputy administrator for the Veterans Administration. He currently resides in Maryland and owns a consulting firm.

Robbie and Stockdale

Although brutality continued in the North, the interrogators were a bit more sophisticated than their Viet Cong cousins. In fact, after 1970 the treatment gradually became less harsh. At least for some. The senior officers, or SROs, often paid for their subordinates' sins by being beaten and thrown into solitary. But the prisoners were still in the military, and command structure was necessary to good order, even when prison life was so harsh. The Code of Conduct, which decreed how American prisoners should act, had to be adhered to. Some of the more noted of these senior officers were Commanders James Stockdale and Jerimiah Denton—classmates at the Naval Academy—and Air Force Lieutenant Colonel Robbie Risner. Stockdale would, after his broken back and nearly severed leg had healed enough for him to become an inspirational command factor, exercise a strong hand and later get the Medal of Honor, just as Rocky Versace did for unrelenting opposition in the face of brutal retribution. Stockdale had earned a graduate degree from Stanford University, which included studies of communism and the Korean War prisoner experience. Thus, he was better prepared than most of the others, philosophically, for what he was convinced would be a long stay. The dynamic Risner, a Korean War ace who had set a transatlantic speed record commemorating the thirtieth anniversary of the Lindbergh flight, quickly made his presence known. Shortly after arrival when the guards were out of earshot, he sang to the tune of "McNamara's Band,"

> My name is Robbie Risner,
> I'm the leader of the Group.
> Listen to my story and
> I'll give you all the poop.

No wonder he was an encouraging leader! He lived to retire as a brigadier general in 1976 and currently lives in San Antonio, Texas.

Stockdale's story is truly remarkable! For much of his nearly eight years of confinement, he was the senior naval prisoner. His forbearance as a POW leader is unmatched. He was tortured fifteen times, was in leg irons for two years, and was in solitary confinement for four years! In addition to the Medal of Honor, his awards for valor include four Silver Stars, two DFCs, and two Purple Hearts. Afterward he served two years as president of the Naval War College before retiring as a three-star admiral. As a civilian, he was a college professor, a college president, and a senior research fellow at the Hoover Institution on War, Revolution and Peace. In the unsuccessful 1992 presidential race, Admiral Stockdale was Ross Perot's running mate on the Independent ticket. His full name is quite aptly James Bond Stockdale

The Wild Weasel

Once upon a time there was a batch of fighter pilots and their backseat observers flying F-105Gs Thunderchiefs out of Takhli Air Base in Thailand. Their mission: to fly ahead of a strike force into North Vietnam and entice surface-to-air missile (SAM) radars to come on the air, then try to knock them out. Not only would they be in the air in the target area before the strike, they would remain during the main effort. Only top pilots performed this mission. They were the "Wild Weasel" crews of the 357th Tactical Fighter Squadron.

The boss weasel was Major Leo Thorsness, a thirty-five-year-old jock from Walnut Grove, Minnesota. Riding in his back seat was navigator Captain Harold Johnson. The date was April 19, 1967. The target: a heavily defended army compound near Hanoi. Leading a flight of four Weasels, Thorsness heard the unmistakable rattle of enemy radars well off from the target area. Sending two of his birds north, he and his wingman stayed on course, dividing the enemy's attention. Johnson's scope picked up many SAM sites below as the big F-105 headed into the danger area. Thorsness quickly silenced two of them before the scenario fell apart.

His wingman, Tom Madison, was hit by flak, so he and his backseater, Tom Sterling, had to eject. The boss Weasel hit another SAM site en route to where the two parachutes went down. Then his other element of Weasels ran into some MiGs, and when the afterburner of one of the 105s wouldn't light, they had to head back to Thailand. Thorsness's 105 was all alone in the hostile air of enemy missiles, antiaircraft fire, and MiGs ready to pounce. As he circled the spot where his downed Weasels were located, the major spotted a MiG-17 off to the left.

Thorsness shot him down with his 20 mm cannon, then, as he tried to shake a MiG on his tail, he saw that his fuel was getting low. He pointed the 105 "down and lit it up," meaning he kicked in his afterburner and ran away from the enemy jet. After a short rendezvous with a tanker, he headed back to the rescue scene. A prop A-1E Skyraider (Sandy) and two Jolly Green Giant rescue helicopters had arrived at the rescue scene. Now he was down to some five hundred rounds of ammunition, but knowing there were at least five MiGs in the area, he turned back to fly cover for the inbound attack force. Using his last ammo, he hit and probably shot down one of the MiGs. With the other four MiGs hot on his tail, he once more lit it up and got away.

By the time he got back to the rescue scene, one of the Sandys had been shot down. He was about to decoy other MiGs away when the attack force arrived. But he still wasn't finished. Thorsness was headed back to the tanker for more fuel when one of the strike force pilots radioed that he was lost and low on gas. Thorsness quickly figured he could never make it back to his home base, so he decided to vector the tanker to the lost pilot, then head for Udorn Air Base, a forward base in Thailand that he "might" reach.

As soon as he departed the hot area, the major throttled back and coaxed his big bird to the airfield. His tanks ran dry as he touched down.

But he may have used up his luck. Eleven days later, Thorsness was on his ninety-third mission (he could rotate home with just seven more missions) when he and Captain Johnson were shot down. Actually, they ejected at around 600 knots, and Leo suffered severe injuries that wouldn't completely heal during the prison camp ordeals ahead of him.

Leo wound up in the Hanoi Hilton, where he strongly resisted the efforts of the North Vietnamese army to get him to feed their outlandish propaganda machine. This nonsense was bizarre to anyone with any amount of logic, but not to the Communist world that gobbled it up and spread it to the antiwar protesters in America. Leo spent some six years as a POW, three of which, he says, were brutal, and the last three—boring. But he still limped when he walked out of the prison on release day.

Due to quite a bit of exposure recently—one instance being a story by Senator John McCain (himself a Vietnam POW) that has made the rounds of the Internet—another naval aviator POW has become quite famous. His name was Michael Christian. This is what Leo Thorsness had to say about him in a speech:

> You've probably seen the bumper sticker somewhere along the road. It depicts an American Flag, accompanied by the words "These colors don't run." I'm always glad to see this, because it reminds me of an incident from my confinement in North Vietnam at the Hao Lo POW Camp or the "Hanoi Hilton," as it

became known. Then a Major in the US Air Force, I had been captured and imprisoned from 1967–1973. Our treatment had been frequently brutal. After three years, however, the beatings and torture became less frequent. During the last year, we were allowed outside most days for a couple of minutes to bathe. We showered by drawing water from a concrete tank with a homemade bucket. One day as we all stood by the tank, stripped of our clothes, a young Naval pilot named Mike Christian found the remnants of a handkerchief in a gutter that ran under the prison wall. Mike managed to sneak the grimy rag into our cell and began fashioning it into a flag. Over time, we all loaned him a little soap, and he spent days cleaning the material. We helped by scrounging and stealing bits and pieces of anything he could use. At night, under his mosquito net, Mike worked on the flag. He made red and blue from ground-up roof tiles and tiny amounts of ink and painted the colors onto the cloth with watery rice glue. Using thread from his own blanket and a homemade bamboo needle, he sewed on the stars. Early in the morning a few days later, when the guards were not alert, he whispered loudly from the back of our cell, "Hey gang, look here." He proudly held up this tattered piece of cloth, waving it as if in a breeze. If you used your imagination, you could tell it was supposed to be an American flag. When he raised that smudgy fabric, we automatically stood straight and saluted, our chests puffing out, and more than a few eyes had tears. About once a week, the guards would strip us, run us outside, and go through our clothing. During one of those shakedowns, they found Mike's flag. We all knew what would happen. That night they came for him. Night interrogations were always the worst. They opened the cell door and pulled Mike out. We could hear the beginning of the torture before they even had him in the torture cell. They beat him most of the night. About daylight, they pushed what was left of him back through the cell door. He was badly broken; even his voice was gone. Within two weeks, despite the danger, Mike scrounged another piece of cloth and began another flag. The Stars and Stripes, our national symbol, was worth the sacrifice to him. Now whenever I see the flag, I think of Mike and the morning he first waved that tattered emblem of a nation. It was then, thousands of miles from home, in a lonely prison cell, he showed us what it is to be truly free.

It was in the Hilton that Leo Thorsness also knew Paul Galanti, another naval aviator who bucked the interrogators for several years.

Galanti was shot down on July 17, 1966, while flying an A-4C Skyhawk, the Navy's main ground attack aircraft at the time, from the carrier USS *Hancock*. An Army brat, he had graduated from Annapolis in the class of 1962 and had gone straight into flight training. He was held in ten camps during his captivity, although most of his nearly seven years as a prisoner were spent in the Hilton. He spent one year in solitary. His greatest fame came as a result of a visit by East German Communists. He was photographed on a prop-aganda movie set bed in an attempt to make it look as if the POWs were being treated humanely, but he sabotaged the shooting by holding his middle fingers down like a baseball catcher's sign, an obscene message, when his captors weren't looking. Somehow the photo made it to the West and appeared on the cover of *Life*. How-ever, the offending fingers were airbrushed out.

Galanti retired from the Navy as a commander with the Silver Star, the Bronze Star, and two Purple Hearts. Currently he is the director of the National Services Officers for American Ex-POWs, and resides in Richmond, Virginia. For a number of years Galanti lived in Virginia Beach, where his good friend Mike Christian was a successful restaurateur. (Christian died in a tragic apartment fire in the 1980s.) And to give this circle of intertwining comradeship an even more interesting twist, Paul Galanti was cochair, along with Mike's widow, of John McCain's Virginia presidential campaign.

☆☆☆☆☆

John McCain. He was the grandson of a four-star admiral and the son of a four-star admiral, so it would seem he would have an easy path in the Navy. Born in 1936, he graduated from Annapolis in 1958 and became a naval aviator. With glory and honor a major part of his family history, it was only natural that he would find a war to define his own courage. He was assigned to the carrier USS *Forrestal* and was about to take off on a mission over North Vietnam when a horrible fire struck the huge ship. McCain, lucky to escape without serious burns, volunteered to continue in the war from another carrier, the USS *Oriskany.*

On October 26, 1967, while on a raid over Hanoi, McCain's Skyhawk was struck by a SAM, and he was forced to eject from the spiraling wreckage. Both of his arms and a leg were broken. He regained consciousness as angry North Vietnamese pulled him from the lake where he had landed and began to beat him. His shoulder was broken when a rifle butt was slammed into it. Soon the smashed-up lieutenant commander was the Hilton's newest resident—and without medical aid.

A few months after he became a guest of North Vietnam, his father, Admiral Jack McCain, became CINCPAC, commander of the Pacific fleet. Of course, John's captors knew who he was, and they rubbed their hands together at the propaganda prospects. They offered him early release. Citing the Code of Conduct's decree that prisoners would be set free in the order in which they were captured, he firmly refused the offer over and over. This insolence brought repeated beatings. Off and on, McCain spent nearly two years in solitary. When he came home with the other prisoners in 1973, over five years of his life had been spent in the rags of Ho Chi Minh's beasts of prey.

John McCain, of course, retired as a captain and turned to politics. He won a seat representing Arizona in the House in 1982, and followed Barry Goldwater into the US Senate in 1987. His run at the White House was aborted in 2000, when the George W. Bush juggernaut forced him to back off. As of this writing, Senator McCain is a strong proponent of many constructive programs and is one of the foremost congressional leaders in national defense.

The McCain admirals would be very proud of him.

Many other POWs were heroic in the Vietnam War. There were fewer of them than in the Civil War, both world wars, and the Korean War, but the privations they endured or died from are beyond comprehension.

THE BRAVE NURSE

She was born in Nassau County, New York, on May 5, 1946, and graduated from Hampton Institute in 1968 with a degree in biology and nursing. She had been a member of the Army Student Nurse Program. On November 30, 1967, she pinned on the gold bars of a second lieutenant and went on active duty in the Army. Then it was on to Fort Sam Houston in San Antonio, followed by a short stay at Wilson Army Hospital, Fort Dix, New Jersey. As First Lieutenant Diane Lindsay (she had married Captain John Lindsay), she was serving with the 95th Evacuation Hospital in Vietnam when one day a disturbed soldier on her ward brandished two hand grenades. He pulled the pin on one and threw it, but it didn't go off.

As he prepared to do the same with the second grenade, Lieutenant Lindsay approached him, speaking quietly, asking him for the explosive weapon. A doctor saw what was happening and sidled up next to her, joining in the attempt to disarm the distraught young man. Lieutenant Lindsay slowly held out her hand, convincing the soldier that he didn't wish to kill or harm so many already wounded patients. The doctor chimed in. After what seemed an incredible amount of time, the man, wide-eyed and sobbing, handed over the grenade.

On July 1, 1970, Lieutenant Lindsay was awarded the Soldier's Medal for bravery. She was the first black nurse in the history of the Army to receive the medal.

Tango Mike/Mike

Latino, Hispanic, Mexican American; they're all labels. Tango Mike/Mike was one of the many of their ethnicity who have served bravely, honorably, and often heroically in the military over the years. The service, in wartime or peacetime, has long been a popular place for the patriotic young people of Latin American descent. This is the story of one of them, Roy P. Benavidez.

But let's back up to the war for independence from Mexico, when one of Roy's forbears fought as a captain in the Texas Army during the siege of Bexar (San Antonio) prior to the the famed Battle of the Alamo. On the other side, Roy's mother was a full-blooded Yaqui, an Indian tribe considered every bit as fierce as the dreaded Apaches.

With this warrior blood coursing through his veins, Roy came into the world on August 5, 1935. By the time he was in his teens in Cuero, he was a typical South Texas Mexican kid: full of hell and ready to fight at the drop of a sombrero—a typical candidate of the time for prison or worse. But he joined the National Guard and made corporal, then decided the Regular Army was the life he wanted. He enlisted in 1954, wanting to become a paratrooper, but frequent fights and mouthing off at the wrong time kept him from jump school. After two overseas jaunts, he married his childhood sweetheart, Lala, and began his second romance with the parachute. This time he was accepted and earned his coveted silver jump wings.

Following more than fifty jumps, he was off to the new conflict in Vietnam as a sergeant assigned as an adviser to the Vietnamese 25th Infantry "Tigers." There, he had numerous adventures before stepping on a land mine that wounded him so badly that he didn't awaken until after he was medevaced to Fort Sam Houston, Texas. And then he was confused, but his main problem was his back. With a spine twisted like a corkscrew, he was told he would never walk again and would be discharged with a 100 percent disability. But all he wanted was to stay in the Army. *Paraplegic*—the word wasn't in his vocabulary. Lala listened patiently as he rambled on about his destiny not including a wheelchair.

He decided, come hell or high water, he was going to walk again—and before the discharge paperwork had a chance to catch up with him. Throwing himself out of bed the first night, he managed to crawl to the wall in intense pain. Night after night, teeth gritted, he improved by inches. But he fell every time. He heard his fellow patients start making bets, "Hey, look at the Mexican. I'll bet a beer he falls."

Finally he could stand. Not move, just stand. Amid more bets by his ward-mates, themselves often missing a limb or immobile in their beds, he began to move his feet. The pain was excruciating, but he overcame it. And slowly he got better, walking farther and farther until he was finally approved for active duty. The day he said good-bye to the other guys on the ward, the orthopedist, there to warmly see him off, referred to all of the betting he'd created by saying, "Sergeant, you've left me with a whole ward of alcoholics."

It had taken him six months, but he'd made it.

Still in much pain in the 82nd Airborne Division at Fort Bragg, North Carolina, he was assigned to nonjump status as a clerk, but faked his way onto a manifest and returned to jumping. His next bluff was in getting his old request for Special Forces, the famed Green Berets, approved. He even ran it through the washer a couple of times to make it look as if it had been pigeon-holed for two years. It worked.

Running five miles a day with a seventy-pound backpack, accompanied by his continuing pain, he went through the rigors of Special Forces training at Bragg. The training was all the more difficult because he had dropped out of school, and because he had first chosen the intelligence specialty of a Special Forces twelve-man team. Then he switched to light and heavy weapons. In 1968 he received orders sending him back to Vietnam.

Assigned to the Fifth Special Forces Group, then to B-56, an intelligence gathering unit, Benavidez picked up the radio call sign of "Tango Mike/Mike," the phonetic abbreviation for "That Mean Mexican." And he liked the handle.

On May 2 the unbelievable spirit that Roy Benavidez had inherited and developed through his many trials was given the ultimate test. In the longest citation for a medal I've ever read, this is a summary of what happened on that steamy day:

> …a 12-man Special Forces Reconnaissance team was inserted by helicopters in a dense jungle area west of Loc Ninh to gather

ROY P. BENAVIDEZ

intelligence information about confirmed large-scale enemy activity... the team met heavy resistance and requested extraction. Three helicopters were unable to land due to intense enemy small arms and anti-aircraft fire. Sergeant Benavidez was in the forward operating base in Loc Ninh monitoring the operation by radio when these helicopters returned to off-load wounded crew members. He voluntarily boarded a returning aircraft to assist in another extraction attempt.

Realizing that all the team members were dead or wounded, and unable to move to the pickup zone, he directed the aircraft to a nearby clearing where he jumped from the hovering helicopter, and ran approximately 75 meters under withering small arms fire to the crippled team... he was wounded in his right leg, face and head. Despite these painful injuries, he took charge, repositioned the team members and directed their fire to facilitate the landing of an extraction aircraft... under intense enemy fire, he carried and dragged half of the wounded men to the waiting helicopter. He then provided protective fire by running alongside of the aircraft... he was then severely wounded in the abdomen and back.

At this moment the aircraft crashed. But Tango Mike/Mike wasn't finished. In intense pain, he helped the wounded out of the downed chopper and formed them into a small defensive perimeter. Under heavy automatic weapons and grenade fire, he moved around distributing water and ammo. With enemy fire increasing, he called in tactical air support and directed fire from gunships. He was then hit in the right thigh while administering first aid, and still he managed to ferry wounded comrades to a new extraction chopper that had managed to land. On his second trip with wounded, he was clubbed from behind by the rifle butt of an enemy soldier. In the ensuing hand-to-hand combat, he sustained additional wounds to his head and arms before killing his enemy with his Special Forces knife. He then continued to carry wounded to the helicopter. Still firing at the enemy, he made one more trip to the perimeter to collect any remaining classified material and bring in the remaining wounded.

Only then did he permit his bloody body to be hauled into the aircraft.

He came to later on the ground outside the bullet-ridden helicopter just as he was about to be inserted in a body bag. He couldn't see, his intestines were exposed, his jaws were broken, and blood was oozing from *thirty-seven* puncture wounds. Only a shout from one of his buddies kept the green bag from being zipped up.

In February 1981 the South Texas Mexican who barely escaped the gangs as a teenager took his wife, Lala, and his three children to Washington, where in spite of stepping on the president's foot during the ceremony, he swelled with pride as Ronald Reagan presented him with the five-pointed Medal of Honor.

Master Sergeant Roy P. Benavidez had earned his stripes.

He passed away November 19, 1998, in San Antonio, Texas.

HACK

He simply couldn't wait to get into it. At fourteen, he went into the US Merchant Marine. At fifteen he lied his way into the Army. Five years later he was given a battlefield commission in Korea. There, when the valuable Ranger companies were disbanded, the Twenty-seventh Wolfhound Raiders regiment formed a special "intelligence gathering" element to go through enemy lines in much the same manner as the later long-range patrol-type did. Hack, with already a fearless reputation, was given command of it. For the bravery he continuously exhibited in these dangerous missions, he was awarded the first *five* of his Silver Stars. It would take pages to recount his heroic acts.

He finished his Korean War exploits as its youngest captain.

After completing his college degree in history and being granted a Regular Army commission, his next big war came along. He served five years in three tours in Vietnam and was the Army's youngest full colonel. His exploits were legend there, and he piled up many more medals—enough to fill a book, which he wrote. In fact, he has since written several books and hundreds of newspaper columns. At the end of his last tour in Vietnam, he got into a scrap with the top brass, which he claims cost him general's stars. He also hints that following his disagreement there were attempts on his life by unnamed assailants.

All of this is quite uncongruous for a man who unflinchingly faced incredible numbers of bullets, grenades, shrapnel, knives, and all the other killing instruments a warrior of his experience has encountered.

Regardless of his clashes with the good guys, his conflict with the bad guys of North Vietnam was incredibly heroic. When he retired, his decorations for valor included two DSCs, *ten* Silver Stars (though he claimed one of them was unearned), eight Bronze Stars (seven for valor), and eight Purple Hearts! Now, as a popular journalist who likes to continue attacking the military brass, he claims to be the country's most highly decorated living hero.

He's well known as "Hack"—Colonel David H. Hackworth.

Colonel Bud Day

Who determines who the most decorated member of the military is? Let's look at the phenomenal career of a man who entered the Marine Corps at age seventeen in 1942. The young George "Bud" Day then served thirty months in the South Pacific as a noncommissioned officer. After the war, the high-school dropout from Sioux City, Iowa, earned a BS, and then graduated from law school—joining the Army Reserve along the way. He was called to active duty as a lieutenant in 1951. After completing jet pilot training, Day served two tours in the Far East in the cockpit of fighter-bombers. He was destined for bravery, honor, and fame almost beyond comprehension.

As he piled up thousands of hours of jet-flying time, along came Vietnam. Following seventy-two missions with the 31st Tactical Fighter Wing, the Iowan organized and commanded the "Misty

Super FACs," an F-100 squadron with the mission of directing air strikes. Major Bud Day was shot down over North Vietnam on August 26, 1967, suffering three arm breaks, damage to one eye, and a dislocated knee. Captured and viciously tortured by Viet Cong, he managed to escape and head south to the American lines. Following an incredible trek in which he almost made it, Day was again captured.

The beatings continued. Arriving at the Hanoi Hilton, and still badly injured, Day quickly proved that his spirit was indomitable. On one occasion, facing severe torture, he rose and began to sing "The Star-Spangled Banner." Other prisoners joined in and soon the singing spread throughout the camp.

Bud Day spent sixty-seven months as a POW, and was awarded the Medal of Honor upon his release. He retired after thirty years of service as a colonel. He holds nearly seventy military decorations and awards, of which more than fifty are for combat. Topping them are the Medal of Honor, the Air Force Cross (DSC), the DSM, Silver Star, Legion of Merit, DFC, Bronze Star for Valor, ten Air Medals, and three Purple Hearts. That's more than equal to Audie Murphy's chestful of ribbons.

Bud Day claims the smartest thing he ever did was marry his childhood sweetheart, Doris. They reside in Florida, where he has a law practice. He has served on numerous boards, often as president, and continues to contribute public services. His major project as of this writing is trying to secure the medical benefits military retirees have lost in the past years—benefits they were promised while serving.

IN SHORT

The war continued to escalate as the number of US forces in Vietnam progressed toward the peak strength of 542,000. In 1968 what was called the "Tet Offensive" hammered provincial capitals, American forces, and even the barely defended US embassy in

Saigon on January 31, the lunar New Year. It was a huge risk taken by the brilliant North Vietnamese general Giap, but it worked. Although US and South Vietnamese forces collected themselves and turned the enemy offensive into an allied victory, American media mistakenly painted Tet, as it became known, as a defeat. This irresponsible reporting shook Washington, encouraged the antiwar demonstrators, and influenced a no longer confident President Johnson to decide against running for reelection. General William Westmoreland, commanding in Vietnam, would not get more forces, but fewer, as de-escalation began.

Ho Chi Minh died in 1969, but his deeply ingrained philosophies continued to drive North Vietnam.

The war would continue for five more years, primarily because of North Vietnam's haggling at the peace table in Paris. President Nixon finally brought it to a close and by the end of 1973 there were almost no US military elements left in the country. In early 1975 the North Vietnamese marched unopposed into Saigon, and the name of the capital was changed to Ho Chi Minh City.

Due to political vacillation and incompetence, it had all been for naught.

CHAPTER THIRTEEN

POST-VIETNAM

Brush Fires

They weren't brush fires to anyone who was wounded or killed in them, but in the scope of previous wars they are quite minute: Grenada, Panama, Desert Storm, Somalia, Bosnia, Kosovo... Iraq II. There were heroes, as in any conflict, no matter how small, but their stories are more obscure. First, Grenada. The US invasion of Grenada and the overthrow of its Marxist government was once more a matter of wrestling a Communist tentacle, this one from Castro's Cuba. On October 13, 1983, the Grenadan army, controlled by former deputy prime minister Bernard Coard, seized power in a bloody coup. Coard's hard-line Marxism caused deep concern among neighboring Caribbean nations, as well as in Washington. Additionally, there were nearly one thousand American medical students in Grenada at the time of the coup.

In the early morning of October 25, 1983, the United States invaded the island of Grenada. The initial assault consisted of some twelve hundred troops, and they were met by stiff resistance from the Grenadan army and Cuban military units on the island. Heavy fighting continued for several days, but as the invasion force grew to more than seven thousand, the defenders either surrendered or fled

297

into the mountains. Scattered fighting continued as US troops hunted down stragglers, but for the most part the island quickly fell under American control. By mid-December, US combat forces went home and a pro-American government took power.

One of the acts of heroism in this short conflict resulted in an aircrewman of Marine Medium Helicopter Squadron 261 getting the Bronze Star for valor. When his CH-53D chopper landed on a bullet-swept beach on October 26 to rescue some American civilians, Corporal Robert Myers saw their confusion and fear and ran down the beach through a hail of bullets to lead them back to the aircraft. With mortar and automatic-weapons fire all around, he hurried many of them along, including several small children, bolstering their courage, until he could usher as many as possible into the huge helicopter. Only then did he climb aboard the rapidly departing aircraft.

When the pro-Cuban regime was overthrown, a government friendly to the United States was installed and some of Castro's Marxist influence was stymied.

A Poker Game

The first Gulf War, Operation Desert Storm, lasted only one hundred hours, but one mostly unknown action stands out. It was related to me at lunch one day in 1997 by the then commanding officer of the Third Armored Cavalry Regiment, Colonel Bob Wilson.

When the 1st Infantry Division (Mechanized) moved into combat in Kuwait in February 1991, it had as its screening element and contact with the 1st Cavalry Division to the east, a squadron of cavalry known as the 1st/4th . The squadron was roughly equivalent to a battalion in strength, but it had some M1A1 tanks and was heavy on helicopters. It was commanded by then Lieutenant Colonel Bob Wilson. Its reconnaissance in force and screening role quickly changed into an aggressive attack mission in the extremely fluid front. The squadron was highly successful, moving rapidly and taking over two thousand prisoners by the time Saddam's Iraqis were ready to consider terms.

A ceasefire was called so the coalition forces could talk it over.

At 2:40 in the morning on March 1, the commanding general of the division sent an urgent call to Wilson, "How long until you can move your squadron north 15 km into Iraq and secure Safwan airfield?"

The departure was delayed until 6:15, then the 1st/4th scrambled north and crossed into Iraq. With helicopters overhead, Wilson elected to bypass the town of Safwan and proceed directly to the airfield. He knew the peace talks would take place there, but the objective *had* to be in American hands beforehand. But as the dust settled when he reached the airfield, Wilson quickly discovered he wasn't alone—a strong force of enemy tanks and other vehicles were in prepared positions just north of the airstrip. It was a short time after 10:00. Wilson boldly moved to the position of several Iraqi armored vehicles and dismounted, facing a neatly dressed enemy colonel. He knew at once that this was no ragtag militia officer—it had to be a brigade commander in the elite Republican Guards!

"What are you doing in Iraq?" the colonel asked brusquely.

Wilson was on his own, out in front, with no signs of his division, but he told the enemy colonel this was the site for the peace talks, and that the Iraqi forces had to move five miles north by noon or the 1st Division would attack. The colonel responded angrily and said he'd have to talk to his general. He then repositioned four T-72 tanks within fifty meters of Wilson, who looked around, wondering how much he could bluff. He was certain he was outnumbered by a full brigade, but he quickly decided to play the hand out. He moved some three hundred meters away and ordered his ground troop commanders to reposition their tanks forward and show more combat power. He also had the Cobra helicopters aggressively overfly the Iraqi positions. Wilson observed through his binoculars, glancing at his watch. *What would the Iraqis do?* Cat and mouse. Then, at 11:00, the Iraqis flinched and began moving out. Over two hundred armored vehicles headed north along the road to Basra. The enemy force wasn't just a brigade—the lieutenant colonel had faked out the entire Hammurabi Division with a single squadron of armored cavalry!

At this writing, Bob Wilson is a major general commanding the Seventh Infantry Division and Fort Carson, Colorado.

ON TO SOMALIA

It was in a place called "the most dangerous city in the world." It's real name—Mogadishu. Background: When the United States in cooperation with the UN intervened in Somalia in 1993 to relieve widespread starvation caused by fighting warlords, an operation was planned in which a special army ranger force would hit a meeting place in the heart of Somalia's capital city and abduct several leaders of a warring faction. It turned into a nightmare in which bravery was commonplace. This fierce battle within its small scale over a nineteen-hour period equaled nearly anything in the huge past of American combat. As mentioned at the beginning of this book, the battle was portrayed in *Black Hawk Down*. The following was part of it:

> *Citation:* Master Sergeant Gary I. Gordon, United States Army, distinguished himself by actions above and beyond the call of duty on 3 October 1993, while serving as Sniper Team Leader, United States Army Special Operations Command with Task Force Ranger in Mogadishu, Somalia. Master Sergeant Gordon's sniper team provided precision fires from the lead helicopter during an assault and at two helicopter crash sites, while subjected to intense automatic weapons and rocket-propelled grenade fires. When Master Sergeant Gordon learned that ground forces were not immediately available to secure the second crash site, he and another sniper unhesitatingly volunteered to be inserted to protect the four critically wounded personnel, despite being well aware of the growing number of enemy personnel closing in on

the site. After his third request to be inserted, Master Sergeant Gordon received permission to perform his volunteer mission. When debris and enemy ground fires at the site caused them to abort the first attempt, Master Sergeant Gordon was inserted one hundred meters south of the crash site. Equipped with only his sniper rifle and a pistol, Master Sergeant Gordon and his fellow sniper, while under intense small arms fire from the enemy, fought their way through a dense maze of shanties and shacks to reach the critically injured crewmembers. Master Sergeant Gordon immediately pulled the pilot and the other crewmembers from the aircraft, establishing a perimeter which placed him and his fellow sniper in the most vulnerable position. Master Sergeant Gordon used his long-range rifle and sidearm to kill an undetermined number of attackers until he depleted his ammunition. Master Sergeant Gordon then went back to the wreckage, recovering some of the crew's weapons and ammunition. Despite the fact that he was critically low on ammunition, he provided some of it to the dazed pilot and then radioed for help. Master Sergeant Gordon continued to travel the perimeter, protecting the downed crew. After his team member was fatally wounded and his own rifle ammunition exhausted, Master Sergeant Gordon returned to the wreckage, recovering a rifle with the last five rounds of ammunition and gave it to the pilot with the words, "good luck." Then, armed only with his pistol, Master Sergeant Gordon continued to fight until he was fatally wounded. His actions saved the pilot's life. Master Sergeant Gordon's extraordinary heroism and devotion to duty were in keeping with the highest standards of military service and reflect great credit upon him, his unit and the United States Army.

"... *Another sniper, a fellow sniper, his team member...*" Who was this other person? Why was the citation written this way? Rather odd, isn't it? That's because this is the first time that a team of two men, fighting together on the ground, earned the Medal of Honor for a combined feat of incredible bravery in the same action!

Gary Gordon's fellow sniper was Sergeant First Class Randall D.

Shughart, from Newville, Pennsylvania. Oddly, Gordon was born in the town of Lincoln in Penobscot County, Maine—while Shughart was born in the city of Lincoln in Lancaster County, Nebraska. Part of his MOH citation reads:

> Sergeant First Class Shughart and his team leader were inserted one hundred meters south of the crash site. Equipped with only his sniper rifle and a pistol, Sergeant First Class Shughart and his team leader, while under intense small arms fire from the enemy, fought their way through a dense maze of shanties and shacks to reach the critically injured crewmembers. Sergeant First Class Shughart pulled the pilot and the other crewmembers from the aircraft, establishing a perimeter which placed him and his fellow sniper in the most vulnerable position. Sergeant First Class Shughart used his long-range rifle and side arm to kill an undetermined number of attackers while traveling the perimeter, protecting the downed crew. Sergeant First Class Shughart continued his protective fire until he depleted his ammunition and was fatally wounded. His actions saved the pilot.

AFGHANISTAN AND OPERATION IRAQI FREEDOM

Following the great tragedy of 9/11, American forces were sent into the backward, war-torn country of Afghanistan in search of the leader of al Qaeda, Osama bin Laden. Since the Russians had thrown up their hands after a decade of trying to conquer the country in 1989, the fiercely fundamentalist Islamic sect known as the Taliban had held the country by the throat. Atrocious restrictions on women were but part of their inhuman practices as they reduced human life to unimaginable poverty and oppression. Fighting the Taliban called for a strong element of unconventional warfare requiring the use of what has become known as Special Operations—a combination of Army Green Berets, Navy Seals, Marines, and Air Force Special Ops. The latter provides gunships for support of the other elements.

The difficult mission of training and fighting with the various coalition (spelled warlord) forces is an Army Green Beret requirement. These have been the fiercely bearded Americans in native garb whose photos have slipped into the newspapers. As usual, their heroic feats go unrewarded and unrecognized because of the clandestine and classified nature of their activities. Many are in those Afghan mountains for extended periods. It's what they do.

We can rest assured that all of the forces who fought there had their share of heroics and will continue to have them. The Afghanistan conflict was also the beginning of the word "embedded" for journalists being attached to frontline outfits. Ernie Pyle, who was killed covering combat in WWII, immortalized the role of the reporter living in the same foxholes as the GI Joes, but in this conflict the media made itself more visible. However, when the news dwindled down to the drudgery of everyday Special Ops or guard duty, the cameras and pens of the media moved on to the excitement of the Iraqi campaign.

I waited and waited for inspiration as to how I should handle the Afghanistan and the Iraq wars. Suddenly, it came, in the form of a relentless NFL defensive back. It was the springboard. These were different conflicts from those that have brought us our heroes in the past. *The courage and heroic acts are essentially the same, but the settings are different.* Media coverage was different, so daily awards of medals didn't reach us as readily. So much of everyday combat was collaborative and the equipment was so sophisticated that no Sergeant Yorks, no Eddie Rickenbakers, no Robert E. Lees or Audie Murphys surfaced. But, as always, they were there: the 82nd Airborne has had its share of heroic acts, as have all of the other major units. Army Special Forces Major Mark Mitchell earned the first DSC since Vietnam. A photo surfaced of a couple hundred soldiers reenlisting at the 101st Airborne Division headquarters in Iraq. At this writing, there have been over 140 awards of the Silver Star.

Sergeant Major Michael B. Stack's Army Special Forces team came under fire on April 11, 2004, when it was traveling from Baghdad to Al Hillah. Ambushed, Stack, forty-eight, immediately covered the end of the convoy so his team could escape the kill zone. He organized a security force and was preparing a counterattack when he was killed. A father of six and grandfather of three, he was awarded the Silver Star posthumously. It could easily have been a DSC.

In May of 2004 Marine Captain Brian Chontosh, Marine Sergeant Marco Martinez, and Marine Lance Corporal Joseph Perez were awarded Navy Crosses for extraordinary heroism in Iraq.

Marine Corporal Thomas W. Kuster, twenty-eight, was awarded three Purple Hearts for wounds he suffered in Iraq. In one case, a bullet was removed from the back of his knee and he walks with a limp, but he's back on duty. "My parents begged me to come home," Kuster said, "but I felt like if I was to go, I'd be turning my back on my Marines."

And the perception of heroes had changed in the previous thirty years. Undoubtedly the Vietnam conflict that raged at home had a distinct bearing on the country's view of heroes—the term itself almost became a dirty word, so brainwashed by the antiwar proponents was the country. Political correctness and expediency came into play. By the time operation Iraqi Freedom was launched, the very term *hero* was given a looser interpretation. Just being there and doing one's duty was considered heroic.

The rules were different. But true heroism wasn't.

Every day, service personnel performed unheralded heroic acts in both of these wars. Imagine the courage it took to daily face an enemy whose identity and location was unknown, and whose motivation was fanatical terrorism—as it is in Iraq on a large scale, or in Afghanistan, where Pat Tillman was blitzed. In many cases, there was simply no one to recommend individuals for medals, or to bring their stories to the American public. And we didn't hear of the awards for valor except in passing. Most of the media was too busy reporting casualties, following the headline axiom "If it bleeds, it leads." Journalist Kate O'Beirne in the *National Review Online* wrote, "All villains and victims, no valor." A perfect example was those

Green Berets operating daily in Afghanistan; they *lived* the fight as guerrillas in remote mountains, immersed, bearded, living as supposed friendly tribesmen in small teams. Surely, there are some Mogadishu-type heroes there—and they aren't alone.

THE SEALS

Glory and honor and fame; the pomp that a soldier prizes;
The league-long waving line as the marching falls and rises;
Rumbling of caissons and guns; the clatter of horses' feet,
And a million awe-struck faces far down the waiting street.

But better than martial woe, and the pageant of civic sorrow;
Better than praise of to-day, or the statue we build to-morrow;
Better than honor and glory, and History's iron pen,
Was the thought of duty done and the love of his fellow-men.
—Richard Watson Gilder, "The Burial of Sherman" (1891)

With so much about the Green Berets in this collection, it may appear that the Navy SEALs have been overlooked. SEAL (sea, air, land) are the US Navy's elite Special Operations teams. With the motto "Failure is not an option," the SEALs were a John F. Kennedy offspring. They were formed to fight in teams of one to sixteen men. Most of their missions are clandestine in nature, planned in exacting detail and executed with precision and swiftness. They are the Navy's commandos, deadly efficient in missions so clandestine that our public has seldom known about their operations—from Vietnam to Iraq.

Their history dates back to 1942 at Little Creek, Virginia, when "Amphibious Scouts and Raiders" training began. The mission of these teams was to identify and reconnoiter objective beaches, maintain a designated position on the specific beach, and guide the assault waves in. These groups saw action during the North African landings and in Sicily, Salerno, Anzio, Normandy, and southern France.

Special Services Unit #1 operated in the Pacific and its teams were a vital cog in numerous landings.

A third Scouts and Raiders group operated in China. One element of what was code-named "Amphibious Roger" conducted a survey of the Upper Yangtze River in the spring of 1945. Disguised as Chinese coolies, they conducted an extended exploration of the Chinese coast from Shanghai almost to Hong Kong.

In 1944 NCDUs (Naval Combat Demolition Units—another forebear of the SEALs) were vital in the Normandy invasion. Taking 50 percent casualties, these teams cleared large areas of underwater obstacles the Germans had planted offshore. They cleared seven hundred yards of landing area at Utah Beach in two hours, and another nine hundred yards later in the day. At Omaha Beach they blew ten gaps in the German defenses. It's hard to estimate how many thousands of Allied lives were saved by their heroic actions.

Another designation for SEAL predecessors was adopted in the Pacific: UDT, Underwater Demolition Teams. Many of their operations were equally heroic.

Korea. It's improbable that MacArthur's brilliant Inchon invasion would have been successful were it not for the UDTs that were employed. UDT 1 and 3 provided personnel who went in ahead of the landing craft, scouting mud flats, marking low points in the channel, clearing fouled propellers, and searching for mines. Four UDT personnel acted as wave-guides for the Marine landing.

Vietnam. In this war that involved so much river and jungle warfare, the SEALs came into their own as feared warriors. The Viet Cong operated as if the Geneva Convention never existed, and the SEALs fought fire with fire. It was said that the "most feared animal in the jungles of Vietnam was a Navy SEAL." The VC and the NVA lived in terror of the "men with green faces," who would materialize suddenly, often in the night, from nowhere. The enemy hated the SEALs so much that the current Vietnamese government has brought suit against former senator Bob Kerrey for war crimes.

Unbelievable! That would be like the Nazis suing us over the

Nuremburg trials. But then, the Communist mind has never been rational anyway.

Three SEALs were awarded the Medal of Honor for action in Vietnam—Lieutenant Thomas Norris for the three-day rescue of two downed pilots that involved great danger, and to Petty Officer Michael Thornton, who, during an extremely hazardous operation, braved intense enemy fire to save his wounded commander, an act that culminated in Thornton towing his lieutenant out to sea for some two hours before being rescued.

The third and most famous is, of course, Bob Kerrey. In 1968, Lieutenant (Junior Grade) Kerrey led his SEAL team on an extremely hazardous mission on an island in Nha Trang Bay to capture high-ranking Viet Cong political leaders. In the course of the operation, he received massive injuries when a grenade exploded at his feet. Though bleeding profusely and in intense pain, as well as being in a nearly unconscious state, Kerrey continued to calmly command the mission to its successful completion. Later, part of his right leg was amputated.

Schooled as a pharmacist, which should make him a superhero to the pill counters of the world, Kerrey established a chain of restaurants after leaving the Navy and served as governor of his home state of Nebraska from 1982 to 1986. He became a US senator in 1988 and served two terms. He was also an unsuccessful candidate for the Democrats in the 1982 presidential campaign. He is currently president of the New School University in New York City.

Another famous SEAL was Master Chief Rudy Boesch, who retired from the US Navy after completing over forty-five years of continuous activity. He was honorably discharged on August 1, 1990. Boesch was awarded the Bronze Star for heroic action during more than forty-five combat operations.

Two Navy SEALs have received the Navy Cross for valor in Afghanistan, but their actions are still classified. They are Senior Chief Britt Slabinski and Chief Bosun's Mate Stephen Bass.

AFGHANISTAN

As in the case of the Navy SEALs, reports of heroic action in Afghanistan have been mostly classified. So many of these acts have been conducted by Special Operations personnel—Air Force, SEAL, and Army Special Forces and Rangers—that the reports are still classified. Public Affairs controls what will be fed to the public, other than what embedded reporters have written or broadcast. I'm sure the awards in many cases have been released to hometown newspapers. We know this: the war isn't over, and we have servicemen of different services and ranks performing heroically every day. An action that might have produced a Bronze Star in earlier wars might today be considered routine. The Special Ops guys, many in their beards and civilian garb, are in there as advisers and cave probers, performing a major mission.

Little mention has been given in this collection about the Rangers. From well before the Revolution, there have been units of tough special fighting men called Rangers. In fact, they date back to the American frontier in 1670. In 1754 the famous Major Robert Rogers formed the first official Ranger force. It fought effectively during the French and Indian War, gaining wide fame. In the Revolutionary War we had Morgan's Rangers, described by one British general as "the most crack shots in the American army." Swamp Fox Francis Marion's men were Rangers. In 1813 the Army register listed officers for twelve companies of Rangers.

During the Civil War, the famous Colonel John Singleton Mosby put his Rangers to daring use, as did Colonel Turner Ashby. The unheralded Mean's Rangers on the Union side once captured General James Longstreet's ammunition train and also disrupted Mosby at one juncture.

Moving up to WWII, we encounter William Orlando Darby, a 1933 graduate of West Point. As a second lieutenant, he was assigned to the First Battalion of Field Artillery in the 1st Cavalry Division at Fort Bliss. In 1941 he went through amphibious training that would be valuable later. In 1942 he was based in Northern Ireland as a captain and aide to the commanding general of the 34th Infantry Division. Major General Lucian Truscott Jr. selected him to form a commando-type unit. The new Rangers came into being. Darby had his pick of thousands of volunteers, and a grueling training course was begun. Some of these new Rangers accompanied the British and Canadian commandos on the ill-fated raid on Dieppe, France—the first Americans to fight on the Continent in WWII.

The 1st Ranger Battalion under Lieutenant Colonel Darby led Patton's drive to capture El Guettar in North Africa in March 1943, and Darby won his first DSC. During the Italian campaign, two more Ranger battalions joined Darby's command and fought with distinction. During the Normandy landings, the 2nd Ranger Battalion assaulted the perpendicular cliffs at Omaha Beach under intense enemy fire and destroyed a large gun battery that would have devastated the offshore Allied fleet. Throughout the ensuing campaigns until the end of the war, Darby's Rangers covered themselves with glory in one valorous action after another.

Colonel Bill Darby, age thirty-four, was killed by an artillery round just a few days before VE Day. He was the only Army officer promoted to brigadier general posthumously in the war.

The modern-day Seventy-fifth Ranger Regiment traces its history to the famous Merrill's Marauders of the China-Burma-India theater in WWII. Under Brigadier General Frank Merrill, this command fought heroically in numerous actions, usually behind Japanese lines.

During the Korean War, several Ranger infantry companies were formed. These highly motivated units of 112 men were attached to divisions to be used as needed. (As a side note, three officers who had commanded such Ranger companies were friends of mine in the 10th Special Forces Group in Bad Tölz, Germany, in 1955–56— Black Jack Striegel, Dorsey Anderson, and the notorious John C. Scagnelli. There was a good "Scag" story in *True* magazine many years ago, relating to Korea and battlefield commissions: told by a Ranger first sergeant, it went,

Two new second lieutenants reported in for duty one day wearing starched khakis. I told them to wait, that the company commander was out on patrol. He finally arrived in his dirty, sweaty fatigues with grenades strung across his chest. One officer stepped forward, saluting, "Sir, Lieutenant Smith, West Point, Class of Fifty."

The second one did likewise, "Lieutenant Brown, West Point, Class of Fifty, Sir!"

The captain looked up from his field desk, returned their salutes, and growled, "Scagnelli, Omaha Beach, '44."

Ranger exploits in Vietnam and later wars could fill another book. Companies of the Seventy-fifth Ranger Regiment are hard at it daily in Iraq and Afghanistan, but the Rangers are even more widespread. Each arduous training class gets dozens of officers and enlisted men who will proudly wear the thin black-and-gold Ranger tab forever—the little black and yellow semicircular patch that marks them as a cut above the rest—but may never serve in a Ranger outfit. Many Special Forces members and other Special Ops types have also endured the difficult training course.

At this writing, only one Distinguished Service Cross has been awarded for Afghanistan valor. In late November of 2001, five hundred Taliban prisoners took over the old stone fortress of Qala-I-Jangi near Mazar-e-Sharif. They gained access to two fully stocked armories and staged a bloody revolt. A team of sixteen American and British Special Operations personnel, led by Major Mark E. Mitchell, sped to the fortress to rescue two American CIA agents. Armed with an M4 rifle and an M9 pistol, Mitchell led three of his soldiers, via the unwound turban of a Northern Alliance soldier, thirty-plus feet to the top of the fortress. From there, while fighting with small arms, he directed air strikes on the main body of the rebels. Mitchell pulled his team out at dark, but brought them back the next day to continue the battle. An incoming bomb wounded nine of his men, and he spent most of the day evacuating them. Mitchell still wasn't finished; that night he led five men back to the fortress and under more heavy fire directed AC130 Air Force gunship attacks that eventually broke the enemy's spine.

As of this writing, Lieutenant Colonel Mitchell is redeployed in Afghanistan.

IRAQ

Sergeant First Class Paul R. Smith seemed to have a date with destiny ever since he returned from the Gulf War to Germany in the spring of 1991. Before that, he'd been a lousy soldier to whom partying was more important than duty. But something happened to him in that conflict that made him such a dedicated NCO that he became known as a "hard-ass." Over the next several years, as he rose to the rank of platoon sergeant in a combat engineer company, he dished out punishment to soldiers who goofed up as readily as he trained himself to perfection.

But let's go back to Bamberg, Germany, on the night he met the young German woman Birgit. After an evening of getting to know each other, he serenaded her from the street below, singing a love song from the movie *Top Gun* while she tossed rose petals to him. The tall, slender soldier from Tampa, Florida, had enlisted in the Army following his high-school graduation in 1989, a nondescript and hell-raising youth. In January 1992 he married Birgit and became a loving father to her three-year-old daughter. Two years later, a son, David, was born to the Smiths. Paul's way was clear—he would rise to the top as an NCO and retire as a sergeant major.

Then 9/11, Saddam Hussein, and Iraq all came together in March of 2003 when the 11th Engineer Battalion, as part of the 3rd Infantry Division, was part of the Coalition invasion of Iraq. By dawn on April 4, Smith's men were battle-tested, grimy, weary, homesick, and insect-plagued. The two weeks of war seemed like an eternity, but Smith's men knew the war couldn't last too much longer when they reached Saddam International Airport. The SFC was given the mission of setting up a roadblock on the highway between the airport and the city of Baghdad. His men were part of a force of about one hundred assigned to guard the eastern flank of the army at that position.

At 9:30 an infantry contingent radioed that they needed a place to put a handful of prisoners. Smith had seen a courtyard nearby that would be just the ticket. He had a bulldozer knock out the south wall by the highway and strung concertina wire in a corner to hold the POWs. A low tower outside the courtyard would serve as the guard post. He manned the position with two squads—sixteen men. A couple of infantrymen joined him later.

A half hour later, some one hundred Iraqi soldiers armed with RPGs (deadly rocket-propelled grenades) were advancing on the position. Smith called for a Bradley, a heavily armed tracked vehicle, which arrived shortly. It took up a position just outside the courtyard and fired its cannon at the Iraqis. Smith killed a couple of Iraqis with his rifle, then grabbed a bazooka-type rocket launcher and boldly fired it from in front of the Bradley. But by now the Iraqis had climbed into the small tower and were firing down into the court-yard. An M113, a tracked armored personnel carrier, pulled into the position and its .50 caliber machine gun was brought into the fight.

Then inexplicably the Bradley backed out and rumbled away. The men couldn't believe it. This left only the M113 with its trailer. And soon all three of its crew members had been wounded and its .50 was unmanned. After consulting with his first sergeant, Smith got the M113 in position in the middle of the courtyard. There were infantrymen at the nearby roadblock, men from a mortar platoon, medical corpsmen at an aid station, and a command center con-taining several officers not far away. It's believed that Smith made the decision to stay and fight to protect these elements. He climbed up into the gunner's hatch of the 113 and began pouring .50 rounds into the enemy. To fire the gun, the sergeant's upper torso was fully exposed. Private Michael Seaman, who was sheltered in the hatch, kept belts of ammo fed into the machine gun. But every time Smith had to stop firing for reloading, the Iraqis fired back. They still had RPGs and mortars. One of Smith's squad leaders tried to get him to fall back, but the Floridian kept pouring fire into the enemy. Seaman tried to get him to leave, but Smith kept firing.

Then suddenly the gun went quiet. Smith had been hit in the head. He died in the aid station a short time later. His men found letters to Birgit and his parents on his laptop. They had never been sent.

Sergeant First Class (E7) Paul R. Smith was the first service person in Operation Iraqi Freedom to be recommended for the Medal of Honor. At this writing, no decision has been made about its approval.

DARING RESCUE BY APACHE PILOTS*

For two AH-64D Apache Longbow pilots, the night of October 16, 2004, was just a regular night flying a reconnaissance mission around southern Baghdad. Then a distorted cry for help came across the emergency radio, shattering the chatter of all other communications. They recognized the call sign; they recognized the area; and a few minutes later, they were en route to perform what would become a heroic rescue. "I really couldn't make out at first what was going on. The transmission over the radio was broken up and weak, but I could make out that it was a distress call," said Lodi, California, native Army Chief Warrant Officer Justin Taylor, an Apache pilot with Company C, First Battalion, 227th Aviation Regiment, of the 4th Brigade Combat Team.

Then a call sign familiar to Taylor and Captain Ryan Welch, the air mission commander, came across the guard, or emergency, channel. The two men now knew that Army OH-58D Kiowa helicopter pilots were down. "We're in zone 43," came the weak transmission.

---

*Adapted from a fine piece of reporting by Army Corporal Benjamin Cossel, 122 Mobile Public Affairs Detachment, Iraq.

"I recognized the area and immediately made the decision that we were going to break from our sector and go over to the area," said Lebanon, New Hampshire, native Welch. "Those were our guys on the ground, and we had to help. My first thought was we would provide aerial security."

The team changed flight paths, and when they arrived in the area of the crash site, they began trying to contact the pilots on the ground. Then came a call from one of the downed aviators. The wounded pilot explained that the pilot who had called previously was now unable to respond, that two other pilots had been killed in action, and that he and the other survivor were trying to make their way to a defensible position but were having difficulty because one was unable to walk. "When we flew over the sector, we immediately picked up the heat signature of a burning fire," said Welch. "But at first we weren't sure what it was. It kind of looked like one of the many trash fires you see all over Baghdad," Taylor added.

While the two were flying over the fire trying to get a better look at the ground, an excited call came up. "You just flew over our position," the transmission informed.

Welch's wingman noticed the emergency strobe on the ground and notified Welch of the positive identification. "Once we had identified the crew on the ground, I made the call that we were going to land and get those pilots out of there," Welch said. "I had no idea of the situation on the ground or what the landing zone looked like, so I informed my wingman to fly a tight defensive circle around our position to provide cover if needed. As we landed and I got all the cords off of me, I looked back at (Taylor) and told him if he started taking fire, (he should), 'Get this bird out of here, leave me, and we'll collect all of us later.'"

Welch had landed his Apache approximately one hundred meters from the crash site. Armed with his 9 mm pistol and an M4 Carbine rifle, he set out to collect the downed pilots. The captain contacted the pilots and asked if they were able to come to him themselves. The radio response was that one of the pilots couldn't walk. They would need help getting out of their location. "I basically had to stumble my way through an open field. It was treacherous, with potholes and low brush. I stumbled a couple times," recalled Welch. "But I finally came up on the crash site about ten minutes later."

When Welch arrived on the scene he saw one pilot standing and one sitting. The two had been able to get a fair distance away from their downed aircraft. "As I came up on them, I noticed they looked pretty bad, multiple cuts on their face and both looked like the early stages of shock had set in. I called out to Army Chief Warrant Officer Chad Beck, who was standing, to get him to help me with Chief Warrant Officer Greg Crow," Welch said. "It took a few seconds to get Mr. Beck's attention as he was visibly shaken and dazed."

Both of the downed pilots were assigned to the First Battalion, Twenty-fifth Aviation Regiment of the 25th Infantry Division. Their unit is attached to the 4th Brigade Combat Team, Welch's unit. As the two got Crow up and began the long trek back to Welch's Apache, the mess of tangled cords attached to their equipment nearly tripped them up. "We stumbled initially with all those wires just everywhere," Welch said. "I pulled out my knife and just cut them all away, and we took off."

Assisting two wounded men over the treacherous one hundred meters to his waiting Apache, Welch said the time seemed to slow down to an absolute crawl. They inched their way back, working carefully not to further injure Crow. "We had to move kind of slow," he explained. "I swear it probably took us like ten minutes to get back, but it seemed like we were out there for hours. I was never so relieved to see Taylor and my bird sitting there."

Four personnel to get out and only two seats in the Apache posed a problem. Self-extraction was a maneuver the pilots had been told about in flight school—a maneuver considered dangerous enough that no practical application was given, just the verbal "here's how you do it."

Hanging from every pilot's flight vest is a nylon strap attached to a carabiner. On the outside of the Apache there are handholds bolted on primarily to assist maintenance crews as they work on the birds. But, they also have another purpose—to be used in the event of a self-extraction. The general idea is for the pilot to wrap a nylon strap through the handholds and then connect the strap to the carabiner. The aircraft then flies off to a safe location with the person attached to the outside of the aircraft. "I knew getting back to my bird that Mr. Crow was in no position for self-extraction—that I would have to put him in the front seat," explained Welch. "I radioed to (Taylor) and told him what I intended to do—Crow in the front seat, Beck and I strapped to the outside."

At first Taylor just looked at Welch. "The plan kind of surprised me at first. And then I just thought, "Cool, that's what we're going to do.'"

Beck and Welch worked to get Crow into the front seat as Welch explained what was next to Beck. "At first Beck really didn't want to leave. His commander had just been killed, and he still wasn't thinking 100 percent clearly."

"I can't go; I just can't go," pleaded Beck, but soon enough he understood the situation.

And then another problem surfaced. "The mechanism Kiowa pilots use for self-extraction is different than the setup Apache pilots use," explained Welch. "But we finally got it worked out, got Beck hooked up, and then secured myself to the aircraft."

Secured and assuming a defensive posture with his rifle, Welch gave Taylor the thumbs-up sign and the Apache lifted off. "I was a little bit freaked out," explained Taylor. "You just don't fly an Apache by yourself; it's definitely a two-man aircraft."

At 90 miles per hour the helicopter flew twenty kilometers to Forward Operating Base Falcon, the closest base with a combat support hospital. "I had only my night visor on," Welch said. "I thought my eyes were going to rip out of their sockets and that my nose would tear from my face, the wind was so strong."

Landing on the emergency pad, Welch and Taylor helped medical personnel take Beck and Crow inside for treatment. "One of the medics asked me if I was a medical flight pilot," chuckled Welch.

"You should have seen the look on his face when I told him, 'Nope, I'm an Apache pilot.'"

With the patients safely delivered to the hospital, the two exhausted Apache pilots looked at each other with the same thought. "We both climbed back into our bird," Welch said, "and almost simultaneously said to each other, 'Let's go home.'"

NOT EVERY HERO IS BORN IN AMERICA

Sergeant Rafael Peralta, twenty-five, was born in Mexico and entered the US Marine Corps from San Diego. He acquired US citizenship after entering the Corps. On November 15, 2004, in the vicious battle for Fallujah, he gave his life to save half the men in a fire team. Peralta was assigned as a scout in the First Platoon, Alpha Company, Third Marine Regiment. He wasn't even a member of the assault team that entered the insurgent safe house that day, but it was typical of him to volunteer to join such missions.

One of the first Marines to enter the Iraqi safe house, he was immediately hit in the face by enemy rifle fire. He fell to the floor with other Marines seeking to escape the fusillade. A few moments later, an insurgent rolled a fragmentation grenade into their midst. Without hesitation, the wounded Peralta grabbed the grenade and cradled it into his body.

One Marine was badly wounded by shrapnel from the blast, but the lives of several others were saved by Peralta's heroic act. In past wars such an act has won the Medal of Honor. Time will tell if Sergeant Rafael Peralta is awarded one. He certainly deserves it.

A proud Marine, Peralta had a history of helping his fellow infantrymen. He was perhaps the ultimate example of a foreign-born service member becoming dedicated to the military of the United States. He is a credit to Mexico and to all Hispanic immigrants fighting in our armed forces.

Corporal Yeager

This Marine was in 3/5. His name is Corporal Joel Yeager. As the Marines cleared an apartment building, they got to the top floor and the point man kicked in the door. As he did so, an enemy grenade and a burst of gunfire came out. The explosion and enemy fire took off the point man's leg. He was then immediately shot in the arm as he lay in the doorway. Corporal Yeager tossed a grenade in the room and ran into the doorway and into the enemy fire in order to pull his buddy back to cover. As he was dragging the wounded Marine to cover, his own grenade came back through the doorway. Without pausing, he reached down and threw the grenade back through the door while he heaved his buddy to safety. The grenade went off inside the room and Corporal Yeager threw another in. He immediately entered the room following the second explosion. He gunned down three enemy all within three feet of where he stood and then let fly a third grenade as he backed out of the room to complete the evacuation of the wounded Marine. You have to understand that a grenade goes off within five seconds of having the pin pulled. Marines usually let them "cook off" for a second or two before tossing them in. Therefore, this entire episode took place in less than thirty seconds.

Aside from this Marine's heroic action is the fact that perhaps it's in his bloodlines. Corporal Yeager is the grandson of Brigadier General Chuck Yeager, the Air Force hero whose feats are legendary. Chuck Yeager came out of the hills of West Virginia, uneducated and unworldly, to become the superb pilot who flew the X-1 through the sound barrier.

As a fighter pilot in Europe, he was shot down the day after his first kill in 1943. He evaded capture and, with help from the French Resistance, made a phenomenal escape over the Pyrenees to neutral Spain. Army policy at the time prohibited his return to combat, but he appealed all the way to General Dwight Eisenhower, who allowed him to fly combat missions again.

Chuck Yeager flew sixty-four missions in that war, and by its end he had thirteen kills, five in one day. Staying in the Air Force, he became a leading test pilot. He broke the sound barrier on October 14, 1947, just days after cracking several ribs in a horseback accident. He became America's most famous test pilot, and later commanded the 405th Fighter Wing during the Vietnam War.

He retired as a brigadier general with a chestful of medals in 1975, and became a household name when the movie *The Right Stuff* came out in 1983. His retirement has been marked by a constant demand as a consultant and speaker.

Is it any wonder that Corporal Yeager is one of today's unsung heroes in Iraq?

PAT TILLMAN

We all know his story—listening to some inner voice known only to him, to a sense of responsibility so rare among professional athletes at the time, wanting to follow the heritage of the men in his family, he walked away from the fame of the gridiron to a personal glory that shocked the nation. We heard over and over about him turning down $3.6 million to enlist with his younger brother, Kevin, a promising minor-league baseball player. They went on to rigorous Ranger School, where the failure rate has always been high, and graduated. And throughout, Pat Tillman put a chop-block on interviews and any personal appearances. What he was doing, his contribution to his country, was strictly personal.

It didn't even have a whiff of humility; it just wasn't anyone's business but his own. After serving in Iraq, he was sent with the Second Battalion of the 75th Army Ranger Regiment to help beef up the campaign Special Operations forces had been conducting for over two years near the Pakistan border. His brother also went with the battalion, and they were within shouting distance in those hostile mountains where will-o'-the-wisp al Qaeda and Taliban fighters slipped in and out of the rugged terrain. Just three weeks after their arrival, Pat was on a night operation that had been compromised by a Taliban sympathizer. Suddenly Tillman's patrol was led into a trap and his truck was hit by what may have been friendly fire, probably a miscommunication problem with the Friendlies. He died a few minutes later.

Gary Smith, in the May 3, 2004, issue of *Sports Illustrated*, wrote it so succinctly: "The news whistled through America's soul and raised the hair on the back of its neck. It tapped into people's admiration, their awe, their guilt...a man had sacrificed the biggest dream of all. The NFL."

But was that really his biggest dream?

Kevin White, athletic director at Notre Dame, stated, "To me, Pat Tillman is without question the biggest hero of my lifetime."

Pat Tillman, all-star football player, found his true calling—he brought home through the sacrifice of his life the purest meaning of patriotism, responsibility, and heroism. He will forever be the icon of the many who also gave their lives in untrumpeted sacrifice.

There is an interesting sidelight to Pat Tillman's sacrifice. The Ranger's unit commander, First Lieutenant David Uthlaut, was seriously wounded in that same operation. Uthlaut was First Captain of the Corps of Cadets at West Point in his class of 2001—the highest distinction a cadet can achieve. A strong candidate for a Rhodes scholarship, he instead chose to serve in Iraq.

He placed his patriotism before self.

And now we are at that word again: *patriotism*, a term that nearly became a taboo during and after the Vietnam conflict. Webster's defines a patriot as one who strongly supports his or her country and is willing to defend it. The heroes who have crossed our stage in this narrative never lacked for a feeling of responsibility toward their place as Americans. The term *patriot* would have made them proud, or perhaps, as in Pat Tillman's case, not have been a conscious issue—it was just natural. Yes, patriotism is back. Ask the troops who have served in Iraq.

Actor John Wayne once said, "Sure I wave the American flag. Do you know a better flag to wave? Sure I love my country with all her faults. I'm not ashamed of that, never have been, never will be."

Journalist Charlie Edgren in the *El Paso Times* wrote, "Patriotism is a positive, ongoing, hopeful, persevering, restorative, healing, progressive experience. Or should be. And it's not a short-term, fair-weather commitment. Or it shouldn't be."

Enough said.

The death of beloved (by most of America) President Ronald Reagan just before D-Day, 2004 brought up another use of the word *hero*. "Ronnie," as his wife, Nancy, liked to call him, enlisted in the reserve cavalry program before the war. Commissioned a second lieutenant in Iowa, he moved on to a successful screen career in Hollywood. In 1942 he was called to active duty as a captain of cavalry. In his inimitable humor, he liked to say, "I couldn't see well enough for the horses, so they transferred me to the Air Corps." Reagan was the last cavalryman to occupy the White House. Yes, he was a hero, perhaps one of our grandest of all, because in a time of uncertainty and darkness after the Vietnam debacle he brought back patriotism and faith in America. He glared back at the Soviets and called them an "evil empire." His steadfastness was a strong factor in bringing down the Berlin wall, the demise of Communist rule in the Soviet Union, and the end of its threat to the Western world. The pomp and ceremony of his magnificent funeral proceedings reminded America that, yes, heroes are important... and beloved.

CHAPTER FOURTEEN

THE CLOSING ACT

I t's been said, "Where there's life, there's hope." That statement could almost have been made during our war years beginning with WWII. Some pretty remote spots on the globe that had US military life saw hope, Bob Hope! He may have put on a show from the back end of a truck for fifty servicemen, or on a big sound stage for many thousands, but he brought life, laughter, and, usually, girls. No comprehensive story of American military heroes would be complete without mentioning the different kind of courage, the different kind of heroism of Bob Hope for over fifty years.

Born Leslie Townes Hope in the London suburb of Eltham on May 29, 1903, Bob was the fifth of seven sons. His father immigrated with the brood to Cleveland, Ohio, four years later. Bob later quipped, "I left England when I found out I couldn't be king."

Hope was a busy kid at East High School, trying many jobs. He was a shoe salesman, a soda jerk, and he hustled loose change in the local pool halls. Following high school, he took dancing lessons from hoofer King Rastuws Brown. He tried his hand briefly as a newspaper reporter, and then came his big amateur boxing career as Packy East. Bob liked to make fun of his boxing stint; he said he quit when he "was not only carried out of the ring, but *into* the ring."

The siren song of vaudeville captured him and he did a dance act with a girlfriend when he was eighteen for the princely sum of $8 a night, until his partner's mother caught up with them. But he soon teamed up with first one male partner then another until he began to get decent bookings in New York. After a long run in *Sidewalks of New York* with Ruby Keeler, Bob found success as a single doing comedy. *Major Bowes' Amateur Hour* was his introduction to what would be a long and successful marriage with radio. It was there that he first met Der Bingle, Bing Crosby.

But we're getting ahead of perhaps the biggest duets of his life. Back in 1933 he met a singer six years his junior, fell madly in love with her, and married her in February 1934. She is the same Dolores Hope who has been on many of his Christmas shows, and upon his death had been married to him for nearly seventy years! They adopted four children, the first of which was Linda, who now steers the vast empire of Hope Enterprises.

In 1937 Bob traveled to Hollywood to film *The Big Broadcast of 1938*, a movie that introduced him to filmgoers. The next year he signed with Pepsodent to do the NBC weekly show that brought his flip humor into American homes every Tuesday night for the next eighteen years. His cast included the bug-eyed, mustachioed Jerry Colonna; Vera Vague; and Skinny Ennis and His Orchestra. Later, Les Brown and His Band of Renown joined the show to provide music for such great singers as Judy Garland, Doris Day, and Frances Langford. This show rocketed him to number one in radio, as listeners across the nation stayed home on Tuesday nights so as not to miss a single episode.

In the meantime, the famous *Road* pictures with Bing Crosby and luscious Dorothy Lamour made Bob the master of quip and cowardice—and a major star. They also made Paramount Pictures a lot of money. Those old films are still popular on television for audiences of all ages.

In May 1941 Hope went to March Field, near Riverside, California, to do a show for the Air Corps personnel there. It was the beginning; in just a few short months, Pearl Harbor was bombed and a whole new life opened for Bob. Throughout World War II, his radio shows were performed on American military installations around the world. He put together a small USO troupe in 1943 that consisted of singer Frances Langford, old friend Jack Pepper, and one-man music maker guitarist Tony Romano. They started playing US military facilities in England, then went on to Africa and Sicily. Getting marvelous responses from the guys and gals in uniform put him in his glory. From the lowest private to commanding generals, they laughed at his jokes and loved him. "Humor is good for you," he liked to say. "Did you ever hear of a laughing hyena with heartburn?"

He performed before hundreds of thousands before the war was over—never before had a onetime vaudeville hoofer had such rapport with so many. And it was only the beginning.

In December 1948 Hope and his wife, Dolores, went to Germany to entertain the troops involved in the Berlin Airlift. It was the start of Christmas away from home. With various ensembles and stars, he performed Christmas shows with the troops for so many of those holidays that his kids thought he'd never be home. Finally, he decided 1972 would be the last one. But he was still a sucker for the folks in uniform—every following Christmas found him doing a show at some military installation, on a ship, or in some veterans hospital. (I met him during the Korean War in a hospital in Osaka, Japan, just before I was evacuated to the States, then again at Camp Atterbury, Indiana, the following year when he was playing that hospital. Jerry Colonna and I got half-bombed at the officer's club, while the mustachioed one missed one of the performances. As usual he had beautiful starlets with him, such as Marilyn Maxwell and Mary Murphy.)

When Vietnam came along, Bob went right back into action—quite literally in fact, for on many occasions he entertained troops so close to Charlie, as the Viet Cong were called, that they had to keep his performances secret. His troupes by now, with all the electronics and other showbiz needs to entertain as many as twenty thousand troops at one time, were quite large. And beauties—he wrote a book about them entitled *Five Women I Love: Bob Hope's Vietnam Story*—who sang, danced, joked, smiled, and rocked their beautiful bodies throughout Nam, Thailand, and even in the Central Highlands where the fierce but friendly Montagnards greeted them with interest. In his book Bob was referring to Anita Bryant, Janis Paige, Kaye Stevens, bombshell Joey Heatherton, and blonde beauty Carroll Baker. There were others—Anna Maria Alberghetti, Ann Sydney, Miss USA Diana Lynn Batts, and Raquel Welch, to name a few. And some guys, including Jack Jones, Eddie Fisher, Jerry Colonna, and Les Brown and his musicians, writers, soundmen, grips, the whole gamut...including an always present golf club.

Bob could get a laugh from the humor-hungry servicemen with almost any line. One of his dialogues was about the show's flight to Nam in an Air Force C-141:

> I love the *esprit de corps* among the crew, the way they carried the pilot aboard, it took five of them...he fights!
>
> But it was inspiring to meet the crew...pilot, copilot, navigator, and chaplain.
>
> But I'm a little worried about our navigator. He got lost on the way to file our flight plan.
>
> I'm kidding, he was really good. After we'd been flying about five hours, he stuck his head in the cabin and said, "What's all that water down there?" I said, "That's the Pacific." And he turned to the co-pilot and said, "See? You owe me ten bucks!"
>
> But they're really great flyers, and I especially like the way they landed the plane...right side up!

He liked to incorporate commanding officers into his jokes. At one forward base he quipped, "The colonel got all the cast together in our magnificent dressing room in the base operations hut. It was divided into men's and women's by an army blanket, five feet high. We used the honor system. The girls promised not to look at me."

About the carrier, the USS *Ticonderoga*, "This ship really is a beauty. I understand half the whales in the Pacific are trying to get her to go upstream."

But the man who always played the coward manifested his bravery in a different way. Often he visited wards in hospitals where the worst burn cases or the most badly wounded patients were. He almost always managed to keep a light air to amuse them, but on many occasions had to tear himself away when other members of his cast were in tears. Colonna said, "His guts to do this in ward after ward was a true sign of his courage."

He took a troupe to the Middle East during Desert Storm, went back to England to commemorate the fiftieth anniversary of the end of WWII, and finally, with age ninety approaching, decided it was time to hang up his fatigues. He became the most honored member of show business in history. Military ships and aircraft were named for him; some two thousand awards and citations including fifty-four honorary doctorates were granted him. But his remarkable giving of himself to those in harm's way was his greatest accomplishment.

No one ever really knew how much the man with the flip attitude really cared about those servicemen of his.

He wrote, "I must be a sucker for a uniform. I have no other way of explaining how I became Mary Poppins to the military...somewhere inside me there's a cherished and indestructible memory of my first soldier audience. I looked at them, they laughed at me, and it was love at first sight."

He was honored by the United States Congress five times, and in October 1977 he was feted in the Capitol Rotunda by its members. In perhaps the most moving of his tributes, Resolution 75, passed unanimously by both Houses, Bob Hope was made an honorary veteran. Not even having been knighted by Queen Elizabeth meant as much to him.

Yes, he brought laughter.

And there can be no more fitting note on which to end this journey of our wars and our heroes, our paladins. Let it join with our memory of the compelling sound of "Taps" drifting sadly over

graveyards, whether they be Arlington or any other national cemetery, or even on foreign shores, perhaps mingling with these
immortal words of Major John McCrae:

> *Take up our quarrel with the foe:*
> *To you from failing hands we throw*
> *The torch; be yours to hold it high.*
> *If ye break faith with us who die*
> *We shall not sleep, though poppies grow*
> *In Flanders fields.*